THE USBORNE YOUNG SC
ARCHAEOLOGY

Barbara Cork and Struan Reid

Designed by Iain Ashman

Consultants Dr Anne Millard
and Kevin Flude

Contents

Illustrated by Joseph McEwan, Peter Dennis, Kuo Kang Chen, Iain Ashman
Rob McCaig, Ian Jackson, Penny Simon,
Jeremy Gower, Gerard Browne, Graham Smith, David Wright

   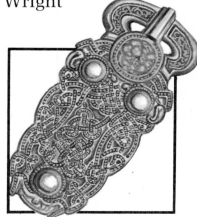

Detectives of the past

Archaeology is about building up a picture of how people lived in the past from the clues they have left behind. The word archaeology means "the study of everything ancient" but many people think archaeology begins the moment you throw something away. Archaeologists work like detectives, gathering evidence from the remains of pottery, bones, buildings and writing, carefully piecing the evidence together and suggesting theories to explain their discoveries. Modern archaeology is a mixture of careful observation, recording and analysis, scientific techniques for finding and examining remains, hard physical work, imagination and guesswork.

Hunting for treasure . . .

Until the end of the 19th century, many people were interested in the past only for the treasure or beautiful works of art they might find to add to their collections. They often destroyed as much as they saved.

Giovanni Belzoni smashed and looted his way through the temples and tombs of Egypt in the early 19th century. In the picture to the left, you can see Belzoni's men dragging part of a statue of Ramesses II to the Nile to be shipped to England.

. . . and legends

Heinrich Schliemann tried to prove some of the people and places in Homer's Greek legends really existed. He found this gold mask in a grave at Mycenae (S. Greece) and believed it belonged to King Agamemnon. But it is 400 years too old for this to be true.

The first archaeologists

Some people in the ancient world investigated and recorded evidence of their past. The first archaeologists were probably the Egyptians, who recorded inscriptions that were already many hundreds of years old.

In the 18th and 19th centuries, many ancient burial mounds were examined. A few people carried out careful and well organized investigations.

Stonehenge

A few curious scholars sketched and recorded monuments from the 16th to the 19th century. William Stukeley recorded British monuments, such as Stonehenge, in the early 18th century but had some strange ideas about why it was built.

Scientific investigators

In the early 19th century, people in Europe and North America became more interested in ancient civilisations, especially those that shed some light on the Bible. By the end of the century, some people began to carry out more detailed and accurate investigations of all the evidence they discovered and this laid the foundations for scientific archaeology in the 20th century.

William Flinders Petrie introduced scientific methods of recording into the study of ancient Egyptian remains, such as pottery.

In the 1920s, Sir Leonard Woolley unearthed the Sumerian city of Ur, one of the greatest cities of ancient Mesopotamia (now Iraq). He carried out detailed investigations and restored objects that would otherwise have crumbled into dust.

This room is called the "treasury".

In 1922, after years of careful searching, Howard Carter caught the first glimpse of the incredible burial treasure of Tutankhamun, which was nearly 4,000 years old. It took almost six years to record and preserve the thousands of valuable objects in the tomb. In the first room alone there were 171 objects and pieces of furniture and Carter worked on these objects for nearly three months before he opened the chamber where the king's body lay.

Science and technology

Archaeologists today may call on a team of scientists and other experts to help them decide where to look for remains of the past and work out the age of the objects they find, what they are made of and how to preserve them. The techniques they use are often borrowed from other sciences (such as medicine and engineering) and a lot of equipment is very expensive. You can find out more in the rest of the book.

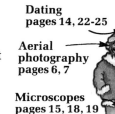

Dating
pages 14, 22-25

Aerial
photography
pages 6, 7

Microscopes
pages 15, 18, 19

X-rays
pages 17, 26, 27

Sonar
page 7
Aqualungs
pages 10, 11

Chemical tests
pages 15, 19, 26, 27

Computers in archaeology

Computers can help archaeologists store and analyse their records, draw 3D plans, reconstruct buildings and test theories about how people lived in the past. It may take some time to convert records into a form a computer can understand. But once the information has been fed into a computer, it saves time in sorting and comparing the records and doing complex calculations. Computers produce accurate results and are not influenced by believing in one particular idea, as an archaeologist might be.

Buildings can be drawn by a computer from measurements archaeologists make on the ruins that survive.

Technology for the future

In the future, archaeologists may be able to use equipment such as the deep-sea robot on page 10, to examine evidence of the past in places where people cannot go. They may also be able to use faster and more accurate dating equipment and distance-measuring instruments that use laser beams. Electronic calculators may be programmed for use in mapping.

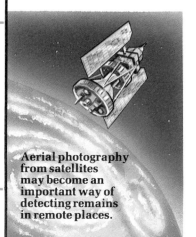

Aerial photography from satellites may become an important way of detecting remains in remote places.

Things you can do

A good way to learn about archaeology is to keep a notebook with sketches, notes and photographs of the objects you find and places you visit. You could also collect newspaper reports of the latest discoveries and scientific techniques. You may even be able to go on a dig – turn to page 31 for more information about this.

Look for pieces of pottery, old bottles and coins in gardens and on country walks.

Visit local museums, ancient ruins and burial mounds that are open to the public.

Look carefully at the buildings in towns to see how they have changed over the years.

For future archaeologists...

You could bury some evidence about your life in the 20th century for future archaeologists to find. Include things like coins, newspaper cuttings, broken china and dried flowers. Seal everything in a watertight container.

The future of the past

The huge sandstone temple of Abu Simbel was cut into more than a thousand blocks and moved to higher ground.

The remains of our past are constantly under threat from new buildings, roads, dams, mining, farming, wars and lack of money to discover, investigate and preserve what has survived so far. One way forward for large, expensive projects has been through international co-operation. People all over the world gave their money and skills to save the temple of Abu Simbel, which would have been covered by the lake behind the new Aswan dam in Egypt.

What to do if you find something

Many young people have made important discoveries. If you find any evidence of the past you think is particularly unusual or valuable, you must tell the police or someone at your local museum. As well as being honoured for your find, you may also receive a reward.

Metal detectors

It is not a good idea to use metal detectors or dig holes to look for objects in places of historic interest. It is illegal in some countries and you will destroy valuable information.

Clues from the past

Only a small fraction of the buildings and objects from the past ever survive the natural processes of decay and destruction by people. If they do survive, it is usually because the material they are made of does not break down easily or because they are buried in conditions (such as very dry, wet or cold conditions), which help to preserve them. So archaeologists often have large gaps in the evidence they collect and cannot build up a complete picture of the people they are studying.

Natural decay

Natural forces, such as the wind, rain, floods, volcanoes and chemical processes all help to destroy evidence of the past. Some materials decay faster than others.

Bacteria, fungi and some animals feed on organic (plant or animal) materials, such as bone, wood and leather. This breaks them down and may destroy them completely.

Bones and teeth take hundreds of years to decay and are often left when other organic materials have disappeared.

Most metals are broken down by chemicals, but gold survives best as it does not join up with chemicals easily. The bronze blade of this dagger has been eaten away by chemicals but the gold design is as bright as ever.

This Mycenaean dagger is over 3,000 years old.

Stone and pottery can survive for thousands of years but even they can be damaged and eaten away by chemicals and pollution. Plants can also break up stonework.

Tree roots have cracked this statue of a Khmer god.

How clues are destroyed

By building work . . .
Buildings are often knocked down to ▶ make way for new buildings, roads, farms or forests. Some of the stones or bricks may be rescued and used again in other buildings. The top of a Roman column has been used as part of this wall.

. . . in storms and battles at sea
◀ Storms and battles have destroyed many ships. After they sink, the remains may be broken up by the currents and tides and eaten away by sea creatures and chemical processes of decay.

. . . by robbers
Many ancient peoples buried their ▶ dead with the goods they thought they would need in the next world. Some of these items were very valuable and robbers often stole the contents of tombs.

. . . by religious fanatics
◀ People with strong religious beliefs sometimes destroyed the statues and temples of people with different beliefs. In this picture, you can see the Spanish conquistadors supervising the destruction of the Aztec temple at Tenochtitlan in Mexico.

. . . by war
Cities and villages are destroyed in wars and their contents burned or stolen. Fires may also start by accident.

This Iron Age village of about 350BC has been attacked by neighbouring people.

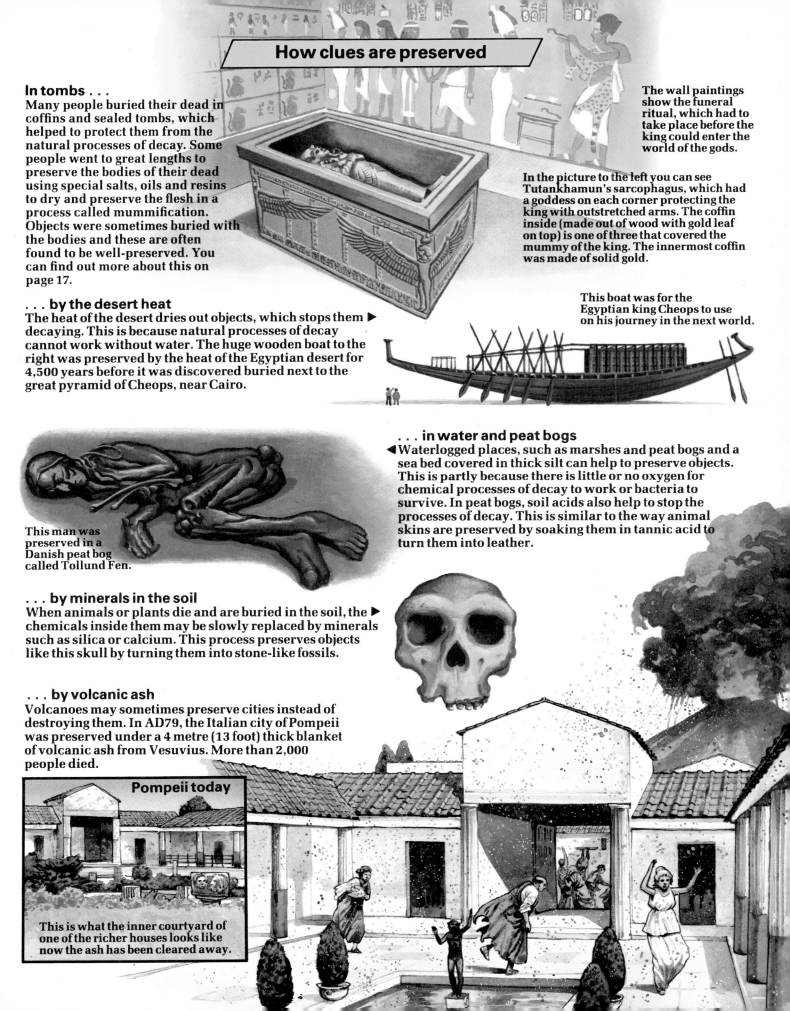

How clues are preserved

In tombs . . .

Many people buried their dead in coffins and sealed tombs, which helped to protect them from the natural processes of decay. Some people went to great lengths to preserve the bodies of their dead using special salts, oils and resins to dry and preserve the flesh in a process called mummification. Objects were sometimes buried with the bodies and these are often found to be well-preserved. You can find out more about this on page 17.

The wall paintings show the funeral ritual, which had to take place before the king could enter the world of the gods.

In the picture to the left you can see Tutankhamun's sarcophagus, which had a goddess on each corner protecting the king with outstretched arms. The coffin inside (made out of wood with gold leaf on top) is one of three that covered the mummy of the king. The innermost coffin was made of solid gold.

. . . by the desert heat

The heat of the desert dries out objects, which stops them ▶ decaying. This is because natural processes of decay cannot work without water. The huge wooden boat to the right was preserved by the heat of the Egyptian desert for 4,500 years before it was discovered buried next to the great pyramid of Cheops, near Cairo.

This boat was for the Egyptian king Cheops to use on his journey in the next world.

. . . in water and peat bogs

◀ Waterlogged places, such as marshes and peat bogs and a sea bed covered in thick silt can help to preserve objects. This is partly because there is little or no oxygen for chemical processes of decay to work or bacteria to survive. In peat bogs, soil acids also help to stop the processes of decay. This is similar to the way animal skins are preserved by soaking them in tannic acid to turn them into leather.

This man was preserved in a Danish peat bog called Tollund Fen.

. . . by minerals in the soil

When animals or plants die and are buried in the soil, the ▶ chemicals inside them may be slowly replaced by minerals such as silica or calcium. This process preserves objects like this skull by turning them into stone-like fossils.

. . . by volcanic ash

Volcanoes may sometimes preserve cities instead of destroying them. In AD79, the Italian city of Pompeii was preserved under a 4 metre (13 foot) thick blanket of volcanic ash from Vesuvius. More than 2,000 people died.

Pompeii today

This is what the inner courtyard of one of the richer houses looks like now the ash has been cleared away.

Looking for evidence

How do archaeologists decide where to look for evidence that has survived from the past? Trained archaeologists have their own instinct and experience to help them and usually search for information about just one particular country or period of history. They piece together clues from written evidence, chance finds, obvious remains and careful searches in likely areas. Some scientific techniques, such as aerial photography, may also be helpful, although they are not always necessary.

People digging a well stumbled on thousands of pottery soldiers and horses buried to guard the tomb of China's first emperor, Ch'in Shih-huang-ti.

Chance discoveries

Evidence of the past often comes to light by chance. Natural forces, such as the wind, rain and burrowing animals may uncover remains. Many accidental discoveries have been made by people when they were ploughing, fishing, quarrying or carrying out building work.

Obvious remains

Some evidence is fairly easy to find because there are obvious remains, such as buildings or mounds of earth, above the surface of the ground. You can see some examples on the right.

Industrial buildings
Nineteenth century brick kiln, Somerset England.

Ancient temples
The pyramid of the Soothsayer, a Maya temple at Uxmal in Mexico.

Stone statues
Gigantic statues on Easter Island. No one knows why these figures were carved.

A bird's eye view

Aerial photographs can reveal signs of ancient towns, fields, roads, tombs and monuments both above and below ground. Three main kinds of marks show up on the photographs – crop marks, soil marks and shadow marks. Different features show up according to the time of year and the weather. Extreme weather, such as droughts or snow, makes it easier to spot remains.

Crops over a wall

Crops over a ditch

Bank over a wall

Crop marks
Ditches, pits and stone walls can be picked out from the air by the way the crops grow over them. Crops grow taller and greener over pits and ditches where the soil is deeper, richer and holds more water. Over stone banks and walls, the crops cannot root so deep or find as much water, so they tend to be shorter and ripen (turn yellow) earlier.

Shadow marks
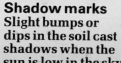
Slight bumps or dips in the soil cast shadows when the sun is low in the sky in early morning or late evening.

Electrical clues

Buried walls and ditches can be found by measuring the resistance to an electric current passed through the ground. This is called resistivity surveying. Damp soils (such as those in ditches) are less resistant to electricity because water conducts electricity well. They give lower readings on the meter.

 ◄ wet
dry ►

Dry soils (such as those over walls) are more resistant to electricity and give higher readings on the meter.

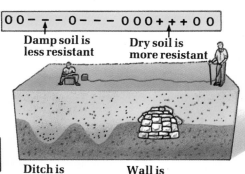

`00 – – – 0 – – – 000 + + + 00`

Damp soil is less resistant

Dry soil is more resistant

Ditch is more magnetic

Wall is less magnetic

`+ + + 0 + + + 000 – – – 0000`

Magnetic clues

Some buried remains can be found because they change the strength of the earth's magnetic field. Iron objects, pottery kilns and pits or ditches filled with soil or rubbish all make the magnetic field stronger because they contain magnetic minerals. Stone walls do not contain magnetic minerals and are less magnetic than the soil around them. An instrument called a proton magnetometer measures the magnetic field and a map is built up from the results. This technique can also be used to detect remains underwater.

On the legend trail

Legends of how people lived in the past are often based on fact and have sometimes helped archaeologists to make spectacular discoveries. In Greek legend, a monster called the Minotaur – half man and half bull – lived in a labyrinth (or maze) at Knossos on the island of Crete. An archaeologist called Arthur Evans uncovered a vast palace at Knossos with a layout as complex as any maze. There were many pictures and statues of bulls in the palace and bulls played an important part in the religious life of the people. Knossos has suffered many earthquakes, which can sound like an angry bull.

A painting of a strange bull-leaping ceremony, which was found at Knossos.

A space shuttle to the same scale as the picture of Silbury Hill.

Hill forts
The hill fort of Maiden Castle in Dorset, England, built between 300BC and AD70. It once sheltered 5,000 people.

Mounds of earth
The largest man-made prehistoric mound in Europe is Silbury Hill, Wiltshire, England. It is 40 metres (131 feet) high and about 4,500 years old but no one is sure why it was built.

Pieces of broken pottery on the surface can indicate where people used to live.

Deep shadow

Hollow over a ditch

Ploughs may bring building stones to the surface.

Dark marks show up over pits and ditches where the soil is damp.

Banks and hollows can be recognized on the ground but larger areas can be seen from the air and patterns are clearer.

Soil marks
If the soil has been disturbed below ground, it can affect the colour of the soil at the surface. This may be because people have dug the soil over or added soil from another area or sometimes because of the way the soil holds water. These soil marks can be picked out most easily when the land has been ploughed.

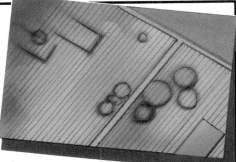

Infra-red photographs

Infra-red film is sometimes used to take the aerial photographs. This picks out changes in temperature caused by buried features. In the picture above, the circles of Bronze Age burials show through the fields, which appear red.

Written evidence
Old documents, inscriptions and maps may help archaeologists to discover evidence of the past. Spanish records 350 years old helped to find the Spanish treasure galleon Nuestra Señora de Atocha, which was wrecked off the Florida Keys on a voyage from Havana to Spain.

Echoes from the deep

Underwater remains can be found using sonar equipment. Sound waves are sent down from a ship on the surface and the time they take to bounce back reveals the shape of the sea bed. Side-scanning sonar draws a picture of the sea bed as it would appear if you were standing on the bottom. Sub-bottom "pingers" record the shape of anything solid in the mud below the sea bed. But it is not always easy to find remains buried deep in the mud or decide which of the many lumps and bumps on the sonar picture might be archaeological remains.

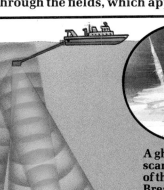

A ghostly side-scan sonar image of the ship Breadalbane, 104 metres (341 feet) below the Arctic Ice in Canada.

Digging into the past

Archaeologists often have to dig into the ground to uncover buried remains. This is called a "dig" or an "excavation" and the place is called a "site". A dig is a carefully planned and highly organized investigation. The methods used depend on the depth of the remains and the amount of time and money available.

Planning a dig

Once the site has been chosen and any landowners have been consulted, the dig itself can be planned. The first step is for archaeologists to walk over the site to get an idea of its size and examine the type of soil and rock in the area. This helps them to work out the number of people and sort of digging equipment they will need. They also look for pieces of pottery, stone or flints that might indicate the best places to start digging.

Clearing the whole area

Some sites may have been used by people for only a short time so that all the remains are in a shallow layer of soil near the surface. In this case, a large area is gradually cleared to provide an overall plan of the site. The different features can be easily compared.

How layers build up

If people have lived on the same site for hundreds or thousands of years, there will be many layers of remains on top of each other. This is known as a stratified site – strata means layer. The oldest layers are at the bottom and the newest at the top, though worms, burrowing animals and plant roots may disturb the layers.

Digging through the layers

In the scene to the right, you can see archaeologists working on a site with many layers of soil and human remains. They have dug deep trenches and are carefully removing one layer at a time to uncover every tiny piece of pottery, bone or metal that might help them to build up a picture of the people who lived on the site.

What happens on a dig

The objects that are uncovered are called the finds. Each type of material (such as bone, metal, or pottery) is put in a separate container according to the layer it was found in. At the end of each day, the finds are collected together in one place. The pottery is washed and dried and all the objects are marked in ink with numbers that indicate the site, the year and the layer and trench they were found in.

Pottery being washed and sorted.

Keeping records

The most important job during a dig is to record exactly where everything was found and what it looked like when it was discovered. This helps archaeologists to work out what the different parts of the site were used for and where buildings once stood.

The records include written descriptions and accurate drawings (to scale) of all the important objects and features, such as walls, pits and floors. Small computers are often used to keep records on many sites. As new features are uncovered, they are added to the plan.

Drawing the layers

The sides of the trenches, known as sections, are drawn to scale to record all the layers and any important objects or features.

Tape measure

Equipment

Trowels and brushes are used to uncover finer details and fragile objects. Sometimes a sieve is used to collect very small objects.

Sieve

Labels

Trowel

Brush

Surveying the site

The site is carefully surveyed before and during the dig and often at the end of the dig as well. Surveying involves measuring distances, directions and angles using equipment such as the theodolite in the picture to the right. The exact shape and size of the surface of the ground can then be worked out so an accurate plan of the site can be drawn up. The plan may be divided into trenches or a grid of numbered squares.

Seeing underground

When hundreds of Etruscan tombs were discovered, archaeologists used a long probe with a light and camera on the end to see into the tombs to help them decide which ones to excavate.

Earth from trenches (spoil heap)

Rescue digs

With the building of new houses, offices and roads, many new sites are being discovered. However, the time available to excavate them may be limited because the builders want to start their own work. This type of dig is called a rescue or salvage dig.

On a rescue dig, archaeologists try to gather as much information as they can in a short time. They may choose a few small areas to excavate thoroughly and work faster in other areas.

Photographs

Three main types of photographs are usually taken on a dig.
1. Photographs of the parts of the site included in the section and plan drawings. (This allows the information on the drawings to be cross-checked later on.)
2. Photographs of the site and the finds that will be needed when the work is published.
3. Colour slides that might be needed for lectures.

Labels to mark layers and features such as floors.

Measuring pole (called a ranging pole) for working out the scale of features.

Industrial archaeology

Industrial buildings and machines can reveal interesting information about industrial processes and working conditions in our more recent past. Many buildings have been uncovered and some have been repaired, restored or adapted to new uses. This is a lead smelt-mill being repaired.

Drawing frames

A drawing frame divided into squares is used on flat surfaces to help the archaeologists record the positions of most of the objects accurately by eye.

Turn over for underwater digs

The underwater detectives

Until recently, any clues to the past that fell or were thrown into deep water were lost forever. But since the 1940s, diving equipment and instruments for finding underwater remains have opened up a new world to archaeologists. An underwater dig may be up to 25 times as expensive as a land dig and it is difficult for archaeologists to raise enough money for the latest equipment.

Archaeologists work in much the same way underwater as they do on land, but they have to learn how to use all the diving equipment and think about safety rules as well as carry out the excavation. The dig has to be planned carefully because the divers can spend only a few hours underwater. It may also be difficult for them to see very far and they cannot communicate easily.

High-tech archaeology

In the future, a few archaeologists may be able to use expensive equipment, such as the special diving suit and robot below, to investigate underwater remains in places too cold or deep for rubber suits and aqualungs.

This revolutionary diving suit, called WASP, keeps the air pressure inside the same as on land. It allows people to work at depths of up to 600 metres (1,968 feet) at any water temperature. It was used in 1983 to examine the wreck of the Breadalbane, which sank under the Arctic ice in 1853.

This robot is controlled from a TV monitor on the surface ship. It can hover just above the bottom without churning up silt. It was used in 1983 on the wreck of the Hamilton, which sank in a storm on Lake Ontario in 1813.

On an underwater dig

In the picture below, you can see archaeologists investigating the wreck of a Roman ship in the Mediterranean. They began the excavation by digging trenches outside the hull to see how much of the ship had survived, if any, and if it was safe to excavate. Now they are working inside the hull to remove the mud and measure, record and recover the cargo. If the ship had broken up and the remains had been scattered over the sea bed, they would have gradually cleared the whole area, just as they do if there is a shallow layer of remains on land. Often nothing survives of the ship itself, only parts of its cargo.

Photographs from submarines

Mini-submarines are sometimes used to take photographs. This is much quicker than using divers. Computers can plot 3D plans of the site from the photographs.

Surveying and recording

A grid of tapes or poles is laid out and the overall shape of the site and the exact positions of all the objects recorded on photographs or drawings. Each object is given a code number for future reference.

Passing messages

Divers can pass on simple messages using hand signals, but sonic helmets like this one use sound waves to allow the divers to talk to each other and people on the surface.

Excavating

Archaeologists remove loose silt by waving their hands or using soft brushes. Trowels are used for harder material. They may have to stop from time to time to let the mud and silt settle.

Poles to mark out grid.

Watch to time air supply in aqualung.

Code numbers on the cargo of wine jars (amphorae).

Sonic helmet

Raising the Mary Rose

In 1982, the Mary Rose (Henry VIII's flagship) was raised to the surface after 437 years on the sea bed.

1 Only half the hull survived. It took 11 years to clear the mud and recover all the objects.

2 Wire ropes were bolted to the hull so the ship could be attached to a lifting frame.

3 The frame was jacked up to lift the ship off the bottom and it was moved inside a steel cradle.

4 The Mary Rose in its cradle, with the lifting frame still attached, was lifted on to a barge and carried ashore.

On the surface

Before they dive, archaeologists discuss previous work, the layout and size of the site and what their particular task for the day will be. Videos were used on the Mary Rose dig to help with these discussions and allow people on the surface to watch the divers at work.

Back from a watery grave

The Swedish warship Wasa sank in Stockholm harbour 350 years ago. Divers used water jets to dig tunnels for steel cables under the ship. The cables were fixed to barges and as the barges were filled with air, the Wasa lifted off the sea bed. The ship was then made watertight and winches pulled it to the surface. After archaeologists had removed some of the objects from inside, the ship floated into dock on its own keel.

Lifting objects

Air-filled bags are used to lift heavy objects. Fragile objects must be packed in sealed containers before they can be lifted.

Extra air tanks to fill lifting balloons.

Metal objects

Metal objects decay in sea water and may become stuck together in solid lumps called concretions. These have to be broken up with a hammer and chisel underwater or in chemical baths on land.

Air lift to suck up mud.

Removing mud

Baskets, buckets and air lifts may be used. Air lifts work like a vacuum cleaner. Compressed air is fed into the nozzle end and as it rushes up the tube, it creates an empty space (vacuum) behind it, which sucks mud up the tube.

Holding back the sea

The ships were sunk to stop pirates sailing into the fjord.

Archaeologists recovered five Viking ships from the Roskilde Fjord in Denmark using this "coffer" dam with the water pumped out from inside. Muddy water and strong currents would have made it difficult to excavate underwater. The fragile wreckage was sprayed with water 24 hours a day to stop it crumbling.

Aqualung

Crayons on plastic sheets are used for recording.

Treasures from the sacred well

Chemicals were used to clear the silt in a well sacred to the Maya at Chichen Itza, Mexico. Divers were then able to recover more than 6,000 items, including incense, copper, jade and gold objects and the bones of humans sacrificed to the water god.

Stone jaguar from the well. It was a symbol of power in the Maya world.

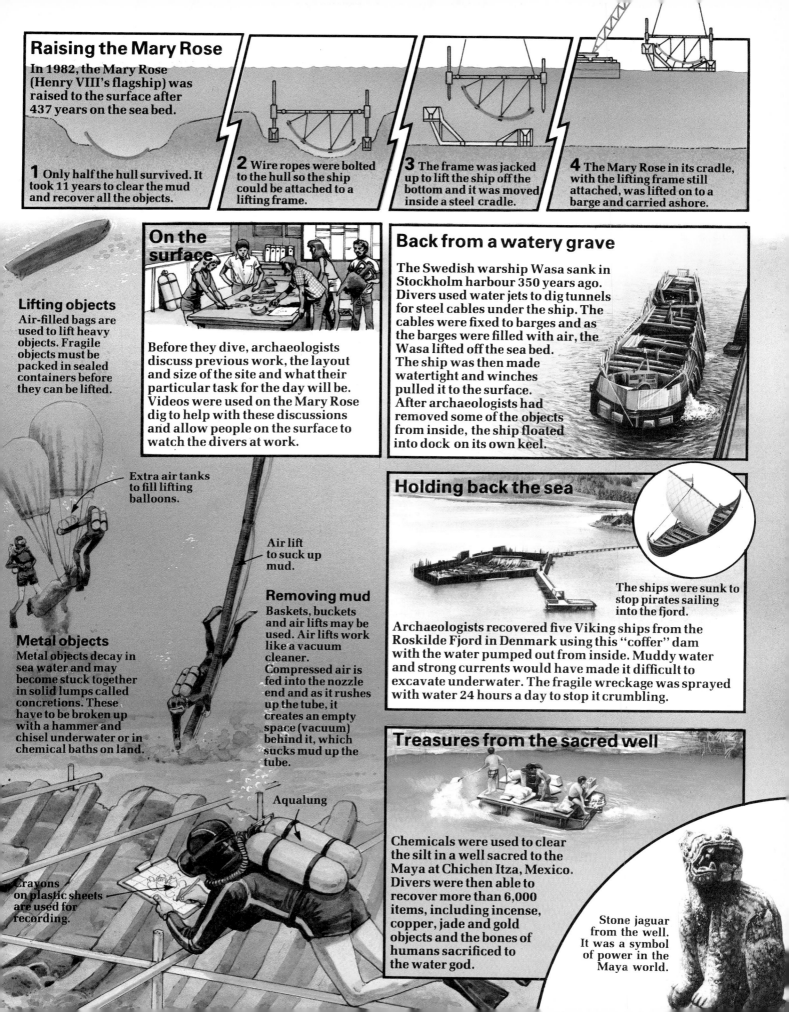

Piecing the evidence together

Across these two pages you can see how archaeologists use all the objects they find on a dig to build up a picture of how the people lived. The first step is to try and sort out all the information into a time sequence. This is known as "phasing" and it forms a basic framework to which information about the economic and social organization of the people can be added.

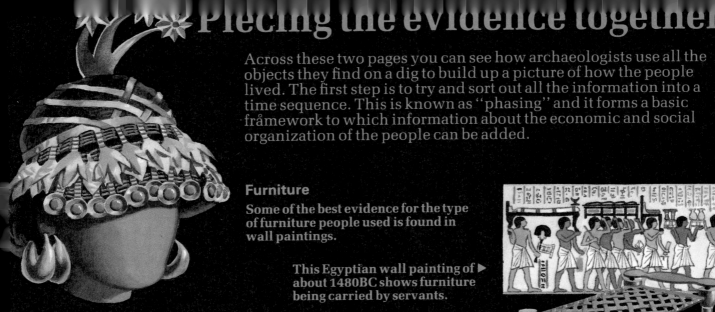

Furniture

Some of the best evidence for the type of furniture people used is found in wall paintings.

This Egyptian wall painting of ▶ about 1480BC shows furniture being carried by servants.

This bronze bed was ▶ made by the Etruscans of Italy in about 350BC.

Social organization

This gold headdress was found in one of the royal graves at Ur, in Iraq, and was worn by a noblewoman buried with her king. When a king died he was buried with his courtiers. They lay down outside the royal chamber in order of importance and killed themselves by drinking poison.

Fashions

This mosaic portrait of a woman from Pompeii gives an idea of hair and jewellery fashions in about AD50.

In the kitchen

This shish-kebab, for grilling meat, dates from about 1200BC and shows one method of cooking in the past.
▼

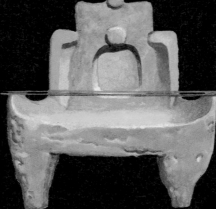

Music and dancing

In the Egyptian wall painting below you can see some women playing a harp, lute, pipes and lyre. Can you work out which is which?

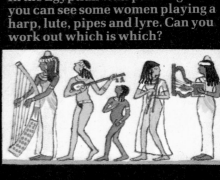

Sport

Evidence shows that the Maya of Mexico played a kind of football with a hard rubber ball. The stone below shows the players dressed in padded hip-guards and knee-pads with feather headdresses.

Toys and games

This clay toy, made in Crete about 1500BC, shows a girl on a swing.

Law

◀ Most societies are governed by a code of law controlled by the rulers. This stone from 1800BC shows King Hammurabi of Babylon receiving the code of justice from a god.

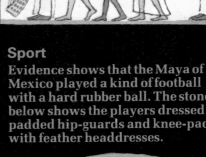

Health and medicine

The person who owned this jaw was losing his teeth, so he had them held together with gold wire by a dentist.

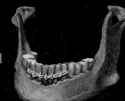

Hunting and farming

This cave painting, at Lascaux in France, shows a Stone Age hunter being attacked by a bison.

This is a clay model of an ox-cart that was used in Mohenjo-daro in Pakistan. It dates from about 2000BC.

Many people asked the gods to help their crops grow. This gold spray of wheat was associated with the corn goddess Demeter. It comes from Syracuse in Sicily and is 2,000 years old.

Religion

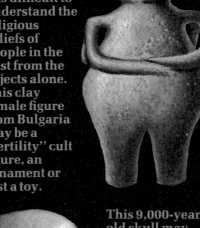

It is difficult to understand the religious beliefs of people in the past from the objects alone. This clay female figure from Bulgaria may be a "fertility" cult figure, an ornament or just a toy.

This 9,000-year-old skull may indicate a form of ancestor worship. It was found beneath the floor of a house in Jericho, Palestine. The face had been rebuilt with clay and shells were used to replace the eyes.

Trade

Trade is usually recognized by the discovery of foreign goods in places far away from where they were made. Trade united the ancient world and helped to build the Assyrian, Persian, Greek and Roman empires. Traders often had a protected status, even when travelling in hostile countries.

Glass was a major item of trade in the Roman Empire.

Coins can show trading connections. These French coins were found in a burial mound at Sutton Hoo, England. They date from about AD625.

Transport

The people of Ur were famous as sailors. This silver model of a boat was made in about 2500BC.

◄ In the Swedish rock carving to the left (which dates from 2000BC) you can see hunters following their prey on skis.

War and weapons

Weapons can tell archaeologists much about the skills of the people who made them and the soldiers who used them.

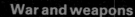

This bronze helmet was found in a grave in Thrace (Bulgaria) and dates from 600BC.

In AD43 the Iron Age fort of Maiden Castle in Dorset was attacked by the Romans. The skeleton of one of the British soldiers was found with an arrowhead still embedded in the spine. ▼

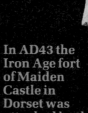

The Celts of Europe were a very warlike race and even their ceremonial objects, like this bronze and enamel shield, were often designed as weapons. This is known as the Battersea Shield and was probably an offering to a god. ▶

Pottery

Archaeologists find a lot of pottery because it does not decay easily, it was not valuable enough for robbers to steal and people threw away broken pots because it did not cost much to make new ones.

The sort of clay the pots were made from and the style and decoration of a pot help archaeologists to work out dates and trade routes and find out about the customs and daily life of the people.

How pots were made

Pottery was first made about 10,000 years ago in the Middle East. One early method was to roll the clay into long "sausages" and coil it round in circles. Another method was to shape the clay on a wheel that potters turned with their hands or feet.

This sort of kiln was used in Mesopotamia (Iraq) about 3500BC.

Archaeologists name some ancient peoples after the pottery found with their remains. The Beaker People of prehistoric Europe were named after their beaker-shaped pots.

The clay pots were dried in the sun and then baked over an open fire to harden them. But higher temperatures were needed to make harder, more delicate pots and so pottery kilns were developed. Baking pottery in a kiln is called firing.

By AD900 the Chinese had made kilns where the temperature was high enough (1450°C/2642°F) to make delicate porcelain cups like this one.

Investigating pottery

Dating

Archaeologists can compare the pottery from different sites to work out which soil layers are probably the same age. If they have enough evidence to date one site, they will then be able to suggest dates for another site where they have no other evidence to help with dating. (See page 23 for more about dating.)

Levels 1 and 3 and 2 and 4 are probably the same age.

Recording

Archaeologists make a detailed record of the different types of whole pots and broken pieces (sherds) they find. This is known as a corpus and includes details of the size, shape, design and decoration. From this record, they can build up a picture of how the shapes and styles of the pots have changed over the years.

Each pot is drawn to scale. One half of the drawing shows the outside of the pot and the other shows a cut-away section.

Using computers

Computers are an efficient way of extracting information from pottery records, especially if large quantities of pottery have been found. They can rapidly compare pottery from different layers and sites and work out changes in the type of pottery over time. They can also be used to search through large amounts of data for a particular type of pottery.

What the pots were used for

The shape, size and decoration of a pot and the quality of the work and the clay used tell archaeologists about the skill of the potter, the cost of making the pot and what it might have been used for.

The Nabataeans of Petra in Jordan were famous as potters and made this very thin bowl for special occasions. It is too delicate to have been used for cooking.

Because of its rough clay and simple design this German pot was probably used for cooking.

This "pithos" from Knossos in Crete is taller than a person. It was used for storage.

Changes in style

Some styles may change quickly while others stay the same for many years. Pottery in daily use, such as these oil lamps, often changed style quickly with the fashions. But pots that were rarely used or had an important meaning in religious rituals often kept the same style for a long time.

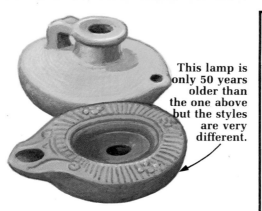

This lamp is only 50 years older than the one above but the styles are very different.

Daily life

The scenes engraved or painted on the sides of a pot can tell archaeologists about the people, their interests and customs, their work and entertainment and how they dressed.

This jug, made in Peru about AD250-750, is shaped like a musician with drum and pipes.

This Greek vase of 520BC shows the olive harvest.

Trading and colonies

This map shows how pottery can indicate trading links and movements of people in the past. If the pots were made some distance from where they were found, this may suggest trade or rule by a foreign power.

Similar clay urns have been found at Carthage on the North African coast and at Tyre and Sidon in Lebanon, showing how the Phoenicians came from Lebanon to establish a colony at Carthage.

This Roman Samian pottery bowl was made in Gaul (France) and exported to Britain.

This vase was made in Cyprus but its design comes from Mycenae on the Greek mainland. Some Mycenaeans may have moved to Cyprus when their kingdom collapsed in the 12th century BC.

Where pots were made

Scientists can work out where a pot was made by examining the colour of the clay and the minerals it contains.

Colour

The colour of the clay is an important clue because clays from different areas turn different colours when they are fired.

The Munsell Soil Colour Chart provides a range of standard colours to which the pottery can be exactly matched. Each colour has a code number.

Minerals under the microscope

Scientists can study the minerals in the clay by examining a thin slice of pottery, about 0.03mm (0.0012in) thick, under a geological microscope. This microscope uses special lighting to show up the minerals in the clay. Scientists can work out where the clay came from, if the pot was made on a wheel and what temperature it was fired at in the kiln.

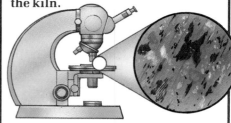

The minerals in the clay show up as different colours under the microscope.

Heavy mineral analysis

In a technique called heavy mineral analysis, a fragment of pottery is crushed and sprinkled on to a liquid that allows the lighter minerals to float and the heavier ones to sink. The heavy minerals are drawn off and examined under a microscope. They are rarer and may indicate the source of the clay.

Burials and bodies

The skeletons and objects found in graves provide valuable information about the beliefs, customs and health of people in the past. The sort of burial people received depended on their position in society. The poor usually received far less attention than the rich and powerful. But most ancient societies buried their dead with the things they believed they would need in the next world and this suggests they believed in life after death.

Bodies

Sometimes a body is preserved by a trick of nature. Doctors in China have examined the 2,000-year-old body of a princess who had been buried in an airtight tomb. Her skin was still elastic and her joints could be moved. In some places, people preserved the bodies of their dead. The most elaborate process of mummification was perfected by the Ancient Egyptians.

Examining an Egyptian mummy

The scientific examination of Egyptian mummies has provided detailed information about the health of the ancient Egyptians. Some of the techniques scientists use and the conclusions they have reached are described across these two pages.

Lungs

The few lungs that have survived show that the Egyptians suffered from breathing problems caused by smoke from fires and by sand from the desert.

Bones

Many Egyptians suffered from arthritis. This is shown by a thickening of the bones at the joints.

Pollution

Lead pollution in ancient Egypt was thirty times less than it is today. This is shown by a technique called optical emission spectrometry in which a piece of bone is burnt and photographed. Different chemicals in the bone are shown by lines on the photograph and the strength of these lines indicates the strength of the chemicals in the bones.

Worms

The Egyptians suffered from worms. In one mummy, worms were found preserved in the body.

Blood groups

It is possible to work out the blood group of a mummy from chemical tests on the flesh and bone marrow. Each person's blood falls into one of four main groups: A, B, O, and AB. These can indicate family connections and have been used to unravel Tutankhamun's complicated family tree.

Burials

An underground palace

In 1977, a tomb complex was discovered beneath a large earth mound at Vergina in Macedonia, Greece. Although no inscription has been found to indicate who was buried there, the chambers contained treasures, including a gold and silver crown and rare wall paintings. Some archaeologists believe that this is the tomb of King Philip of Macedon who reigned in the mid-4th century BC.

The two bodies buried here were cremated and the remains placed in two gold caskets.

It has been possible to reconstruct the head of one of the bodies in a remarkable project described on page 28.

Princes of jade

In 1968, soldiers in Hopei province in China discovered by chance the tombs of Lui Sheng, Prince of Chungshan, and his wife Tou Wan who lived in the 2nd century BC. Their bodies had rotted away but their burial suits had survived. These were made from thousands of pieces of cut and polished jade. Each piece was linked to the next by gold wire.

Jade, a hard green stone, was greatly valued by the Chinese who thought it could prevent the body decaying.

Teeth and gums

Teeth can give some idea of the age of the person. Tutankhamun's jaw had wisdom teeth appearing in it. This shows that he was probably about 18 when he died.

This X-ray picture of the head of Ramesses II shows the bad condition of his teeth and gums. The Egyptians ate a lot of rough bread which wore down their teeth. The kings were affected as much as the poor people.

Skin and brains

The dry, hard skin and flesh on a mummy has to be softened in a salt solution before it can be examined. Narrow blood vessels in the brains of some mummies indicate death from strokes.

Preparing a mummy

The Egyptians believed that the dead person's spirit, or Ka, would die if the body perished. In order to provide a home for the spirit, the body was preserved as much as possible.

After the body was washed, the brain and internal organs were usually removed and stored in special jars, called canopic jars.

The body was then covered with natron (a mixture of sodium salts that absorbed moisture), and dried for about 35 days.

The cuts were sewn up and the body was coated in resin, wrapped in linen and finally placed in a coffin. The whole process took 70 days.

The buried boat mystery

One of the most puzzling burials is the rich ship burial of the 7th century AD at Sutton Hoo in England. Fabulous gold, enamel and silver treasures were found beneath an earth mound with traces of a boat, which the people believed was needed as transport to the next world. But there was no sign of a body. The treasures suggest that the people believed in a mixture of pagan and Christian gods.

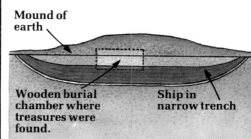

Mound of earth

Wooden burial chamber where treasures were found.

Ship in narrow trench

This solid gold belt-buckle from Sutton Hoo is 13.2 cm (5.2 in) long and has pagan animal designs on it. It was found beside a gold and ivory purse and thirty seven gold coins.

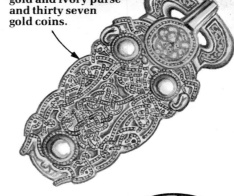

Deep freeze tombs

At Pazyryk in Siberia, Russia, some remarkable Scythian funeral mounds were found in the 1920s. (The Scythians lived in central Asia 2,400 years ago.) The tombs had been robbed soon after the burial and water had seeped into them, freezing and preserving the remains. This picture shows the tomb where the bodies of a Scythian chieftain and his favourite wife and servant were buried.

The tombs were built and decorated like underground houses with carpets, pots, furniture and clothes.

The three bodies buried inside had been preserved by the ice. The arms, legs and backs of the men were tattooed with strange animal designs.

Animal and plant remains

Animal and plant remains can help archaeologists to find out how people hunted animals or farmed the land in the past. They can also help to build up a picture of the climate the people lived in. The most common remains are animal bones and teeth and plant seeds and pollen grains. With the information they provide, archaeologists can find out how people fitted into their environment and used the plants and animals around them to survive.

Animal remains

Archaeologists look for two kinds of information from animal remains – what kinds of animal lived in the area and which animals were hunted or farmed by the people. Teeth, horns and leg bones are the most useful remains because teeth survive for a long time and horns and leg bones are easy to recognize.

The age of animals

Animal teeth are worn down with age and can show how old the animal was when it died.

Young tooth   Old tooth

The efficiency of hunters

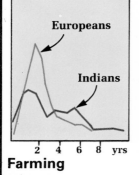

This graph shows that the North American Indians were more efficient hunters than the European settlers. The Indians hunted deer of all ages, whereas the Europeans hunted mostly young deer, which were easier to catch. The age of the deer they killed was worked out from the height of the teeth.

Farming

The bones of wild and domesticated animals are a different size, so archaeologists can work out when people started to farm the animals rather than hunt them.

Foot bone of a wild Auroch.

Foot bone of domesticated cow, descendant of the Auroch.

Bones under the microscope

Under a microscope it is possible to pick out the different cell structure in the bones of wild and domesticated animals.

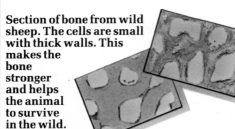

Section of bone from wild sheep. The cells are small with thick walls. This makes the bone stronger and helps the animal to survive in the wild.

Section of bone from domesticated sheep. Long cells with thin walls indicate more fragile bones. They do not need such strong bones because people look after them.

Hunting

This scene shows a Giant Elk being hunted 13,000 years ago. Archaeologists have worked out from its remains that it was about to shed its antlers when it died. This indicates that it was killed in the winter because deer shed their antlers in winter.

Plants and climate

Plant remains can indicate what the climate was like in the past because different groups of plants grow best in particular conditions of temperature and rainfall. There are no trees in this scene because it is too cold.

Farming

Using information from pollen grains, archaeologists can work out where farming sites existed. There is less tree pollen in the soil if the forest has been cut down to make way for farmland.

Crops

If grain is found on a site, this can indicate the presence of a farming community.

Domesticated barley is much fatter than the wild variety.

Bones

Animal bones found on a site have usually been left there by people. It is possible to tell whether people have sliced meat off the bones from the cut marks left by their tools.

Cut marks from a knife

Animals and climate

The remains of certain animals, such as snails, can indicate what the climate was like. This Arctic Fox lives in cold places.

Working animals

Animals used for heavy work often have twisted and swollen bones and teeth worn down by the harnesses.

Meat or milk

The remains of a lot of young animals indicates a meat producing community, where the animals are killed before they are mature. If the bones of a lot of older animals are found, this probably shows a wool and milk producing community where the animals are not killed until they are much older.

Insects

The remains of dung beetles on a site shows there were a lot of plant-eating animals around.

Plant remains

Plants decay quickly in most conditions but in some areas, such as peat bogs or very dry places, they can survive for thousands of years. Plant remains can give archaeologists an idea of the environment of our ancestors and the kinds of food that they ate.

Pollen grains

Each species of plant has a different type of pollen grain, which can be identified under a microscope. This helps to build up a picture of the plants that used to grow in an area.

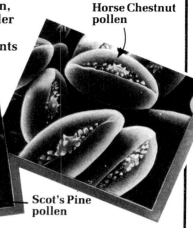

Horse Chestnut pollen

Scot's Pine pollen

Separating the pollen

Samples of soil are collected and the pollen grains are separated off by a process called flotation.

Sample sprinkled on top

Pollen drawn off here

Water pumped in to break up the sample.

Pump

Soil is heavy and sinks to the bottom.

Chambery
Constantinople
Turin
Jerusalem
Possible journey of the Turin Shroud

Tracing a journey

Pollen from seven types of plant that grow near the Dead Sea in the Holy Land, have been found on the Turin Shroud (believed by some people to be the burial cloth of Jesus). This shows that the cloth might have been made in the area.

Funeral flowers

People often placed flowers on the graves of their dead. At Shanidar in Iraq, a Neanderthal (Stone Age) man's grave was found to contain a lot of pollen. His body had been covered with eight different types of flower, including hollyhocks.

A garland of flowers was found on Tutankhamun's second coffin.

Buildings

The remains of buildings help archaeologists to find out how skilled people were at working in wood, brick or stone and how much they knew about building techniques. The size of houses and the equipment inside reveals information about the numbers of people, their living conditions and their wealth. Larger monuments, such as temples, help archaeologists to find out about religious beliefs, the power of the leaders and the organization of workers.

Even if the buildings themselves have disappeared, their foundations below ground or marks on the surface can still give some idea of the shape and purpose of buildings.

At Terra Amata in southern France, archaeologists have discovered traces of the oldest known buildings in the world, built near the sea about 400,000 years ago.

Lines of holes show where strong posts would have been and circles of large stones mark the size and shape of each hut.

The sand on the floor of the huts is not very tightly packed down and this suggests people lived in them for just a short time each year.

Clues in the ground

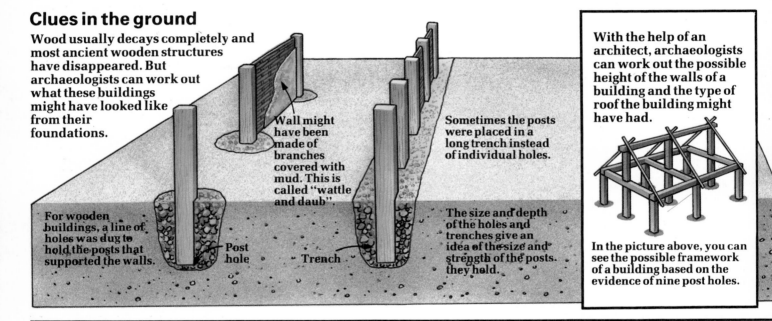

Wood usually decays completely and most ancient wooden structures have disappeared. But archaeologists can work out what these buildings might have looked like from their foundations.

Wall might have been made of branches covered with mud. This is called "wattle and daub".

For wooden buildings, a line of holes was dug to hold the posts that supported the walls.

Post hole

Trench

Sometimes the posts were placed in a long trench instead of individual holes.

The size and depth of the holes and trenches give an idea of the size and strength of the posts they held.

With the help of an architect, archaeologists can work out the possible height of the walls of a building and the type of roof the building might have had.

In the picture above, you can see the possible framework of a building based on the evidence of nine post holes.

Writing

Written evidence helps archaeologists to understand the ideas and thoughts of people who lived thousands of years ago. It is also much easier to date the past when people have left written records, such as letters, lists of kings and inscriptions on buildings.

Some early forms of writing, especially Greek and Latin, are still understood today so archaeologists have been able to find out a great deal about Greek and Roman history. Many ancient scripts however had to be decoded before the information they contained could be revealed.

Ancient writing used today

The Greek alphabet is the origin of all European writing. Ancient Greek and Latin have been spoken for more than 2,000 years and they are still taught today. Many inscriptions and much literature has survived.

In 474BC, a Greek called Hiero defeated the Etruscans near Kyme (S. Italy). One of the helmets he captured was inscribed with a dedication of thanks to Zeus.

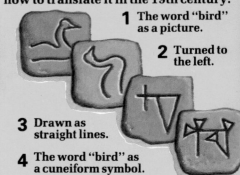

"Hiero, son of Deinomenes, and the Syracusans, to Zeus, from the Etruscans, from Kyme."

The first writing

Writing was first developed in Mesopotamia in about 3500BC. It is known as cuneiform (wedge-shaped) writing because of the marks made by the pen in the clay tablets the people wrote on. No one could read it until Henry Rawlinson worked out how to translate it in the 19th century.

1 The word "bird" as a picture.

2 Turned to the left.

3 Drawn as straight lines.

4 The word "bird" as a cuneiform symbol.

Stone buildings

Stone lasts much longer than most other building materials. Archaeologists can often work out the different stages of building on a stone wall, as you can see in this picture of an English church wall.

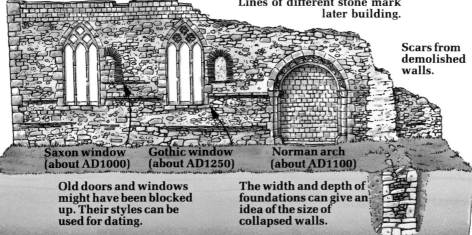

Lines of different stone mark later building.

Scars from demolished walls.

Saxon window (about AD1000)

Gothic window (about AD1250)

Norman arch (about AD1100)

Old doors and windows might have been blocked up. Their styles can be used for dating.

The width and depth of foundations can give an idea of the size of collapsed walls.

Brick buildings

Hand-made bricks, dried in the sun, can be difficult to recognize and early archaeologists often demolished brick walls buried in the soil thinking that they were clearing away the earth.

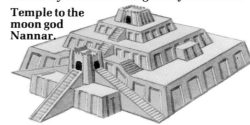

Temple to the moon god Nannar.

This ziggurat in Iraq was buried under a huge mound of earth from decomposed bricks, and archaeologists had to dig very carefully to uncover the lines of bricks. It was built about 2500BC with mud bricks inside and a protective skin of fired bricks in tar.

Models of houses

Archaeologists can sometimes find out about buildings that have disappeared from pictures and models. For example, ancient Chinese wooden houses no longer exist, but pottery models from about 200BC have been preserved in tombs. Tombs themselves often resemble houses.

Town planning

The cities of Mohenjo-daro and Harappa in Pakistan were built in about 2500BC and show a very organized form of town planning. The streets and an elaborate drainage system were laid out in straight lines. Many of the houses were the same size and design.

Built to last

The Romans built the Pont du Gard aqueduct in France to carry water to the city of Nimes. It is still standing after 2,000 years.

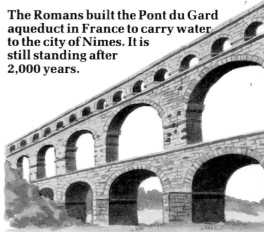

This is one of the world's oldest medical texts, which dates from 2500BC. It is written in cuneiform and lists 15 remedies for illnesses.

"Pulverise pears and the roots of the manna plant: put in beer and let the man drink."

Cracking the code

The text on this stone (found at Rosetta, Egypt) was written in 196BC in three different forms of writing: Egyptian hieroglyphs (writing in pictures), demotic Egyptian (a kind of shorthand) and Greek. In 1822, Jean-Francois Champollion was able to use the Greek writing to translate the hieroglyphs and unravel the mysteries of Egyptian inscriptions.

Hieroglyphs

Demotic Egyptian

"Ptolmys"

Greek

Hidden secrets

Many ancient scripts have still not been decoded, even with the help of computers.

This is part of an astronomy book written by the Maya of central America. The symbols (called glyphs) remain a mystery.

How old is it?

Archaeologists need to know the age of the things they find so they can put people and events into some sort of order. Dates help them to work out possible links between different peoples (through trade for example) and how technology, ideas and beliefs might have developed. Sometimes it is only possible to work out if one object is older or younger than another. This can be estimated from the style of objects, their position in the soil layers and the amount of certain chemical elements they contain. But archaeologists can also work out reasonably accurate dates from written records, the dates on coins and a variety of scientific techniques. Many scientific techniques are expensive and can only be carried out in a few laboratories with special equipment.

Working out dates

This chart summarizes the different dating techniques that archaeologists may use. It tells you how they work, what sort of material they can be used on and the age range they can provide dates for.

10,000,000 years
1,000,000 years
60,000 years
9,000 years
5,000 years

Written records

Historical documents, government and religious records, inscriptions on temple walls, clay tablets or papyrus.

Potassium/argon dating

Measures the amount of these two chemical elements in volcanic rocks. Older rocks have less potassium and more argon.

Fission track dating

Counts the number of tracks made by radioactive elements as they break down. Older objects leave more tracks. Used on rocks, pottery, glass.

Tree ring dating (dendrochronology)

Counting annual (yearly) tree rings and matching up ring patterns to make a dating sequence. Used on wooden objects.

Magnetic dating

Comparing magnetism in an object with changes in the earth's magnetic field in the past (dated by other means). Used on baked clay and mud from lakes.

Carbon 14 (Radiocarbon) dating

Measures radioactivity given off by carbon 14 atoms or counts the atoms. Older objects are less radioactive. Used on organic remains.

Thermoluminescence

Measures the energy from the breakdown of radioactive elements, which is trapped in pottery and given off as light. Older objects give off more light.

New bones or old?

By measuring the amount of fluorine, nitrogen and uranium in bones, archaeologists can sort out the older bones on a site from the younger ones. As bones get older, the amount of fluorine and uranium goes up and the amount of nitrogen goes down. This does not happen at a fixed rate, so it is not possible to work out a date from these tests. It also happens at a different speed in different places so it is not possible to compare the bones from different sites.

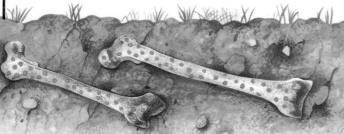

Younger bones have more nitrogen and less fluorine and uranium than older bones.

Older bones have more fluorine and uranium – this seeps into the bones in rainwater and builds up over time. They also have less nitrogen because a chemical in the bones that contains nitrogen (collagen) breaks down.

Magnetic dating

This dating technique is based on the fact that the direction and strength of the earth's magnetic field is constantly changing. In the past, magnetic north has sometimes even pointed south. Scientists have worked out how the earth's magnetic field has changed in the past (in some parts of the world) by measuring the magnetism in samples already dated by other methods.

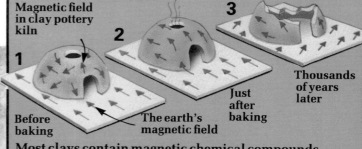

Magnetic field in clay pottery kiln

1 Before baking
The earth's magnetic field
2 Just after baking
3 Thousands of years later

Most clays contain magnetic chemical compounds called iron oxides, which are fixed in the direction of the earth's magnetic field when the clay is baked. This direction does not change as long as the clay is not moved after baking. By comparing the magnetic direction in baked clay with the dated positions of the earth's magnetic field in the past, the age is worked out.

Tree ring dating (dendrochronology)

It is possible to work out the age of wood by counting the growth rings. Each ring is one year's growth but the width of the rings varies with the weather. They are usually wider when the weather is good and narrower when the weather is bad.

Archaeologists look at the pattern of rings on a tree cut down at a known date and compare this with the pattern on a slightly older tree. They look for the point where the pattern matches and count backwards from there. They do the same thing with older and older timber until they build up a master pattern going back many centuries. You can see an imaginary master pattern for the last 44 years in the diagram to the right. The pattern of the rings on pieces of wood found on archaeological sites can then be compared with the master pattern to work out how old they are.

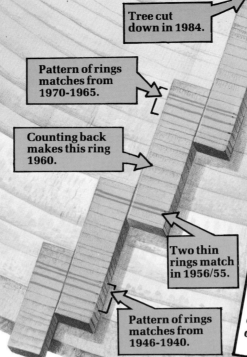

Tree cut down in 1984.

Pattern of rings matches from 1970-1965.

Counting back makes this ring 1960.

Two thin rings match in 1956/55.

Pattern of rings matches from 1946-1940.

Do your own dating

You can work out how old a tree is by counting the growth rings on a tree stump.

One year's growth

The rings are made from the cells that carry water round the tree.

If you rub a piece of sandpaper on the tree stump, it makes it easier to see the rings. Count the darker, more obvious rings, which mark the end of each year's growth. You could also measure the width of the rings to see how this varies from year to year and compare the ring patterns on different species of tree.

The pattern of rings

It has not been possible to work out one master tree ring pattern for the whole world because the pattern of rings depends on the species of tree and the environment it lives in. The technique works best where there are large, long-lived trees, such as the Bristlecone Pines in America. In one tree trunk scientists may be able to trace 6,000 years of tree rings.

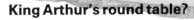

King Arthur's round table?

This round table from Winchester Castle, England, has King Arthur painted in the middle and the names of his knights around the edge. It was painted for King Henry VIII in 1522 but the table itself is much older than this. It is made of 121 separate pieces of oak and tree ring dating suggests it was made in about AD1250-1280. This is about 750 years after the legendary King Arthur is supposed to have lived.

Dating from written records

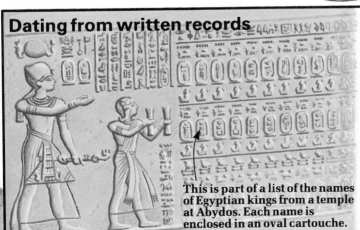

This is part of a list of the names of Egyptian kings from a temple at Abydos. Each name is enclosed in an oval cartouche.

Many ancient peoples took a close interest in astronomy and sometimes the records they made of the stars and planets help with dating. A few Egyptian records give the exact date (day, month and year of a king's reign) when the dog star (Sirius or Sothis) was first sighted just before dawn, after its annual disappearance for 70 days below the horizon. Archaeologists have been able to tie one of these dates in with our present dating system from a record of such a rising in AD139. This took place on the first day of the Egyptian year. The Egyptians used a calendar with 365 days in a year so archaeologists can work backwards through the king lists to fit our dates to the Egyptian records.

The Egyptian priests watched for the rising of the dog star to tell them the new year had begun.

Sometimes archaeologists are lucky enough to find written records to help with dating. They have worked out dates for ancient Egyptian history as far back as 3118BC from carvings and inscriptions listing the order of the kings and the number of years each one reigned for. This has been difficult because the years were counted from one again with each new ruler and, in times of trouble, some kings ruled at the same time as their rivals.

Turn over for radioactive dating

Radioactive dating

Across these two pages you can find out how archaeologists use radioactive chemical elements for dating. The elements may be in the plant or animal remains or pottery they find, or the rocks that objects are found with. Radioactive elements are unstable and tend to break down, giving off energy and radiation. Eventually they change into a different sort of element.

Scientists either measure how much of the original radioactive element is left or how much of the different element has formed. Because each element breaks down at a certain speed, they can work out how old the object is. The speed at which radioactive elements break down is usually measured as the half-life, which is the length of time it takes for half the element to break down. The half-lives of radioactive elements vary from seconds to millions of years.

The carbon 14 revolution

Carbon 14 dating caused a revolution when it was first used in the 1950s because it gave reasonably accurate dates for the kinds of remains that were found on digs all over the world. It could be used to date remains up to 40,000 years old. It is still an important dating technique today and some modern equipment can date remains up to 100,000 years old. But it is not quite as accurate as scientists originally thought and can easily be 'contaminated' by the inclusion of older or younger material.

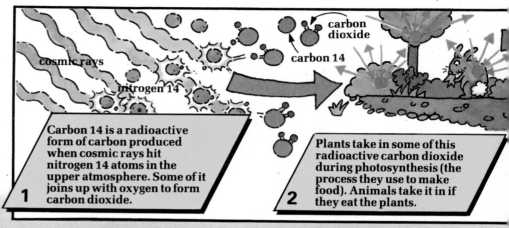

cosmic rays

nitrogen 14

carbon dioxide

carbon 14

1 Carbon 14 is a radioactive form of carbon produced when cosmic rays hit nitrogen 14 atoms in the upper atmosphere. Some of it joins up with oxygen to form carbon dioxide.

2 Plants take in some of this radioactive carbon dioxide during photosynthesis (the process they use to make food). Animals take it in if they eat the plants.

Tree rings change C14 dates

By dating ancient trees using both carbon 14 and tree ring dating, scientists found that the C14 dates were often hundreds of years too young. This is probably because the level of C14 in plants and animals has gone up and down slightly in the past and C14 dating assumes it stays the same. Scientists have worked out a graph to correct C14 dates, although it can only be used on remains up to 8,000 years old.

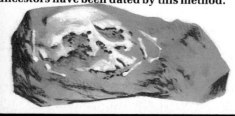

The rocks containing fossils of our earliest ancestors have been dated by this method.

Potassium-argon dating

This technique has been used to date the volcanic rocks that some objects are found in. It is based on the breakdown of a radioactive form of potassium (potassium 40) to form the gas argon 40. Potassium 40 has a half-life of 1.3 million years. In some volcanic rocks, all the argon 40 escapes when they are formed. Any argon 40 produced after this is trapped in the mineral crystals that make up the rocks. Scientists measure how much potassium 40 and argon 40 there is in a piece of rock to work out its age. Older rocks have less potassium 40 and more argon 40.

Fission track dating

Man-made glass, the minerals in pottery and volcanic substances, such as obsidian, can be dated by counting the microscopic tracks made during the breakdown (fission) of a radioactive form of uranium, called U238. Older samples have more tracks for a certain amount of uranium. Scientists know how fast U238 breaks down (it has a half-life of 4,510 million years) so they can work out how old the object is.

How much carbon 14 is there?

Most carbon 14 dating equipment counts the radioactive particles given off as carbon 14 breaks down. The count rate for modern carbon is 10-20 counts per minute and older carbon is less radioactive. As there is not much radioactivity, it takes at least 24 hours to date a sample.

More accurate equipment (first used in 1977), counts the number of carbon 14 atoms in a sample. This is quicker (most samples take only 15-45 minutes) and uses much smaller samples. It can also detect very small amounts of carbon 14, so can be used to date material up to 100,000 years old.

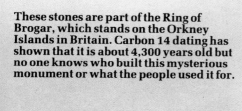

5 If plant and animal remains are preserved, scientists can measure how much of the original C14 is left in them. They know how long C14 takes to break down (it has a half-life of about 6,000 years) so they can work out how old the remains are.

3 As fast as plants and animals take in carbon 14 (often called C14), some of it breaks down. So the level of C14 inside them stays about the same.

4 When plants and animals die, the C14 continues to break down, but they are not taking in any more C14. So the level inside them slowly goes down.

These stones are part of the Ring of Brogar, which stands on the Orkney Islands in Britain. Carbon 14 dating has shown that it is about 4,300 years old but no one knows who built this mysterious monument or what the people used it for.

The age of ancient Europe

Before carbon 14 dating, archaeologists used to think that ideas and beliefs from the great civilisations of Egypt and Mesopotamia spread into western Europe. But carbon 14 dates have now shown that temples were built on Malta before 3000BC (before the great pyramids of Egypt) and some of the stone circles and tombs in western Europe are even older. Some were built about 4000BC and are the oldest monuments in the world.

Archaeologists once thought that these carvings were both the same age because the designs are very similar. But carbon 14 dates have shown that the carving on the left is 1,500 years older than the one on the right.

Spiral carvings from the Tarxien temples on Malta.

Funeral stone from Mycenae, S. Greece.

Using light energy for dating (thermoluminescence)

Scientists can date some objects, especially pottery, by measuring the light energy they give off when they are heated to very high temperatures. Older objects give off more light energy. Most of the energy comes from the breakdown of radioactive elements. This is trapped in the flaws in mineral crystals, such as the quartz crystals in pottery.

2 After firing, energy from the breakdown of radioactive elements is trapped in the pot and this builds up as the pot gets older.

3 When scientists heat the pot thousands of years later, all the trapped energy is released as light. By measuring this they can work out how long ago the pot was fired.

1 Pottery is fired at very high temperatures, which drives out any trapped energy and sets the time clock to zero.

The dates worked out using this technique are reasonably good and it is a useful method because it dates one of the most common objects archaeologists find – pottery. It also provides a date when people made the object, which is something other techniques cannot always do.

Preserving the past

It is very important to preserve ancient objects once they have been excavated so they do not decay any further. This is called conservation. Some objects are so fragile they have to be conserved on the dig itself but most of the conservation work is done in laboratories by scientists called conservators. They have to clean the objects, slow down or stop the chemical and biological processes of decay and protect them so the decay does not start up again. The methods they use depend on what the object is made of, where it was found and how badly it has decayed already.

Conservators also mend broken objects and fill in any missing pieces. They repair the objects so that it is obvious which parts they have added.

Emergency action

As soon as archaeologists opened a 10,000 year old tomb at Jericho in Palestine, all the wooden furniture started to crumble and turn into dust. They had to coat the furniture with wax straight away to seal it from the air and stop any further decay.

Conserving wood and leather

Organic materials (such as wood and leather) that have absorbed water, become soft and weak and should not be allowed to dry out until they can be properly treated. They may be put in tanks of water or wrapped in plastic to keep them damp and seal them from the air.

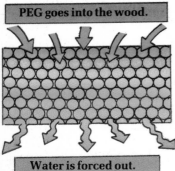

PEG goes into the wood.

Water is forced out.

Polyethylene Glycol (PEG) is often used to preserve wood and leather. It is a liquid wax that slowly replaces the water and then hardens, which strengthens the object. The hull of the Wasa (see page 11) has been sprayed with PEG since it was raised in 1961.

A much quicker way of preserving organic materials is the process used to prepare instant coffee, which is called freeze-drying. The object is first frozen and then placed in a vacuum chamber where the ice turns to gas and is drawn off over a period of weeks.

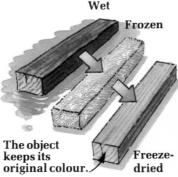

Wet

Frozen

The object keeps its original colour.

Freeze-dried

Backgammon board

Many of the wooden objects from the Mary Rose (see page 11) were preserved by freeze-drying.

Arrows

Beer tankard

Sun dial

Conserving metal

Most metals have decayed badly by the time they are unearthed. They react with oxygen to form metal oxides, such as iron oxide (rust), which breaks down the structure of the metal.

1 When this silver bowl was found, it was covered with black oxides.

2 An X-ray picture showed up the pattern of bulls' heads on the sides of the bowl.

3 The bowl was cleaned by spraying it with a jet of hard particles. The dirt and the particles were sucked out of the sealed cabinet.

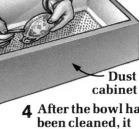

Jet spray

Dust cabinet

4 After the bowl had been cleaned, it was protected with a coat of polyester resin. It comes from Cyprus and is 3,500 years old.

A special oven

The iron guns from the Mary Rose were preserved by heating them in a special oven at 850°C (1,562°F). In the hydrogen atmosphere inside the oven, the iron oxides (rust) are converted to metallic iron. Some people think this changes the structure of the iron and is very bad for the metal.

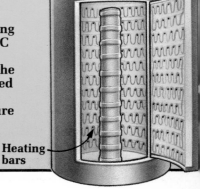

Heating bars

Fitting the pieces together

Pottery objects are often found smashed to pieces. Some of the pieces can be sorted into groups of the same type and then the pieces are matched together like a jigsaw to see if they are from the same pot. If they are, they are carefully stuck together with a special glue (that can be dissolved if any mistakes are made) and the missing sections are filled in with plaster.

The pieces are matched together and glued in position.

The missing sections are filled in with plaster.

The helmet of a king?

Many small fragments of an iron helmet were found in a burial mound at Sutton Hoo, England (see page 17). It may have belonged to the East Anglian King Raedwald. The fragments were carefully fitted together using similar helmets from Sweden as a guide.

The original fragments

The new parts added to make up the shape of the helmet.

Silver eyebrows with garnets along the edge.

Bronze animal heads covered with thin layer of gold.

Iron panel to protect the neck in battle.

Bronze nose, mouth and moustache covered with thin layer of gold.

Cheek pieces that could probably be tied under the chin.

Fakes

Some of the objects archaeologists uncover are very valuable and other people may make copies. Several scientific tests can help to prove if an object is genuine or a fake.

Dating tests

T'ang horse (AD618-906)

In the 1900s, the Chinese uncovered many pottery horses like this one, together with the original moulds that were used to make them. One of the moulds was stolen and copies were made but thermoluminescence dating (see page 25) was able to show which horses were fakes.

Using X-rays

X-rays of objects can help to show if they are fakes without damaging them. An X-ray of this statue of a cat showed that it had been filled with brass filings to make it as heavy as the original bronze statues, which were made in ancient Egypt. The fakes were made of resin.

Chemical tests

A technique called neutron activation analysis (NAA) can identify the chemicals present in a wide range of materials, such as flint, pottery and coins. It can be used to detect fakes because certain chemicals were not included in some materials (such as brass) before a certain date.

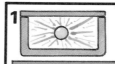

1 Neutrons hit object in metal box.

2 Chemicals in object give off radioactive rays.

3 Energy of rays identifies type of chemicals.

NAA can show tiny chemical differences between modern metals and old metals. The brass of astronomical dials like this one was shown to be identical to modern brass, so they were proved to be fakes.

Proving a theory

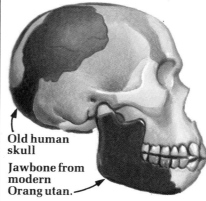

Some fakes may be made to prove a theory or perhaps even as a joke. This skull, found at Piltdown, Sussex, England was claimed for some years to be the "missing link" between modern humans and our ape-like ancestors.

Old human skull

Jawbone from modern Orang utan.

By measuring the amount of nitrogen in the bones (see page 22), scientists showed that the jawbone was not as old as the fragment of the skull. So the two bones could not possibly have come from the same skull. The jawbone had even been stained to make it look old.

Putting theories to the test

To improve their understanding of the past, archaeologists often do experiments to test the theories they have reached from the evidence they have found. They try to work out how and why objects were made, the number of people that might have been needed to make them and how well they might have worked. By making copies of equipment such as pots, tools and weapons and larger items such as boats and buildings, archaeologists can begin to appreciate the amount of work involved and get some idea of how important the objects were to their owners. The results of the experiments can only suggest that certain methods might have been used in the past, they can never prove which techniques were actually used.

Making Roman pots

At Barton-on-Humber in England, archaeologists built a Roman pottery kiln that matched the shape of the remains they had found and produced pottery that looked the same as that the Romans made.

After many experiments, they worked out this igloo design that looked correct and worked well.

The kiln holds about 100 pots.

Bricks for blocking chimney hole during firing.

Making flint tools

It takes great skill to make flint tools and may take years to get the technique absolutely right. Archaeologists often experiment on lumps of flint to see how tools were made and what they might have been used for.

Sharp blades made from this piece of flint.

Using a flint blade to cut up meat.

A face from the past

Techniques used by the police to identify murder victims from their remains have been used to reconstruct faces from ancient skulls. One of the most remarkable of these experiments was that carried out on the skull fragments found in a tomb at Vergina in Greece. This is believed by some people to be the tomb of King Philip of Macedon, father of Alexander the Great (see page 16).

Actual size

This ivory head was found in the tomb at Vergina. It matches other evidence of what Philip may have looked like.

1 Skull fragments were stuck together. Grey plaster was used to fill in the missing parts.

2 On a plaster cast of the skull, pegs were used to mark the position of the muscles.

3 Clay was used to add the muscles and build up the flesh over them.

4 A wax cast was made of the head, and skin colour, false hair and a beard were added. The skull fragments showed an injury to the right eye and Philip is known to have lost an eye in battle. The scar was based on a modern person with a similar injury.

A 2,000 year old recipe

In the 1950s, the contents of Tollund Man's stomach (see page 5) were analysed to see what he had for his last meal. A similar porridge of seeds and grain was made up for people to taste. They found it very bitter.

Testing weapons

To test how weapons were made and how well they worked, exact copies have been made based on the remains archaeologists have found.

A copy of a Roman ballista (a weapon that fired iron missiles) was made to test its range and speed. It was very powerful and could shoot missiles about 250 metres (820 feet).

An experimental farm

At Butser Hill in England, archaeologists have tried to recreate a working Iron Age farm of about 300BC. They are recording its development over many years to understand more about how people lived at that time.

Houses are based on excavated examples and the crops, sheep and cattle are related to prehistoric species. The experiments are recorded in great detail and the results checked with the archaeological evidence.

Fields are used for growing an Iron Age form of wheat called emmer wheat.

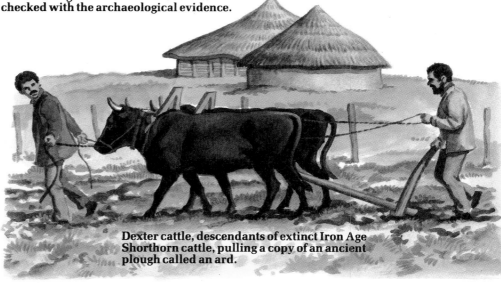

Frame of cedar and maple beams bound together with rope.

Walls thatched with grass.

Copying old houses

Archaeologists in Virginia, North America have built copies of Powhatan Indian houses using the same kind of tools, materials and techniques the Indians themselves used in the 17th century. From this experiment, they have worked out how long it took to build each house and how many people were probably involved.

Dexter cattle, descendants of extinct Iron Age Shorthorn cattle, pulling a copy of an ancient plough called an ard.

Discovering old trade routes

To test his ideas about the boats and trade routes of the Sumerians of Mesopotamia, the Norwegian explorer Thor Heyerdahl built a reed boat called Tigris based on ancient illustrations. He sailed it from the Persian Gulf to the Arabian Sea.

Iraq
Pakistan
Egypt
Route of Tigris

The experiment showed that the Sumerians could have sailed as far as India to set up trading colonies.

Sumerian boat engraved on a 4,000 year old seal. Boats like this are still used in parts of the Middle East.

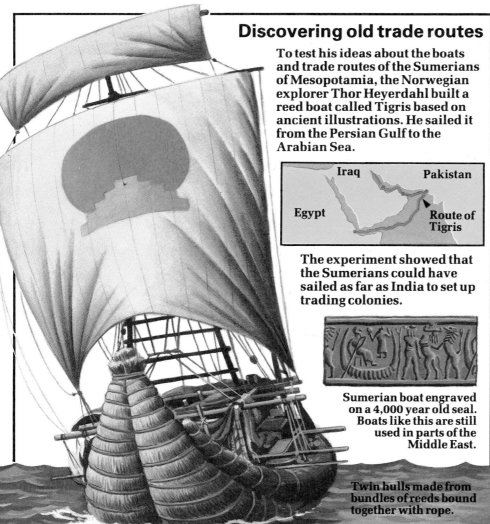

Twin hulls made from bundles of reeds bound together with rope.

Decaying ditches

To work out the original structures on a site, it is important for archaeologists to understand the processes of decay. At Wareham in England, earth mounds and ditches were built to exact measurements. Objects were buried in them and their positions recorded.

New earthworks in 1964

Same earthworks in 1972

The way the soil moves and changes in the positions of the objects can give a clearer understanding of excavated earthworks.

At Lejre in Denmark, copies of Iron Age buildings have been built, burnt down and then examined to see how the remains relate to the original structures.

The uses of pottery to the archaeologist

Large amounts of pottery, much of it broken into pieces (sherds), are usually found on most archaeological sites. This is because pottery has been used for thousands of years and has always been cheap and easy to replace. Although it breaks easily, it does not decay. Because of this, archaeologists can glean much useful information from it.

A check-list of points

Below is a list of the main points archaeologists look out for when they are examining the pottery found on a site.

1. How was it made (by hand, on a wheel or in a mould)?
2. Is the pottery rough or smooth?
3. What is the surface treatment: shiny (glazed, burnished), or matt (unglazed)?
4. Is it decorated or plain?
5. If there is decoration, is it painted, cut into the clay or raised above the surface?
6. If painted, what is the design?
7. If painted, what colour and how many?
8. If the decoration is cut into the clay, what is the design?
9. If the decoration is raised, what is the design?
10. Where is the decoration (inside, outside, both)?

Archaeologists use the answers to these questions to work out the types and dates of the pottery. With these, they should be able to date the site itself.

Description of the pots

Below are descriptions of the pots shown here, not in order.

Wheel-made. Smooth surface. Unglazed. Painted. Leaf-pattern. Red-brown on pink. Inside. **Nabataean** (Jordan, 100-50BC).

Hand-made. Rough surface. Unglazed. Decoration cut in. Line and dot. Outside. **Beaker** (Europe, 2000BC).

Hand-made. Smooth surface. Unglazed. Painted. Geometric. Red/cream. Outside/inside. **Hacilar** (Turkey, 5000BC).

Hand-made. Smooth surface. Unglazed. Painted. Multi-coloured. Outside. **Nazca** (Peru, AD400-500).

Mould-made. Smooth surface. Burnished. Unglazed. Raised decoration. Outside. **Samian** (Roman, 100BC-AD300).

Wheel-made. Smooth surface. Burnished. Painted. Figure on dark ground. Outside. **Attic red-figure** (Greece, 530-400BC).

The names of these pots are on page 32.

The names of these pots are on page 32.

Try-it-yourself

Check-List	
How was it made?	On a Wheel
What is the surface like?	Smooth
What is the surface treatment?	Unglazed
Decoration?	Painted
Design of decoration?	Leaf-pattern
Colour of decoration?	Red-Brown
Where is the decoration?	Inside
Name of pot?	?

Using the check-list, see if you can work out the names of the different pots, in their correct order.

Glossary

Amphora. Storage jar with narrow mouth and two handles.

Artefact. Any object made by humans.

Assyria. Three different empires dating from about 2000 to 600BC.

Aztecs. People who lived in Mexico and built a magnificent capital at Tenochtitlan. Conquered by the Spaniards in AD1521.

Babylon. Ancient capital in Mesopotamia. King Hammurabi made it the capital of his empire in about 1792BC.

Beaker People. Lived in Europe from about 2000 BC.

Bronze Age. Period from about 1800-700BC when bronze was the main material used for tools and weapons.

Cartouche. Oval frame used to enclose and protect Egyptian hieroglyphs of royal names.

Celts. Fierce, warrior race of Europe. In Britain, they were defeated by the Romans in AD43.

Conquistadors. Spanish conquerors of Central and South American Indians in the 16th century AD.

Cultures. Different groups of people and ways of life.

Cuneiform. Wedge-shaped writing on clay invented in Mesopotamia and used from about 3500-500BC.

Domesticated animals and plants. Bred and used by people for work and food.

Element. A substance that cannot be broken down any further. It joins with other elements to form a compound.

Etruscans. People who lived in north and central Italy from about 1000BC.

Glaze. Shiny, glass-like surface on some pottery.

Gothic. Medieval style of architecture with pointed arches, dating from about AD1200.

Henge. Circular area of religious significance found only in the British Isles.

Hieroglyphs. One of the earliest forms of writing in pictures introduced in Egypt in about 3000BC.

Homer. Greek writer who lived in about 700BC and wrote the Illiad (about the Trojan War) and the Odyssey.

Iron Age. Period from about 700-30BC in Europe, and earlier in Middle East, when iron was used for tools and weapons.

Khmer. Empire with capital at Angkor in Kampuchea. Destroyed by the Thais in about AD1400.

Maya. People who lived in the Yucatan peninsula and Belize, Central America. Conquered by the Spaniards in AD1541.

Mesopotamia. Means "land between the two rivers", the area between the Tigris and Euphrates rivers in Iraq.

Mineral. A natural, inorganic substance found in the earth.

Mohenjo-daro. One of the two capitals of the Indus Civilization, dating from about 3000-1700BC.

Mycenaeans. Inhabitants of Mycenae, southern Greece. Height of the civilization was in about 1400BC.

Nabataeans. Rich merchant people based at their capital of Petra in Jordan in the 1st century BC.

Normans. Vikings who settled in France. In AD1066, their leader, William of Normandy, conquered England.

Organic Material. Anything made from substances that once lived, such as wood, leather and bone.

Phoenicians. Lived in the coastal area of the Lebanon and Syria from about 1000BC. Main cities of Tyre, Sidon and Byblos.

Pithos. Large pottery storage jar for oil or grain.

Prehistory. Earliest period before any written records.

Sarcophagus. Large stone container for a human body.

Saxons. People from Germany who settled in England in the 5th century AD.

Scythians. People without permanent homes (nomads) who lived in central Asia from about 750-300BC.

Sherd (Potsherd). Piece of broken pottery.

Stone Age. Period up to the Bronze Age when metals were unknown and tools were made of stone, wood, bone or antler.

Sumer. Area of southern Mesopotamia where people first lived in cities about 3500BC.

Tollund Man. Preserved body of Iron Age man found in peat at Tollund Fen in Denmark. He had been hanged.

Vikings. Inhabitants of Scandinavia from about AD700-1100. Settled all over Europe.

Ziggurat. A rectangular, stepped mound, (with a temple at the top), built by the Sumerians.

Books to read

Children's Encyclopedia of History by A. Millard and P. Vanags (Usborne)
Pocket Handbook to the Ancient World by A. Millard (Usborne)
Discovering Archaeology by I. Barry (Longman)
The Young Archaeologist's Handbook by L. and J. Laing (Piccolo)
Reconstructing the Past by K. Branigan (Hodder and Stoughton)
Introducing Archaeology by M. Magnusson (Bodley Head)
The Archaeology of Ships by P. Johnstone (Bodley Head)
The Penguin Dictionary of Archaeology by W. Bray and D. Trump (Penguin)
A Dictionary of Terms and Techniques in Archaeology by S. Champion (Phaidon)
Archaeology, an Introduction by K. Greene (Batsford)

The World Atlas of Treasure by D. Wilson (Pan)
The Mary Rose by M. Rule (Windward)
Tutankhamun by C. Desroches-Noblecourt (Penguin)
The Bog People by P. V. Glob (Faber)
The Sutton Hoo Ship Burial by Rupert Bruce-Mitford (British Museum)
Voices in Stone by E. Doblhofer (Granada)

Magazines to read

Yesterday's World
3a New Street, Ledbury, Herefordshire, England.
Current Archaeology,
9, Nassington Road, London, NW3, England.
National Geographic,
Post Office Box 19, Guildford, Surrey, GU2 6AD, England or 17th and M Sts. N.W., Washington, D.C. 20036, U.S.A.

Useful Addresses

Your local museum should be able to tell you what to look for in your area and whether there are any excavations you can help on. For more information, look in your local library and write to the addresses below.

Young Archaeologists' Club
Clifford Chambers, 4 Clifford Street, York, YO1 1RD, England. (This is a national club for 9-16 year olds, which organizes activities, competitions and holidays and publishes a magazine with information about excavations to visit or work on.)
Council for British Archaeology
112, Kennington Road, London SE11 6RE, England.
Society for American Archaeology
1511 K Street, N.W., Suite 716, Washington, D.C. 20005, U.S.A.

Index

First published in 1984 by
Usborne Publishing Ltd,
Usborne House, 83-85 Saffron
Hill, London, EC1N 8RT.
Copyright © 1991, 1984
Usborne Publishing

Names of pots on p.30

From top to bottom:
Hacilar, Attic Red-figure,
Beaker, Nazca,
Nabataean, Samian.

THE USBORNE YOUNG SCIENTIST
EVOLUTION

Barbara Cork and Lynn Bresler

Designed by Sue Mims

Consultants Mark Ridley
Anne Hollifield and Gail Vines

Contents

Illustrated by
Chris Lyon, Martin Newton, Bernard Robinson, Chris Shields, Sue Stitt
Christina McInerney, Patti Pearce, Ian Jackson, Jan Nesbitt,
David Webb, Peter Bull, Alan Harris, Phil Weare, Brenda Haw

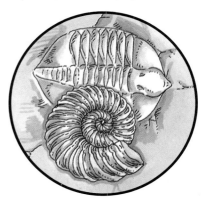

The question of life on Earth

How and when did life begin on our planet? Why is there such an incredible variety of plants and animals living on the Earth today? How did living things come to be suited to their particular way of life? Many people believe that the answer to these questions is that life on Earth developed by a process called evolution. Most scientists believe this is the best explanation for the variety of life today, using the evidence from fossils (the preserved remains of plants and animals) and from studying how plants and animals live today.

The variety of life on Earth

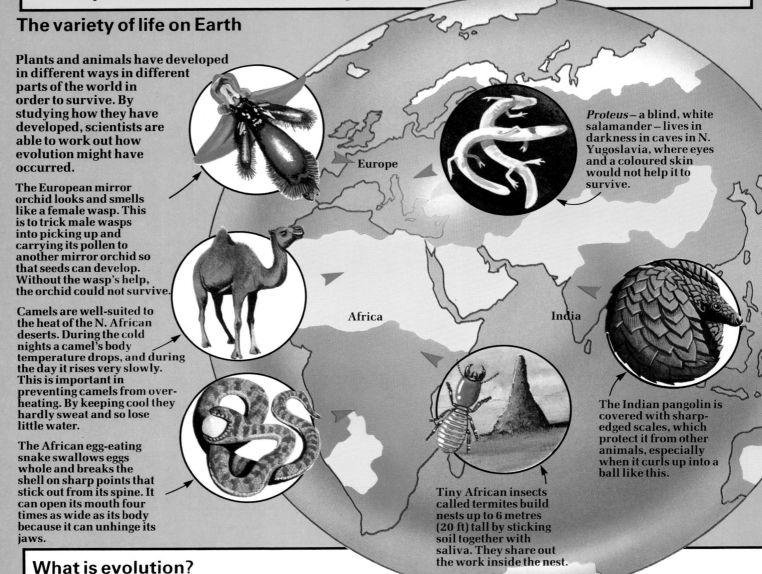

Plants and animals have developed in different ways in different parts of the world in order to survive. By studying how they have developed, scientists are able to work out how evolution might have occurred.

The European mirror orchid looks and smells like a female wasp. This is to trick male wasps into picking up and carrying its pollen to another mirror orchid so that seeds can develop. Without the wasp's help, the orchid could not survive.

Camels are well-suited to the heat of the N. African deserts. During the cold nights a camel's body temperature drops, and during the day it rises very slowly. This is important in preventing camels from over-heating. By keeping cool they hardly sweat and so lose little water.

The African egg-eating snake swallows eggs whole and breaks the shell on sharp points that stick out from its spine. It can open its mouth four times as wide as its body because it can unhinge its jaws.

Europe

Africa

India

Proteus – a blind, white salamander – lives in darkness in caves in N. Yugoslavia, where eyes and a coloured skin would not help it to survive.

The Indian pangolin is covered with sharp-edged scales, which protect it from other animals, especially when it curls up into a ball like this.

Tiny African insects called termites build nests up to 6 metres (20 ft) tall by sticking soil together with saliva. They share out the work inside the nest.

What is evolution?

The theory of evolution explains how plants and animals have gradually changed into new, different kinds of plants and animals over long periods of time. Many different processes are involved in evolution, and this book is designed to show how they all fit together.

DNA

The most important of the processes are:
The chemical code of instructions (called DNA), which is inside every living thing. If mistakes are made to the code, new life forms might evolve. You can read about DNA and how it works on pages 10-13.

The environment (surroundings) in which plants and animals live can affect their chances of survival, which can also lead to change. This is called natural selection, which you can read about on pages 6-7.

   Fossil remains

Looking at rocks and fossils (see pages 20-21) has also helped towards understanding how evolution works, because they provide a record of extinct forms of life, as shown on pages 22-25.

Religious beliefs

All religious beliefs are a matter of faith and cannot be tested scientifically. In some religions (such as the Jewish faith, Christianity, Islam and parts of the Hindu faith), it is believed that a God created all living things and directs their development.

Other religious beliefs (such as Jainism, Buddhism and some Chinese religions) involve a world that is without beginning or end. You can learn more about these different beliefs on the next page.

The Biblical creation story in Genesis is interpreted in different ways, some of which you can read about on page 17. On the same page, you can also see some of the ideas early peoples had about how the Earth was created and developed.

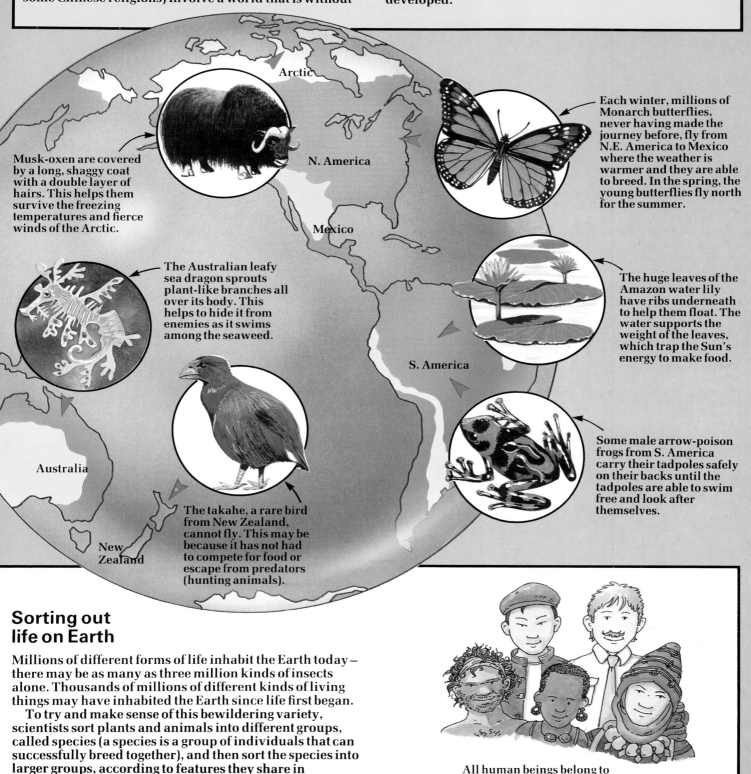

Musk-oxen are covered by a long, shaggy coat with a double layer of hairs. This helps them survive the freezing temperatures and fierce winds of the Arctic.

Arctic

N. America

Mexico

Each winter, millions of Monarch butterflies, never having made the journey before, fly from N.E. America to Mexico where the weather is warmer and they are able to breed. In the spring, the young butterflies fly north for the summer.

The Australian leafy sea dragon sprouts plant-like branches all over its body. This helps to hide it from enemies as it swims among the seaweed.

The huge leaves of the Amazon water lily have ribs underneath to help them float. The water supports the weight of the leaves, which trap the Sun's energy to make food.

S. America

Australia

The takahe, a rare bird from New Zealand, cannot fly. This may be because it has not had to compete for food or escape from predators (hunting animals).

New Zealand

Some male arrow-poison frogs from S. America carry their tadpoles safely on their backs until the tadpoles are able to swim free and look after themselves.

Sorting out life on Earth

Millions of different forms of life inhabit the Earth today – there may be as many as three million kinds of insects alone. Thousands of millions of different kinds of living things may have inhabited the Earth since life first began.

To try and make sense of this bewildering variety, scientists sort plants and animals into different groups, called species (a species is a group of individuals that can successfully breed together), and then sort the species into larger groups, according to features they share in common. This sorting is called classification, and you can read more about it on page 16.

All human beings belong to one species, even though they all look very different.

Thinking about evolution . . .

Across these two pages, you can trace the history of the most important ideas about the origin and diversity of life on Earth. You can see how religious and philosophical ideas of a perfect and unchanging world began to be challenged by scientists from the 16th century onwards. This led to Darwin's theory in the 19th century and to 20th century discoveries in genetics.

Creation myths and religion

The creation myths, dating from about 3000BC, are the earliest written ideas about the origin of the world. A popular idea of the Ancient Egyptians was that the sun god, Re, created the world from a dark, watery chaos. A myth from Mesopotamia tells of a god creating the universe from the body of a dead monster.

There are two accounts of the creation of the world in the Book of Genesis in the Bible, both written more than 500 years BC. The first describes how God created the world in six days; the second concerns the creation of human beings from the first man and woman – Adam and Eve.

18th century

In the 18th century, many people thought that God directed the natural processes that shaped the Earth. Scientific discoveries suggested the Earth was much older than Biblical estimates. Explorers found a huge variety of species not mentioned in the Bible and the discovery of fossils that were unlike any modern forms suggested that God had allowed some of his creatures to become extinct (die out).

Buffon worked out the age of the Earth as at least 168,000 or even half a million years old. He did not believe in evolution, but brought the idea into science by discussing problems such as extinction and how species form.

Linnaeus developed a system of classifying living things, which he thought revealed the order of God's design.

A 17th century scientist

19th century

At the beginning of the 19th century, Lamarck put forward the first theory of evolution, which most people did not accept. They believed in the unchanging, recently created world of the Bible or in a world of natural laws created and controlled by God. In 1859, Darwin published his theory of natural selection, which became the basis for the modern theory of evolution.

This plaice is suited to its environment, the seabed.

Paley suggested that living things were so well suited to their environment, they must have been designed by an intelligent creator.

Cuvier believed in an original creation which was wiped out from time to time by catastrophes in different parts of the world. After each catastrophe, plants and animals from nearby areas filled the gaps.

Lamarck believed living things had evolved gradually from the simplest to the most complex. He suggested that in each generation living things could change their characteristics to cope with the environment, and pass these changes on to their offspring.

In the 1820s and 30s, geologists argued about whether God controlled natural processes. Some thought the fossil evidence showed gradual change through time, others believed in separate creations throughout time, with species becoming extinct and being replaced by new ones.

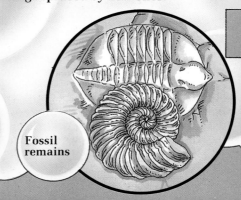

Fossil remains

4

Jainism and Buddhism began about 600BC, and teach that the world has no beginning or end and is ruled by vital energy forces.

Islam began in Mecca about AD600 and its followers believe one God made heaven and earth and human beings.

Hinduism developed about 5,000 years ago. Most Hindus believe the world was created by one or more gods.

Ancient Greeks

The early Greek philosophers were the first to suggest that the world was created and controlled by natural processes and chance rather than by a God. They also believed in a perfect world which stayed the same through all time. So they were interested in the beginning of things but not change or evolution afterwards.

Plato (left) and Aristotle (right)

Their ideas, especially those of Plato and Aristotle, lasted for nearly 2,000 years.

According to Plato, the only things that really existed were "forms", which were fixed forever.

Plato's pupil, Aristotle, was the first to observe a system in nature. He arranged living things according to their degree of "perfection" in a Ladder of Nature. God was at the top and humans were half way down.

17th century

In the 17th century, telescopes revealed that Space seemed to have no limits and early microscopes showed tiny creatures with amazing and complex structures. There was a widespread belief that microscopic creatures could be created from non-living matter. But scientists still tried to make their discoveries fit with the Bible.

16th century

In the 16th century, people began to question religious beliefs. They rediscovered the works of the Greeks, explorers found strange new animals and plants and the first scientific discoveries were made.

A new plant discovery

Middle Ages

In Europe during this period, people believed the world had been created recently by God. Plants and animals had been put into the world to serve people. There was more interest in the purpose and will of God than the study of nature. But Islamic philosophers, such as Averroes, suggested a world in which creation continually took place.

Charles Darwin

Charles Darwin also believed in evolution from simple to more complex creatures, but by natural selection (that is, those individuals best adapted to their environment survive to pass on their characteristics), rather than by the actions of God. Alfred Russel Wallace came up with the same idea.

20th century

Early in the 20th century, discoveries in genetics (how characteristics are controlled and passed on) at first seemed to discredit Darwins's ideas. However, by the 1920s a new "synthetic" theory had been worked out, which brought together genetics, mathematical predictions and an updated version of Darwin's natural selection theory. In the 1950s the structure of the chemical in the genes (DNA) was discovered and by the 1960s the code of instruction carried by DNA was worked out (see pages 10-11). These discoveries led scientists in the 1970s and 80s to think of natural selection as working at the gene level, the most successful genes being those that had the most copies of themselves in the population.

Some people do not believe in evolution. Creationists believe God created every species, each of which has not evolved or died out.

Researchers are still trying to answer questions such as: How did life begin? Does life evolve by gradual or sudden changes, or both? How important is chance in evolution? How do genes control the way living things develop, function and behave?

5

Darwin's theory of natural selection

Charles Darwin put forward his theory of natural selection to explain how evolution could have happened. He realized that plants and animals must be able to pass on their characteristics to their offspring, although he knew nothing about how inheritance[1] works. He thought that the variety between individual members of a species[2] would mean that some members would be better adapted than others to their particular environment, and would be more likely to survive and pass on their helpful characteristics.

However, natural selection does not automatically lead to change. A well-adapted population may stay the same because the most typical individuals are more likely to survive and pass on their characteristics. Natural selection may also keep variety in a population, as a characteristic that is harmful in one situation may be useful in another. Some situations are so complex that other factors, which are not yet understood, may be involved.

Darwin's ideas

1. *Most species produce far more offspring than could possibly survive.* One pair of mice could produce about 40 babies a year and these babies could have offspring of their own after only six weeks. Imagine what would happen if all those mice survived and kept breeding . . .

2. *An individual's chances of survival will be affected by the environment in which it lives.* The environment includes the weather, finding food and a mate, finding somewhere to live, and other animals and plants.

Which mice are more likely to be caught by the owl?

3. *Individuals vary. Some will be better adapted than others to their environment and will stand a better chance of surviving.* Darwin did not know what caused variation – we now know it is caused by mutations and the mixing up of genes during sexual reproduction (see pages 10-13).

The dark-coloured mice stand more chance of surviving to pass on their genes.

4. *If the better-adapted individuals survive long enough to reproduce . . . and if they pass the characteristics that helped them to survive on to their offspring . . . their offspring will also stand a better chance of surviving.* This idea is sometimes called the "survival of the fittest".

Eventually there are more dark-coloured mice than light-coloured mice.

Evidence of natural selection

. . . in S. America   . . . in Africa

Termite nest
Aardvark
Anteater

Both these animals feed on ants and termites. They have strong front legs and claws to dig into the nest, and long noses and sticky tongues to find the insects and lick them up.

Darwin knew that plants and animals that live in similar surroundings look similar and cope with surviving in a similar way (as shown above). He saw this as evidence of adaptation to the environment by natural selection.

An amazing example is the 110 breeds of dog that people have developed from the wolf over 14,000 years. All dogs are still one species though, and can usually breed together.

Darwin found further evidence to support his theory from looking at domesticated plants and animals. People have deliberately changed these by breeding together specially chosen individuals. This is called artificial selection, and shows how the characteristics of plants and animals can be changed over many generations.

1. See page 12 for how inheritance works.
2. See pages 14-16 to find out more about species.

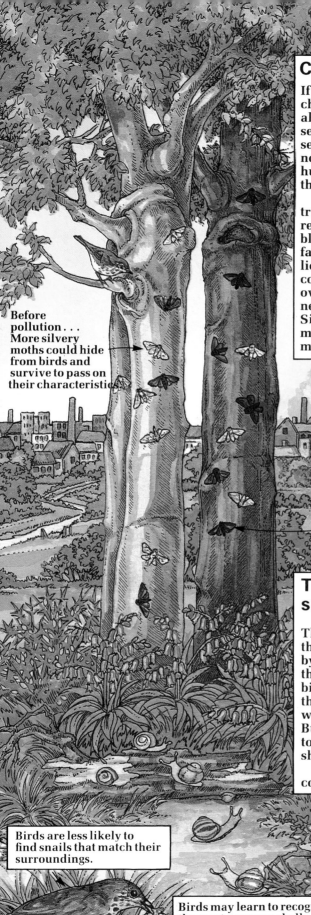

Changing with the times

If the surroundings change, the characteristics of a population may also change as a result of natural selection. This is called directional selection, and the most obvious cases nowadays are caused by the actions of humans. One example is the case of the peppered moths.

In 19th-century Britain, the tree trunks on which peppered moths rested during the day became blackened when pollution from the factories killed off the light-coloured lichens covering the trees. But the colour of the moths' wings changed over the generations to match their new surroundings, as you can see here. Since pollution was reduced in the mid-1950s, the proportion of silvery moths has gradually increased.

Before pollution...
More silvery moths could hide from birds and survive to pass on their characteristics.

After pollution...
More black moths could hide from birds and survive to pass on their characteristics.

The puzzle of the banded snails

The different colours and patterns on the shells of banded snails are affected by the colour of their surroundings, the climate and the behaviour of the birds that eat them. One or more of these natural factors may "select" which snails survive in any one place. But in some places there doesn't seem to be any reason for the huge variety in shell colour and pattern.

This example shows how complicated natural selection is.

Birds are less likely to find snails that match their surroundings.

Birds may learn to recognize the most common shell pattern as their usual food. So out-of-the-ordinary snails are more likely to survive.

Light-shelled snails reflect heat, so survive better in hot places.

Dark-shelled snails absorb more heat, so survive better in cold conditions.

Working in different ways

Sometimes natural selection allows a number of different forms of the same species to exist in a population at the same time.

Male

Male mocker swallowtail butterflies all look the same (probably to help females recognize them during courtship).

Female

Disguised females

But there are at least four types of female. One looks like the male. The others each look like a different species of butterfly which taste unpleasant. The three disguises above probably help to protect the females from being eaten by birds while they mate and lay their eggs. The male does not need this sort of protection.

More about Darwin's ideas

According to the theory of natural selection, animals should evolve features that help them to survive and reproduce. So why does the peacock have such a ridiculous tail? . . . and why do deer have antlers? Darwin argued that features such as these probably evolved to help animals compete for a mate.

Sexual selection

Darwin called his idea sexual selection. The features that helped to win a mate would be passed on from generation to generation, with other animals doing the "selecting" instead of the environment.

Sexual selection mostly works in two ways: competition and choice. In some species, males have to compete with each other to win females; in other species, females seem to choose which male they will mate with, as shown in the pictures on this page.

Animal behaviour

The way in which animals behave affects their chances of survival. Why, therefore, do some animals seem to help others, sometimes at their own expense? According to the theory of natural selection, their helpful behaviour is less likely to be passed on, because animals that help others reduce their own chances of survival.

The answer may be that they are really behaving selfishly by helping their relatives, and so making sure that some of their own offspring or relatives survive to pass on their characteristics. They may also know that they are likely to be paid back later. Or they may be gaining food, experience and protection while they wait for the chance to set up on their own.

How males compete for a mate

Males compete either to gain areas to which females are attracted (such as good places to breed or nest, or where there is plenty of food), or to win direct possession of the females themselves.

Males often try to frighten each other away just by using threatening behaviour. If they do fight, they risk injury or even loss of the females to a third male.

In some species, such as dung flies, the male guards the female after mating, to make sure it is his sperm which fertilizes her eggs. His behaviour prevents other males from mating with her until she has laid her eggs.

Male dung fly holding on to a female. He is kicking out to prevent another male from mating with her.

How females choose a mate

Where females do the selecting, the males have developed various means of making themselves more attractive. Here are some examples.

Leaves stripped off branch

▶ Some birds, such as this blue bird of paradise, use their amazing feathers in spectacular displays to attract females. They even strip the leaves and twigs off the branches, so the females will get a better view.

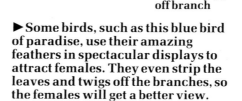

Scorpion fly

◀ Male scorpion flies give their females food (usually an insect) during courtship. Females choose to mate with the males that give them larger-sized insects. They use the protein from their insect gift to lay more eggs.

▶ These small flies, called drosophila, go through a rapid courtship dance before mating. Females are more likely to mate with males that can keep up with them during the last part of this dance. This probably allows them to choose the fittest males as mates.

Drosophila

◀ Male African weaverbirds build nests by weaving strips of leaves into a big hollow ball. Females are more attracted to males with freshly-built green nests than to those with old brown nests.

A newly-built nest

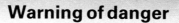

Give and take

Some animals receive help in return for the help they give others (called mutualism or symbiosis). Such animals are more likely to survive together and pass on their helpful behaviour.

For example, cleaner fish pick the parasites off the surface of larger fish. The large fish benefit by getting rid of their parasites and the cleaner fish get a reliable supply of food. Here a wrasse is cleaning a goatfish.

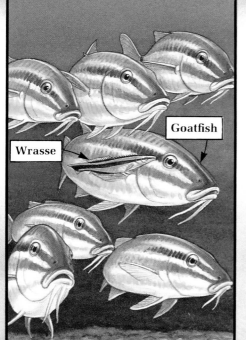

Goatfish

Wrasse

Warning of danger

Some birds and mammals give alarm calls or warning signals if they are in danger. They may be risking their lives to save their fellows. Or they may have selfish reasons for behaving like this.

Springboks leap up and down in this strange way if they spot danger. They may be warning other members of the herd, so that all the herd can escape. Or they may be saying, "Look how fit I am, go after someone else."

How lions help each other

Lions have a complex social life, in which males and females sometimes seem to help each other at their own expense.

The male lions are often related, and help each other to win and defend a pride of lionesses. To avoid injury, or perhaps simply to help a relative, one male may let another mate with a lioness without putting up a fight.

The lionesses are usually related to each other (but not to the males). They help each other to hunt and to look after the cubs. Sharing out the work may help them to survive.

If new males take over the group, they often kill the cubs. The lionesses do not stop them; they may gain more from having cubs with the new males, than by trying to save existing cubs.

The chemical code of life

Darwin worked out his theory of natural selection without knowing how plants and animals are able to produce offspring that are like themselves. He did not know about the chemical code of instructions, called DNA, which is inside the cells of every living thing. But are the offspring exactly the same as their parents? You can begin to see how plants and animals might change and evolve over a long period of time, if you understand how they can change from one generation to the next.

The DNA code of instructions controls the way plants and animals look and the way their bodies work. When plants and animals reproduce, a copy of the instructions is passed on from parents to their offspring. Sometimes these instructions are mixed up, or the code isn't copied exactly, which can lead to change.

Where is the DNA?

All living things are made up of cells. Inside each cell is a nucleus, and inside the nucleus are structures called chromosomes. Each chromosome is made up of sections of DNA, called genes, which instruct the cell what to do. Apart from a few viruses, all living things use DNA, which suggest that all life on Earth might have evolved from the same source.

You are different from a fly or a buttercup because your basic set of instructions, or code, is different from theirs. Different Species can also have different numbers of chromosomes: for example, you have 46, a horse has 63 and some butterflies have 400.

All living things have DNA.

All the cells in a plant or animal contain the full DNA code for that species. But each cell only uses the parts of the code it needs for the job it has to do. It is not yet understood exactly how this process works.

Copying the code

New cells are needed all the time— about 500 million of your body cells die each day and have to be replaced. Every time a new cell is made, the DNA is copied, so that when the cell divides, each of the two new cells has its own copy of the code.

1. The two DNA strands separate.

2. Spare bases are always present and these join up with their matching pairs on the separated strands.

3. Two new strands are formed.

Spare base

How does the code work

The code spells out different words which are built up into sentences. Each sentence is a gene. There are also codes for stop and start. You can see how this works below.

1. DNA consists of two thin strands wound round each other like a spiral staircase.

2. The steps of the staircase are made up of four chemical building blocks (called bases), which are linked in pairs.

3. The bases can only pair up in a certain way: adenine (letter A) with thymine (T): and guanine (G) with cytosine (C).

4. The bases are like a four-letter alphabet and the letters are read in groups of three. Each group of three letters forms a word.

What does the code do?

The code tells the cell to produce different proteins, which control how your body grows and develops. Your body contains at least 10,000 kinds of proteins.

Proteins are made up of chains of substances called amino acids. Each word codes for a particular type of amino acid. The amino acids are then arranged in the order of the words in each gene. There may be hundreds or thousands of amino acids in each protein chain.

Passing on the code

Once the DNA has been copied, the cell is ready to divide and pass on the code. There are two kinds of cell division.

1 The process that creates new cells when you grow, and replaces worn-out cells, is called mitosis. After the DNA has been copied, the cell divides, and the two new cells look the same as the original cell – they each have the same number of chromosomes (which carry the DNA). Only two chromosomes are shown here, to make it easier to understand.

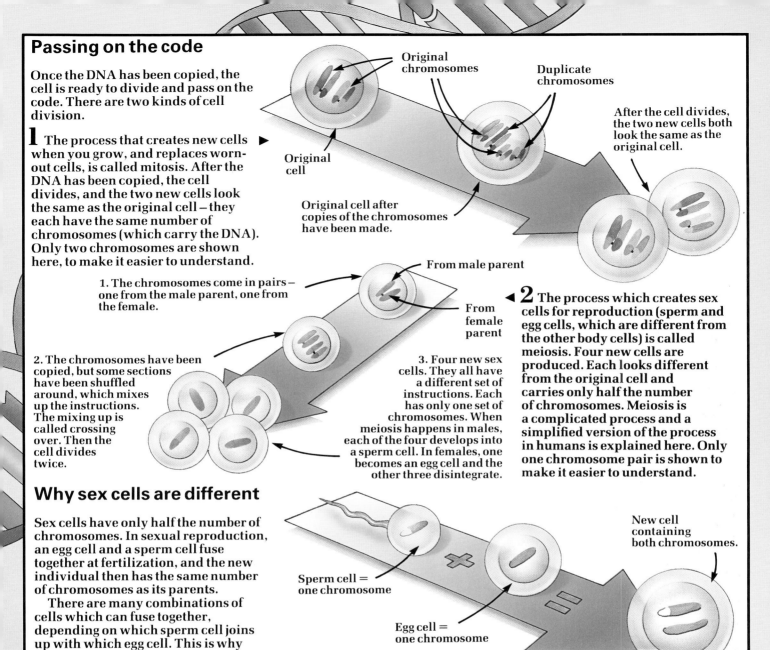

Original chromosomes

Duplicate chromosomes

Original cell

After the cell divides, the two new cells both look the same as the original cell.

Original cell after copies of the chromosomes have been made.

From male parent

From female parent

1. The chromosomes come in pairs – one from the male parent, one from the female.

2. The chromosomes have been copied, but some sections have been shuffled around, which mixes up the instructions. The mixing up is called crossing over. Then the cell divides twice.

3. Four new sex cells. They all have a different set of instructions. Each has only one set of chromosomes. When meiosis happens in males, each of the four develops into a sperm cell. In females, one becomes an egg cell and the other three disintegrate.

2 The process which creates sex cells for reproduction (sperm and egg cells, which are different from the other body cells) is called meiosis. Four new cells are produced. Each looks different from the original cell and carries only half the number of chromosomes. Meiosis is a complicated process and a simplified version of the process in humans is explained here. Only one chromosome pair is shown to make it easier to understand.

Why sex cells are different

Sex cells have only half the number of chromosomes. In sexual reproduction, an egg cell and a sperm cell fuse together at fertilization, and the new individual then has the same number of chromosomes as its parents.

There are many combinations of cells which can fuse together, depending on which sperm cell joins up with which egg cell. This is why there is variety between different members of the same species.

Sperm cell = one chromosome

Egg cell = one chromosome

New cell containing both chromosomes.

Making mistakes – mutations

This white tigress is an example of a mutation – she has no gene to make coloured stripes.

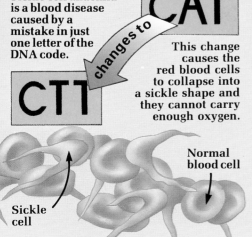

Sickle cell anaemia is a blood disease caused by a mistake in just one letter of the DNA code.

CTT changes to CAT

This change causes the red blood cells to collapse into a sickle shape and they cannot carry enough oxygen.

Sickle cell

Normal blood cell

Mistakes (called mutations) sometimes happen to the code. The bases in the DNA might not be copied exactly, or something might go wrong during crossing over in meiosis (see above). The mutation might have the effect that a different protein is made, which could alter the characteristics of its bearer. If mutations occur in the sex cells, they will be passed on and could provide the raw material for the evolution of new species over time.

Most mutations have only a slight effect, or even none at all, if the change does not alter the protein instruction. But some changes can be harmful, or even lethal, because they upset a life process.

Turn over to see how the genes work

The chemical code in action

When plants and animals reproduce, they pass on their genetic code of instructions (including any change to the code) to their offspring. This is called inheritance. A minority of plants and animals inherit an exact copy of the instructions from just one parent and all the offspring have identical sets of genes (called asexual reproduction). The majority inherit a mixture of the genetic instructions from two parents (called sexual reproduction, see page 11), and each offspring has a slightly different set of genes.

The way in which plants and animals then develop depends partly on their inheritance and partly on the conditions in which they live (their environment). The environment affects the way plants and animals grow up, but it does not affect the DNA code.

The different genes which make up the code control your "characteristics", that is, the way you look, how your body works and how you behave. The way genes do this is very complex and is not yet fully understood. But you can find out how some genes work on the page opposite.

The theory of inheritance

During the last century, Gregor Mendel experimented with breeding pea plants to discover how characteristics such as height, seed shape and flower colour were inherited. He kept careful records of the plants he used and the sort of offspring they produced. After many years he worked out his theory of inheritance. Mendel first published his work in 1866, but the significance of his results and ideas was not recognized for nearly 40 years.

Mendel knew nothing about DNA, but his theory – which applies to all living things, including humans – has formed the basis of all studies in genetics. This example of his theory uses the flower colour of peas.

1 For each characteristic, at least one gene is inherited from each parent.

2 Each gene exists in two forms – dominant and recessive. Either one or the other form is inherited from each parent.

3 For each characteristic, the dominant form will appear in the offspring, unless two recessive genes are inherited.

4 The way dominant or recessive genes are inherited depends largely on chance. Mendel worked out that, on average, ¾ inherit at least one dominant gene, and ¼ inherit two recessive genes.

Parent plant with only purple genes

Parent plant with only white genes

Parent plants each have one purple gene and one white gene.

Purple is the dominant gene, white is the recessive gene. All offspring will be purple, because they can only inherit one recessive gene.

Three flowers are purple, one is white – the ratio which Mendel worked out.

The hidden genes
The way a plant or animal looks (called its phenotype) may differ from its genetic make-up (called its genotype). For example, two of the purple flowers shown here carry the recessive gene for white, which they can pass on to their offspring.

Genes and the environment

The environment cannot change the genetic code, but it does affect how the instructions are carried out in an individual.

Two cuttings from one parent plant (which therefore have the same DNA) grown in different environments will look different. But seeds then taken from these cuttings, and grown in the same environment, will produce similar offspring.

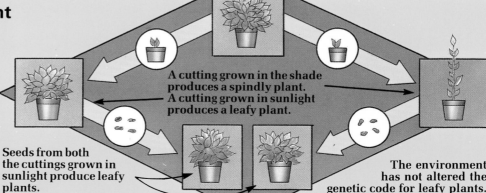

A cutting grown in the shade produces a spindly plant. A cutting grown in sunlight produces a leafy plant.

Seeds from both the cuttings grown in sunlight produce leafy plants.

The environment has not altered the genetic code for leafy plants.

Genes in action

Since Mendel's time, scientists have discovered that very few characteristics are controlled by genes in such a straightforward way as flower colour in peas. For example, genes can exist in more than two forms (as in blood groups, shown on the right). Many characteristics are controlled by more than one gene, whilst some genes seem to switch other genes on and off. If a change is made to a "control" gene, it might affect the way several genes interact with each other, and could lead to a change in characteristics.

Here are a few examples of genes in action in humans, to give you some idea of how complicated the process is.

Children's genotypes

Blood group A

Parents' genotypes

Blood group B

Blood group O

Blood group AB

AB

AO

BO

BO

OO

Boy or girl?

Your sex is controlled by the way the sex chromosomes pair up during fertilization. In humans, each cell has 46 chromosomes, two of which are sex chromosomes. The sex cells have half this amount (see page 11) – 22 plus 1 sex chromosome. Eggs always have an X sex chromosome, sperm have either X or Y. These can pair up as shown on the right, which means that in humans the male determines the sex of the offspring. (This is not always the case; in birds the female sex cells determine the sex of the offspring.)

Genes and blood groups

Your blood group is controlled by a genetic instruction that occurs in three slightly different forms – A, B and O. You inherit one of these from each parent. A and B instructions are both dominant over O, but A and B are neither dominant nor recessive to each other. This is called incomplete dominance.

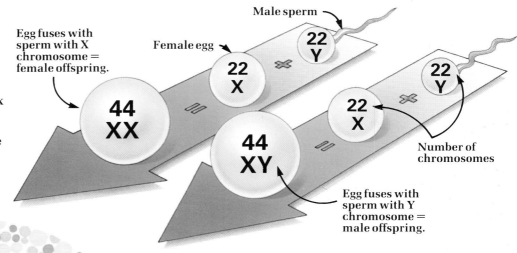

Male sperm

Female egg

Egg fuses with sperm with X chromosome = female offspring.

44 XX

22 X

22 Y

22 X

44 XY

22 Y

Number of chromosomes

Egg fuses with sperm with Y chromosome = male offspring.

If you cannot see the difference between red and green . . .

. . . you will not see a teapot here.

Sex-linked genes

Some human characteristics are inherited on the X and Y chromosomes, so it is possible for males and females to inherit different characteristics: for example, the various kinds of colour blindness.

The gene for colour vision occurs only on the X chromosome. If this carries the recessive form of the gene that causes colour blindness, males will be colour blind. Females would have to inherit the recessive gene on both their X chromosomes – which is much less likely -- to be colour blind.

Making an inheritance chart

You could make a family tree showing various characteristics: for example, eye colour, hair colour and height. (Remember to ask older members of the family what colour their hair was when they were young.)

Remember too, for example, that brown eye colour is dominant over blue; dark hair is dominant over fair; and fair hair is dominant over red.

Father's parents

Mother's parents

Marriage

What are species?

A species is a group of similar-looking plants or animals that can breed successfully together.[1] The processes of genetic change and natural selection, which you have read about so far, suggest that over long periods of time new species might be formed.

Often, new species evolve when an existing species becomes separated into one or more groups. Each group will have organisms possessing a slightly different set of genes. The differing environments of the two groups will favour (select) different genes, so the organisms become different and will eventually no longer able to breed together.

By looking at the reasons why living species are unable to breed together, it is possible to find out how new species might have been formed in the past and might still be being formed today. Laboratory experiments can provide valuable information about the genetic make-up of different species. One unusual way in which new species can form is called polyploidy (see opposite). This can lead to the "instant" formation of new species – mostly of plants – in only one or two generations.

Genetic drift

There is also the possibility of evolution by chance rather than by natural selection. This is called "genetic drift". It is most likely to be important if a very small group breaks away from the main species.

In the small group, the set of genes is much smaller, and it is a matter of chance which genes have been included. It is possible that one or more genes may be lost entirely. There is also a greater chance of any mutation (good or bad) being passed on, since there is less choice of genes in the group as a whole.

How species form in different areas

Darwin illustrated his ideas about species by his study of life on the Galapagos Islands,[2] where there are 13 species of finches found nowhere else. Each has a different shape or size of beak, eats different food and lives in different surroundings. These are five examples of the finch species.

Large ground finch. Blunt, powerful beak for breaking open large seeds. Lives on coasts and lowlands, mainly at ground level.

Vegetarian tree finch. Eats fruits, buds and seeds. Lives in forests.

◄ Warbler finch. Small pointed beak for probing into cracks. Eats only insects. Lives in forests.

Small tree finch. Strong sharp beak for grabbing and cutting. Eats mainly insects. Lives in trees.

Woodpecker finch. Uses cactus spines as tool to fish insects out of cracks in tree bark.

These finches probably evolved from one species that flew to the islands from the mainland. There were few other bird species on the islands, so the finches took advantage of and adapted to a variety of habitats, that is different surroundings, such as lowlands and forests. The finches are all so different now that none of the species can breed with another.

How species form in the same area

A species may split into two, even when all the individuals live in the same area. For example, one of the types of fruit flies which live in N. America.

Hawthorn   Apple

1. At one time, the flies lived on hawthorn bushes, laid their eggs in August and the maggots hatched in October and ate the ripe fruit.
2. Then apple trees were introduced. Their fruit ripens in September. Perhaps some flies already laid eggs earlier (in July) and the maggots hatched earlier and ate the ripe apples.
3. Gradually, more flies followed the "apple cycle". Both flies still look the same but can be regarded as different species. They can no longer breed together, because they now lay eggs at different times.

Instant species

Under certain conditions, two different species can sometimes breed together: their offspring are called hybrids. These are usually sterile (they cannot reproduce), because they inherit a different set of chromosomes from each parent, which cannot pair up during meiosis (see page 11).

Occasionally, however, the number of chromosomes in the cell is doubled (that is, they are copied but not divided into two cells, see page 11). If the hybrid fertilizes itself (this mostly happens in plants), the chromosomes can pair up, and a "polyploid" will result.

Polyploids *are* able to reproduce, and a new species can then build up over one or two generations.

Polyploids always have multiples of a basic number of chromosomes. The number varies from species to species: that for wheat is 7. The wheat first cultivated by people had 2 sets of chromosomes ($2 \times 7 = 14$).

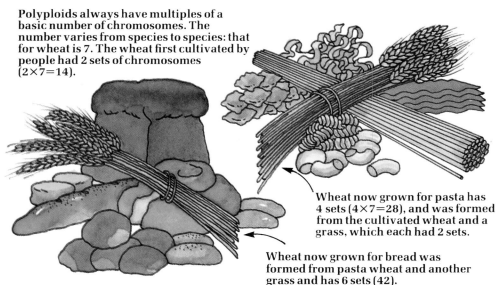

Wheat now grown for pasta has 4 sets ($4 \times 7 = 28$), and was formed from the cultivated wheat and a grass, which each had 2 sets.

Wheat now grown for bread was formed from pasta wheat and another grass and has 6 sets (42).

What keeps living things apart?

Here you can see some examples of living species which can no longer breed together, and the reasons for this. New species usually take a long time to form, so studying living species may provide clues as to how they were formed in the past.

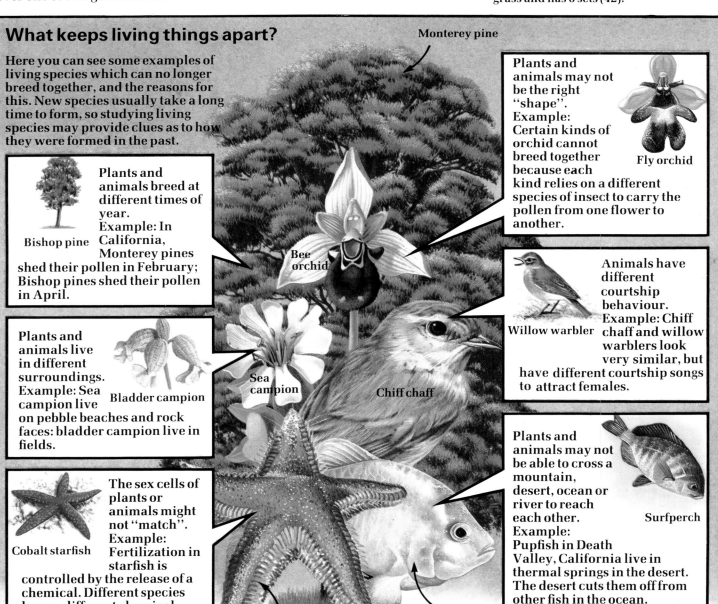

Monterey pine

Plants and animals breed at different times of year.
Example: In California, Monterey pines shed their pollen in February; Bishop pines shed their pollen in April.

Bishop pine

Plants and animals live in different surroundings.
Example: Sea campion live on pebble beaches and rock faces: bladder campion live in fields.

Bladder campion

The sex cells of plants or animals might not "match".
Example: Fertilization in starfish is controlled by the release of a chemical. Different species have a different chemical.

Cobalt starfish

Plants and animals may not be the right "shape".
Example: Certain kinds of orchid cannot breed together because each kind relies on a different species of insect to carry the pollen from one flower to another.

Fly orchid

Animals have different courtship behaviour.
Example: Chiff chaff and willow warblers look very similar, but have different courtship songs to attract females.

Willow warbler

Plants and animals may not be able to cross a mountain, desert, ocean or river to reach each other.
Example: Pupfish in Death Valley, California live in thermal springs in the desert. The desert cuts them off from other fish in the ocean.

Surfperch

Bee orchid

Sea campion

Chiff chaff

Common starfish

Pupfish

Classification

So far, you have read how all forms of life have the same chemical code, and how it works. You have seen various selection processes at work, and how new species can be formed. Here you can see how the enormous number of living species, and those found as fossil remains, can be "classified", that is, grouped together by comparing features they have in common.

This grouping is based on a system worked out by Carl Linnaeus in the 1750s, and arranges plants and animals into larger and larger groups. By comparing similar features between these groups, classification builds up a picture of how all forms of life are related. And shows how different forms of life might have evolved from a common ancestor.

Looking at different features

Plants and animals are sorted into groups by comparing features they have in common. The sorting can be done in various ways, depending on the features being looked at. These are the features most widely used:
- The appearance of plants and animals.
- The skeletons of animals and the flowering parts of plants.
- How plants and animals develop, for example from seeds, eggs, and so on.

Tiger

These two animals look similar, for example, so they can be grouped together.

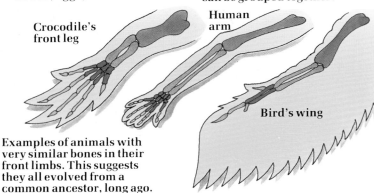

Crocodile's front leg

Human arm

Bird's wing

Examples of animals with very similar bones in their front limbs. This suggests they all evolved from a common ancestor, long ago.

Linnaeus' system of classification

The groups are classified according to Carl Linnaeus' system. Starting with the smallest, he called them: species, genus (pl. genera), family, order, class, phylum (pl. phyla) and kingdom. Here is an example, which shows that a tiger is a flesh-eating mammal with a backbone, belonging to the cat family.

Linnaeus' groups	Subdivision	Meaning of subdivision
Kingdom	Animal	
Phylum	Chordate	Nerve chord running down back
Sub-phylum	Vertebrate	Having a backbone
Class	Mammal	Covered in hair; young feed on mother's milk
Order	Carnivora	Flesh-eating
Family	Felidae	Cats
Genus	*Panthera*	Big cats
Species*	*Panthera tigris*	Tiger

*Species have two-part names which are always written in Latin. The first part gives the genus; the second part the species.

Cladistics

In this method of classification, organisms are grouped into "clades", according to features they all share, but which others do not. For example, a starling is a bird because it has feathers, a feature shared by no other animals. So, birds form a clade.

Similarly, a cow is a mammal because it has mammary glands. All mammals feed their young with milk from mammary glands, a feature shared by no other animals. So mammals form a clade.

Here is a list of animals to be arranged into a group: mouse, starling, cow, goldfish, penguin.

1. The first stage is to identify any shared features:

FEATURE	MOUSE	STARLING	COW	GOLDFISH	PENGUIN
MAMMARY GLAND	✓		✓		
LUNGS	✓	✓	✓		✓
JAWS	✓	✓	✓	✓	✓
FEATHERS		✓			✓

2. The animals are then grouped according to the shared features:

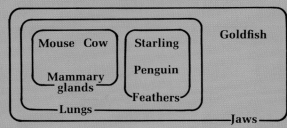

3. Finally, a branching diagram, or "cladogram", is drawn:

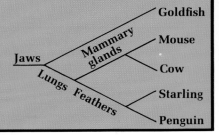

16

The origin of life

The beginning of life on Earth is a mystery that has puzzled people for centuries. On this page, you can read about people's early ideas as to the origin of life on Earth.

The most widely accepted scientific theory as to how life began is shown on page 18. There are other theories, one of which – that life may have arrived from outer space – is described below.

Creation stories

People have always imagined how the world might have begun. The first peoples often had similar ideas – regardless of where they lived – partly because they based their stories on what happened in their own lives.

Ancient Egyptian ideas

For example, one Egyptian myth says the world was originally filled with water, from which a hill arose. On the hill a lotus flower grew, and from it emerged the young sun god who created other gods, the land and all creatures. This "happened" to the Ancient Egyptians every year. The River Nile flooded and, as the water went down, the land reappeared and with it the birth of new things.

"Birth" ideas

Many of the ideas are concerned with birth, such as the world being born out of an egg, or out of the body of a dead monster. Other ideas were similar to the Egyptian one described above, although sometimes the gods themselves actually became the world. Other beliefs are concerned with a god (or gods) "speaking" and the world being created, as in the Genesis story.

Aborigine ideas

For the Australian Aborigines, the earth and sky have always existed. But in ancient times (Dreamtime), so one of their stories goes, beings moved over the Earth and their actions and footprints became the landscape – hills, caves, trees, and so on – and all Aborigines were descended from these ancestral beings.

This picture, based on ▶ an Aboriginal bark painting, shows two spirit beings in the form of humans.

Creationism

Creationism is the belief that God created every living thing, each with its own purpose, although not everyone believes it happened exactly as the Bible says.

You can read about three of the various Creationist beliefs below. In each, God is thought to have created "Man", fully developed and intelligent, by a separate act. Creationists do not think that humans evolved from apes. You can also read about the story of Genesis, as told in the Bible.

Genesis story

The story of Genesis in the Bible tells how God spoke, and so created the world in six days.

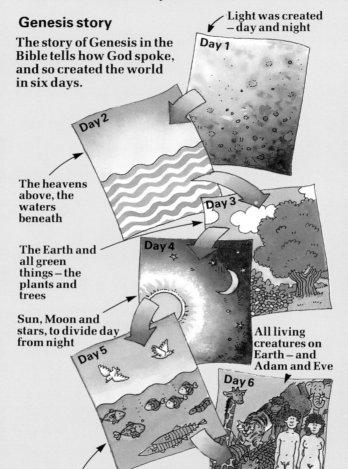

Light was created – day and night

Day 1

Day 2

The heavens above, the waters beneath

Day 3

The Earth and all green things – the plants and trees

Day 4

Sun, Moon and stars, to divide day from night

Day 5

All living creatures on Earth – and Adam and Eve

Day 6

Birds in the sky, and fish in the sea

Creationist beliefs

● God created the world in exactly six days, as told in Genesis, the first book of the Bible. It happened about 4,004 years before the birth of Jesus Christ.

● God created the world in six "days", each of which lasted for thousands of years. Everything that God had created was destroyed by the Biblical Flood (as shown by the fossil remains). God then re-created the Earth as it is today.

● God has created new forms of life at different times (which is why the fossil record seems incomplete), with small-scale evolution happening in between.

Life from outer space

A few people think the Earth's early atmosphere was too hot for the formation of life. But cells might have been formed in the cold depths of outer space, where there are clouds of dust and gas containing many of the raw materials of life. These cells might have made up part of the tails of comets, which are dense masses of gas and dust. As the comets passed close, some cells could have reached Earth where, by chance process, they might have been "assembled" into life forms.

However, if there are any living cells in outer space, most scientists think that they are unlikely to be able to survive in the very different conditions on Earth.

How life began

The scientific theory of the origin of life is based on experiments which recreate the early atmosphere on Earth, and also on the study of simple life forms alive today. Because all forms of life have the same basic chemistry and genetic code, it is thought that life probably arose only once, and may have evolved from lifeless matter, that is from the gases in the early atmosphere. Here you can see the stages of how life on Earth may have begun.

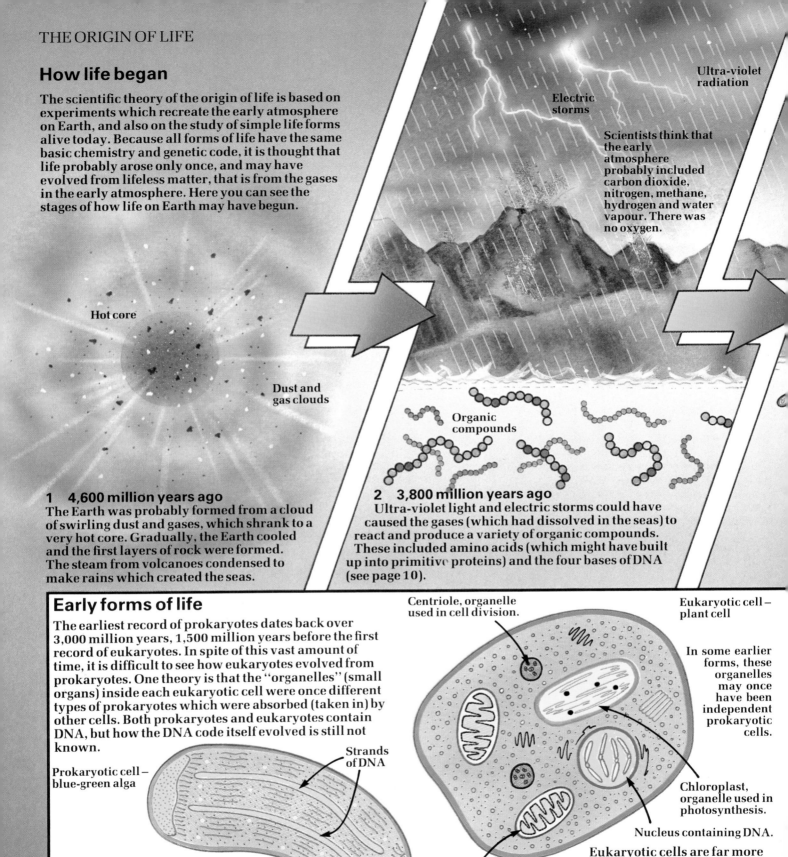

Electric storms

Ultra-violet radiation

Scientists think that the early atmosphere probably included carbon dioxide, nitrogen, methane, hydrogen and water vapour. There was no oxygen.

Hot core

Dust and gas clouds

Organic compounds

1   4,600 million years ago
The Earth was probably formed from a cloud of swirling dust and gases, which shrank to a very hot core. Gradually, the Earth cooled and the first layers of rock were formed. The steam from volcanoes condensed to make rains which created the seas.

2   3,800 million years ago
Ultra-violet light and electric storms could have caused the gases (which had dissolved in the seas) to react and produce a variety of organic compounds. These included amino acids (which might have built up into primitive proteins) and the four bases of DNA (see page 10).

Early forms of life

The earliest record of prokaryotes dates back over 3,000 million years, 1,500 million years before the first record of eukaryotes. In spite of this vast amount of time, it is difficult to see how eukaryotes evolved from prokaryotes. One theory is that the "organelles" (small organs) inside each eukaryotic cell were once different types of prokaryotes which were absorbed (taken in) by other cells. Both prokaryotes and eukaryotes contain DNA, but how the DNA code itself evolved is still not known.

Centriole, organelle used in cell division.

Eukaryotic cell – plant cell

In some earlier forms, these organelles may once have been independent prokaryotic cells.

Prokaryotic cell – blue-green alga

Strands of DNA

Chloroplast, organelle used in photosynthesis.

Nucleus containing DNA.

Prokaryotic cells have a very simple structure, as shown in this blue-green alga cell. The DNA, which is just simple strands, is not enclosed inside a nucleus. The cells reproduce by dividing in two.

Mitochondrion (organelle), the "powerhouse" of the cell.

Eukaryotic cells are far more complex, and contain various organelles, as shown in this plant cell. The DNA is enclosed inside a nucleus (there is a bit of DNA inside some of the organelles too), and the cells reproduce and grow by the processes of meiosis and mitosis (see page 11).

The oxygen formed a protective layer of ozone high in the atmosphere, which screened out harmful ultra-violet radiation.

Anaerobic bacteria (anaerobic means not needing oxygen).

Aerobic bacteria (aerobic means needing oxygen).

3   3,000 million years ago

Although it is not yet known how, some of these compounds came together to create the earliest forms of life, the prokaryotes. These were minute, single-celled organisms, such as bacteria and blue-green algae. These organisms used hydrogen for photosynthesis (energy production).

4   1,500 million years ago

Some bacteria started to use carbon dioxide and water for photosynthesis, and oxygen was given off as a waste product. The release of oxygen caused a dramatic change. Until then, most life forms had lived under water, for protection from the harmful ultra-violet radiation. Now this radiation was screened out by the oxygen, which formed an ozone layer high in the atmosphere. New, more complex, life forms (called eukaryotes) arose, and gradually a greater variety of life evolved on the surface of and near the edges of the seas. Finally, life started to appear on the land.

The life "clock"

This clock face gives some idea of the amount of time taken for life to evolve. Bacteria did not begin until about 20 minutes past the hour, with the earliest forms of animal life, such as jellyfish and plant life, such as algae, not starting until about ¼ to the hour. The first land plants, and animals such as reptiles and amphibians, arrived between ¼ to and 5 to. The dinosaurs arrived about 3 minutes to; the apes about 40 seconds to the hour. Humans first appeared just as the hour strikes.

Humans, 5 million years ago

Apes, 35 million years ago

Dinosaurs, 200 million years ago

Reptiles, 340 million years ago

570 million years ago

Algae and jellyfish

Plants, 500 million years ago

Bacteria

4,600 million years ago

1,500 million years ago

3,000 million years ago

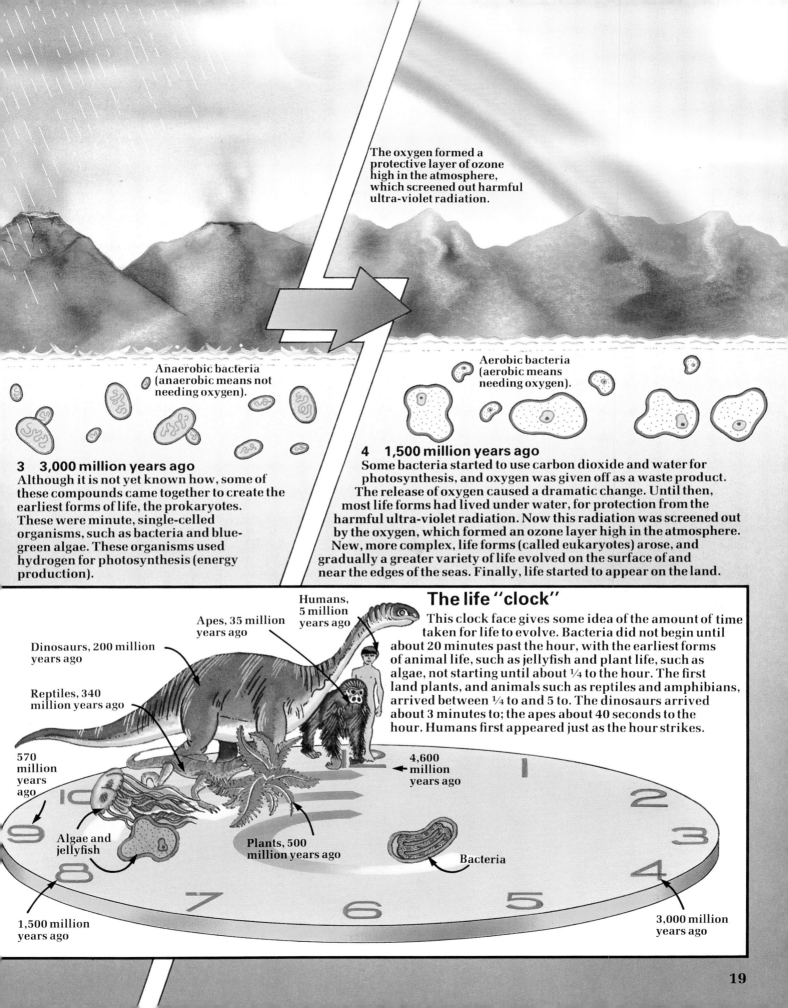

The fossil record

On the previous page, the life clock shows that the earliest forms of life appeared more than 3,000 million years ago. Evidence for these and other life forms can be seen from the fossilized remains of plants and animals. These have been found in the various layers of rock which have been formed over time, although only a few fossils have been found in the earliest layers —

called the Pre-Cambrian layers. The fossil record itself has many gaps, partly because not all plants and animals become fossilized, and partly because it is not possible to find all the fossils "locked" into the rocks. Even so, enough remains have been found to work out a timescale of the evolution of some of the different forms of life.

How rocks are formed

Rocks are constantly being eroded (worn away) by wind, rain and ice. The bits of rock, called sediments, are swept away into lakes and seas by the wind and rain.

The sediments sink to form layers under the water, and

are gradually packed down by the weight of new layers on top. Over millions of years, the sediments harden to form layers of rock, called strata. If plant or animal remains are trapped in the sediment, they may become fossilized.

Rocks of different ages are exposed one on top of the other, with the oldest at the bottom.

The different layers of rock are called strata.

The strata have been pushed upwards from the bottom.

Erosion exposes strata of different ages side by side.

This "slice" through the Earth shows that the strata are not always neatly arranged on top of each other. Sometimes movements in the Earth's crust have disturbed them, which can make it difficult to work out the sequence of fossils. Here you can see how movement has forced the strata upwards.

How fossils are formed

Most plants and animal remains are either decomposed (broken down) by bacteria and fungi or eaten by animals. Plants and animals become fossilized only if they are buried fairly quickly, that is, covered by drifting sand or drowned in mud and silt. These conditions do not exist everywhere, which is why only a small proportion of plants and animals become fossilized.

Here are three examples of how fossils can be formed.

The impression left behind by a brittlestar, after it decayed away.

"Trace" fossils can sometimes be preserved, if impressions have been left by decayed matter — such as leaf imprints, worm trails and even dinosaur footprints — or "moulds" of shells which have dissolved away.

When plants and animals die, the "soft" parts usually rot away, so most fossil remains are the "hard" parts, for example, shells, teeth, bone and wood. Over time, these can be preserved by minerals being formed within them.

Ammonite shells preserved by the formation of minerals.

An ant preserved in amber (hardened resin).

Very occasionally, the soft parts of remains are preserved. Such fossils are usually found in the most recent strata.

20

Continental drift

The continents have not always been in the same position on the globe as they are today. For example, this is probably how the globe looked 200 million years ago.

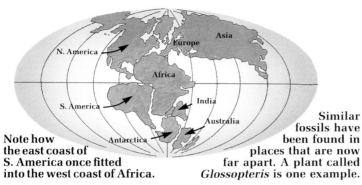

Note how the east coast of S. America once fitted into the west coast of Africa.

Similar fossils have been found in places that are now far apart. A plant called *Glossopteris* is one example.

The continents have drifted. At various times, seas have covered land which is now mountains, and the climate has changed greatly over time (for example, Africa was once covered in ice). This is why fossil remains have been found where, today, similar plants and animals could not survive.

How continental drift works

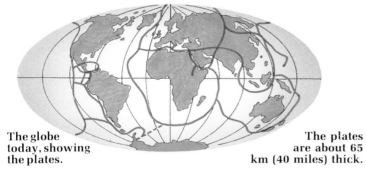

The globe today, showing the plates.

The plates are about 65 km (40 miles) thick.

The Earth's outer layer is divided into sections called plates, which drift past each other at the rate of about 2 cm (½ in) a year. Where plates are moving apart, new hot molten (liquid) rock rises up from inside the Earth to "plug the gap". Where plates meet, one slides down under the other. All this causes pressure inside the Earth, which is one reason for the movement, such as folding, of the strata.

Pre-Cambrian fossils

The first life forms date back to the Pre-Cambrian strata, over 3,000 million years ago. Very few fossils have been found, partly because the creatures were mostly soft-bodied.

From the Cambrian strata onwards, far more fossil remains have been found, and it is possible to picture how life might have looked, as shown on pages 22-25. Not all the plants and creatures shown existed at the same time and in the same place.

These are examples of Pre-Cambrian trace fossils.

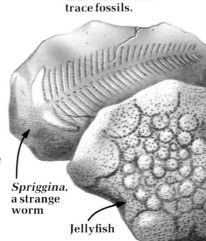

Spriggina, a strange worm

Jellyfish

Timechart of life on Earth

This "cliff" shows the names of the various strata and how long ago they were formed. (The Pre-Cambrian strata covers so many millions of years that it is not possible to include it on these pages.) The strata is divided into eras as shown: Palaeozic (ancient life), Mesozoic (middle life) and Cenozoic (new life).

	million years ago		Today	
Cenozoic	0.01	Holocene		Modern humans
	2	Pleistocene		Early humans
	5	Pliocene		"Ape-people"
	22	Miocene		Grazing animals
	38	Oligocene		Early apes / Modern mammals
	55	Eocene		Early elephants / Early horses
	65	Palaeocene		
Mesozoic	140	Cretaceous		Flowering plants / Small mammals
	195	Jurassic		Dinosaurs
	230	Triassic		Large reptiles / Birds, snakes and lizards
Palaeozic	280	Permian		
	345	Carboniferous		Plant-eating reptiles
	395	Devonian		Amphibians
	435	Silurian		Land vertebrates / Insects
	500	Ordovician		Land plants / Fungi / Vertebrates with jaws
	570	Cambrian		Jawless vertebrates / Molluscs / Crustaceans / Echinoderms
				Worms / Jellyfish, etc.
	3,500	Pre-Cambrian		Bacteria / Blue-green algae

21

Cambrian
570-500 million years ago

The variety of life forms seems to have exploded at the beginning of the Cambrian Period. Life forms were still only to be found in the seas, but the earlier forms now evolved into a variety of invertebrate forms (that is, creatures without backbones), including:

- Brachiopods (hinged shells, fixed to the seabed by a foot).
- Arthropods ("shelled" creatures), such as trilobites, relatives of modern insects, spiders, lobsters and crabs.
- Echinoderms (spiny-skinned) creatures, such as sea urchins.

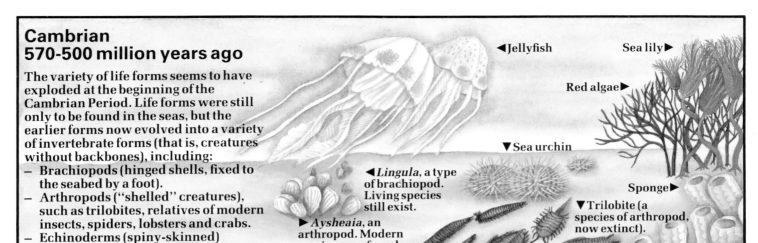

◄Jellyfish   Sea lily►

Red algae►

▼Sea urchin

◄*Lingula*, a type of brachiopod. Living species still exist.

Sponge►

► *Aysheaia*, an arthropod. Modern versions are found in humid tropical undergrowth.

▼Trilobite (a species of arthropod, now extinct).

Ordovician
500-435 million years ago

Life forms still remained in the sea, but the creatures became larger in size, and diversified still further, including:

- Cephalopods such as octopus, nautiloids (which later evolved into ammonites) and squid. These were some of the first creatures that could swim; most of the earlier life forms were fixed to or could only move about on the seabed.
- Vertebrates (creatures with backbones), for example jawless fish covered with bony armour.

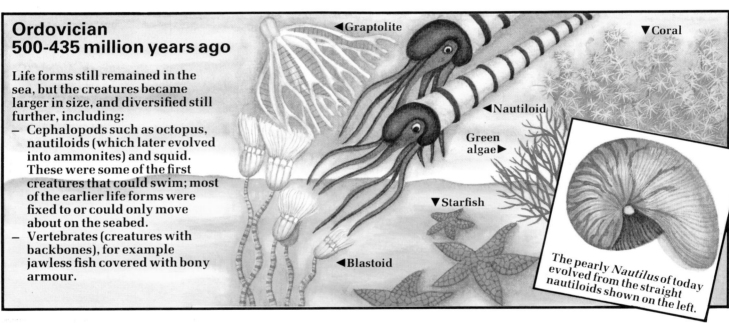

◄Graptolite   ▼Coral

◄Nautiloid

Green algae►

▼Starfish

◄Blastoid

The pearly *Nautilus* of today evolved from the straight nautiloids shown on the left.

Silurian
435-395 million years ago

By the end of the Silurian Period, life had at last appeared on land.

- Marsh plants started to grow at the edges of the sea (they needed to be near water to reproduce). They probably evolved from the algae which started to grow in the Cambrian Period.
- Giant arthropods (sea scorpions) moved onto the seashore.

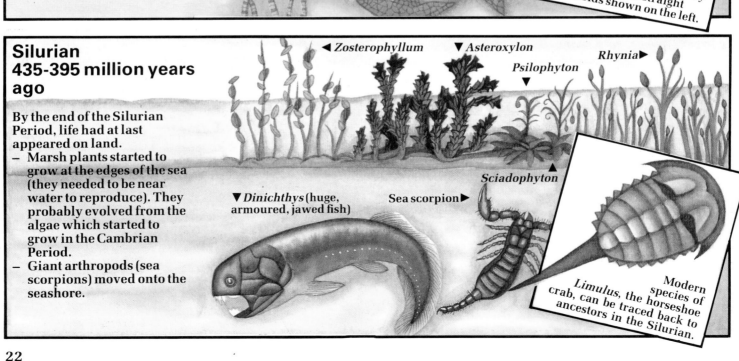

◄*Zosterophyllum*   ▼*Asteroxylon*   *Rhynia*►

Psilophyton
▼

▼*Dinichthys* (huge, armoured, jawed fish)   Sea scorpion►

Sciadophyton

Modern species of *Limulus*, the horseshoe crab, can be traced back to ancestors in the Silurian.

Devonian
394-345 million years ago

The Devonian Period is known as the "Age of Fishes". Plant life also expanded in the swamps and marshes.

- Fish developed bony skeletons and swim bladders (the earliest form of lung). Some fish developed paired fins, which eventually enabled them to "walk" onto land, where their "lungs" helped them to survive out of water.
- Sharks began to develop.
- The first amphibians (cold-blooded vertebrates) evolved from the "lunged" fish. They had to stay near water, in order to keep their bodies moist and to be able to breed.
- The first insects probably appeared.
- Trees and forests began to form.

◄Clubmoss, grew to over 30 m (100 ft) tall. Today, it only grows to a few cm.

▼Seed fern

Cordaite►

◄Horsetail

▲ *Ichthyostega*, an early amphibian

▲ *Eusthenopteron* (bony fish) from which the amphibians developed.

Carboniferous
345-280 million years ago

The climate started to become much drier. Gymnosperm (non-flowering, seed-bearing) plants developed, as did a greater variety of insect and animal life. What we now dig up as coal was formed at this time. (Coal is decayed plant life, fossilized in the swampy sediments.)

- Conifer (cone-bearing) trees first appeared.
- The first reptiles evolved from amphibians. They laid hard-shelled eggs and had dry, scaly skin to retain their body moisture. Therefore, they did not need to stay near water in order to survive. They were herbivores (plant eaters) and, in the Jurassic Period, some developed into warm-blooded mammals.
- Ammonites developed from nautiloids.

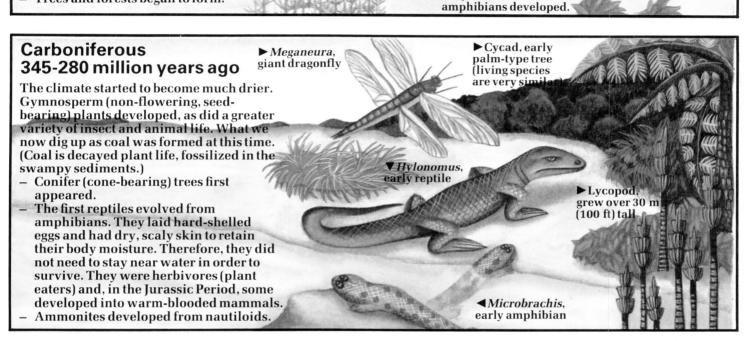

► *Meganeura*, giant dragonfly

►Cycad, early palm-type tree (living species are very similar)

▼*Hylonomus*, early reptile

►Lycopod, grew over 30 m (100 ft) tall

◄*Microbrachis*, early amphibian

Permian
280-230 million years ago

The Permian Period saw the swampy primitive forests being replaced by conifer and gingko (Maidenhair) trees. The Appalachian Mountains and many of the deserts were formed. Amphibians and insects were still developing, but it was the reptile group which really started to expand.

- Sail-backed reptiles appeared. (Mammals, including humans, eventually evolved from these creatures.)
- Trilobites became extinct (died out).

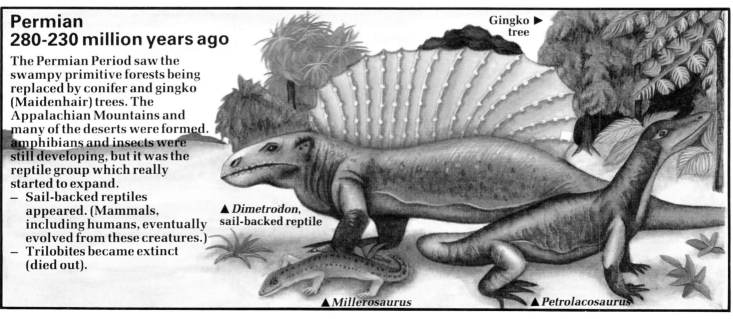

Gingko ► tree

▲ *Dimetrodon*, sail-backed reptile

▲ *Millerosaurus*

▲ *Petrolacosaurus*

Triassic
230-195 million years ago

The Triassic marked the beginning of the "Age of the Reptiles". The spread of the gymnosperms continued.
- Conifers, such as firs, pines and cedars, expanded as the horsetails and seed ferns started to die out.
- Palm-like trees started to develop.
- In the sea, the reptiles included turtles; on land, the ancestors of snakes and lizards.
- Ammonites dominated the seas.

Jurassic
195-140 million years ago

During the Jurassic, the climate was warm everywhere – even the Poles had no ice covering – and shallow seas covered much of the land. The cone-bearing plants (such as conifers) dominated the landscape. The first small mammals appeared; but the reptiles, including the dinosaurs, ruled the air, land and sea.
- In the air were reptile-birds, such as *Rhamphorhychus*; on land, some dinosaurs fed on plants, whilst others fed on mammals and smaller dinosaurs.
- Small mammals (warm-blooded vertebrates) were mostly active at night and fed mainly on insects.

Cretaceous
140-65 million years ago

The continents continued to drift apart, and the Rockies and Andes were formed. The first angiosperms (flowering plants) appeared, which provided a new source of food. The mammals developed still further, as did some of the dinosaurs. But, by the end of the Cretaceous, *all* the dinosaurs had become extinct, as had all the ammonites and most of the microscopic plant life in the seas.
- Three main types of mammals had emerged: monotremes (egg-laying, such as the duck-billed platypus), marsupials (pouched, such as the kangaroo) and placentals (from which humans eventually developed).

Rhamphorhychus
Jurassic

Brachiosaurus
Jurassic

Allosaurus
Jurassic

Archaeopteryx
Jurassic

Parasaurolophus
Cretaceous

Ichthyosaur
Triassic

Palm-type tree
Triassic

Tyrannosaurus
Cretaceous

Pleiosaur
Triassic

Stegosaurus
Jurassic

Alamosaurus
Cretaceous

Ornithomimus
Cretaceous

Crocodile
Triassic

Ornitholestes
Jurassic

Magnolia
Cretaceous

Lizard
Cretaceous

Early mammal
Cretaceous

Turtle
Triassic

*Not all the plants and animals shown here were alive at the same time and in the same place.

Palaeocene
65-55 million years ago

During the Palaeocene, the flowering plants dominated the landscape. The extinction of the dinosaurs enabled the mammals to take over – rodents (such as rats and mice), carnivores (such as cats and dogs) and primates (such as monkeys). They were mostly ground-living and no longer needed to live by night. The continued drifting of the continents cut off some groups of mammals from others, such as the marsupials in Australasia.

Eocene and Oligocene
55-22 million years ago

By the start of the Eocene Period, the variety of flowering plants and mammals had further developed, to take advantage of the different habitats and sources of food. The ancestors of elephants and horses appeared. The primates had evolved into "grasping" tree-climbers, where they fed on the leaves, fruit, nuts and sap. They also had better eyesight than earlier mammals, because the position of the eyes in the skull had changed to face the front. The Himalayas and Alps were formed only about now.

Miocene, Pliocene and Pleistocene
22 million-10 thousand years ago

The climate changed dramatically during the Miocene Period. The temperature dropped and grasslands replaced much of the woodlands and forests. This change led to the emergence of herds of grazing animals. The first apes also evolved.

The first hominids (early humans) arrived during the Pliocene Period, the end of which saw the start of the Ice Age. Many mammals died out; but some survived the cold (such as woolly mammoths), whilst others moved south to warmer weather. The Pleistocene Period began after the Ice Age, about two million years ago.

Baluchitherium, early rhino Oligocene

Poebrotherium, early camel Oligocene

Teratornis, vulture Pleistocene

Deiontherium, early elephant Miocene

Brontotherium Oligocene

Macrauchenia Pleistocene

Uintatherium, six-horned herbivore Eocene

Diatryma, flightless bird Eocene

Duck-billed platypus Palaeocene

Echidna (spiny ant-eater) Palaeocene

Hyracotherium (*Eohippus*), earliest horse Eocene

Megatherium, giant ground sloth Pleistocene

Palaeolagus, early hare Oligocene

Paramys, early rats and mice Eocene

Smilodon, sabre-toothed cat Pleistocene

*This page shows some of the ancestors of modern animals.

Turn over to read about human evolution

Human evolution

Were humans brought onto the Earth fully-formed and intelligent, as told in the Bible? Or do humans share an ancestor with apes? Even for those who believe in the second alternative, there are still many theories about the fossil remains of hominids (early humans): one problem is the gap in the fossil record, between 8 and 4 million years ago.

Shown here is a possible version of human evolution. Until more fossil evidence is found, the complete version will remain unknown.

Classifying the apes

Humans are classified into the primate order in the chordate phylum.[1] Primates are a group of animals which includes apes, that is gibbons, orang-utans, gorillas and chimpanzees. The exact relationship between the apes is difficult to work out, since there are arguments as to which features are most important for comparison.

This is one possible classification, comparing features such as size and shape of skull, brain and teeth.

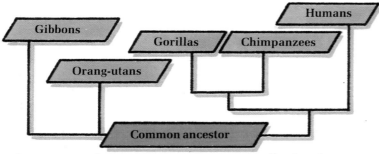

As you can see, humans appear to be more closely related to chimpanzees and gorillas than to the other apes. However, some studies suggest that humans may be more closely related to chimpanzees, while others have indicated that gorillas may be our closest living relatives.

The human element

Although humans are grouped with the apes, they differ greatly, as shown here. But it is by looking for features we share with apes, or with fossil remains, that it may be possible to work out exactly how humans evolved.

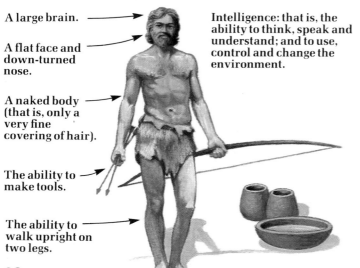

A large brain.

A flat face and down-turned nose.

A naked body (that is, only a very fine covering of hair).

The ability to make tools.

The ability to walk upright on two legs.

Intelligence: that is, the ability to think, speak and understand; and to use, control and change the environment.

The fossil evidence

The map (opposite) shows you where some of the fossil remains have been found. Except for *Ramapithecus* (which is probably not closely related to humans at all), those of earliest date have been found in Africa.

Ramapithecus

The fossil remains are of jaw bones and teeth only, but it is possible that *Ramapithecus* looked like this. Some people now think that they were more closely related to orang-utans than to any of the other apes.

Ramapithecus 14 million years ago was first found in India, and named after *Rama* (a Hindu god) and *pithecus* (the Greek for monkey or ape).

The fossil gap

Fossils have not yet been found for the period between 8-4 million years ago. One possible reason is that much of the land was covered by shallow seas and some apes might have adapted to their new habitat by taking to the water in search of food and shelter. This theory could explain why fossils found after the gap have features which humans do not share with other primates, such as little body hair, a layer of fat under the skin and breath control under water, all of which are helpful when swimming.

Australopithecus ("southern ape")

Evidence of three main species has been found. They walked upright and used bones and stones as tools. However, they shared some features with gorillas and chimpanzees, and this suggests that the split between apes and hominids happened during this period.

Australopithecus afarensis. Parts of a skeleton were found in Hadar, in Ethiopia, and nicknamed "Lucy". This is how she may have looked.

Australopithecus 4 million years ago

Australopithecus gracile

Australopithecus robustus

1. Classification is explained on page 16.

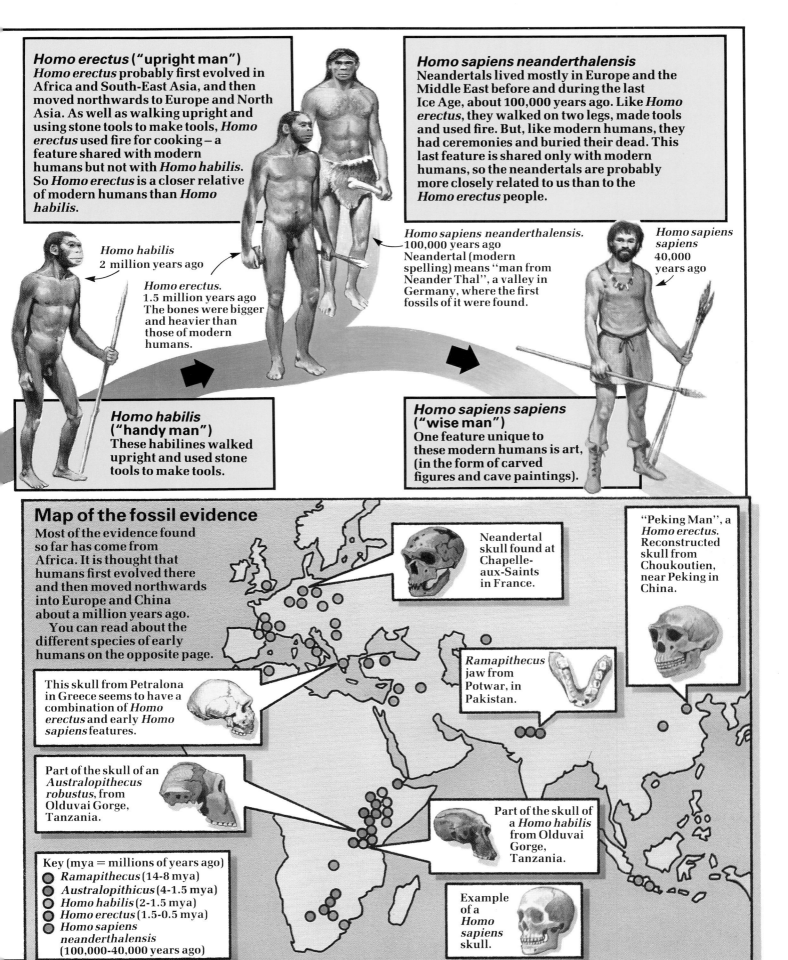

Homo erectus ("upright man")
Homo erectus probably first evolved in Africa and South-East Asia, and then moved northwards to Europe and North Asia. As well as walking upright and using stone tools to make tools, *Homo erectus* used fire for cooking – a feature shared with modern humans but not with *Homo habilis*. So *Homo erectus* is a closer relative of modern humans than *Homo habilis*.

Homo sapiens neanderthalensis
Neandertals lived mostly in Europe and the Middle East before and during the last Ice Age, about 100,000 years ago. Like *Homo erectus*, they walked on two legs, made tools and used fire. But, like modern humans, they had ceremonies and buried their dead. This last feature is shared only with modern humans, so the neandertals are probably more closely related to us than to the *Homo erectus* people.

Homo habilis
2 million years ago

Homo erectus.
1.5 million years ago
The bones were bigger and heavier than those of modern humans.

Homo sapiens neanderthalensis.
100,000 years ago
Neandertal (modern spelling) means "man from Neander Thal", a valley in Germany, where the first fossils of it were found.

Homo sapiens sapiens
40,000 years ago

Homo habilis ("handy man")
These habilines walked upright and used stone tools to make tools.

Homo sapiens sapiens ("wise man")
One feature unique to these modern humans is art, (in the form of carved figures and cave paintings).

Map of the fossil evidence
Most of the evidence found so far has come from Africa. It is thought that humans first evolved there and then moved northwards into Europe and China about a million years ago.

You can read about the different species of early humans on the opposite page.

Neandertal skull found at Chapelle-aux-Saints in France.

"Peking Man", a *Homo erectus*. Reconstructed skull from Choukoutien, near Peking in China.

This skull from Petralona in Greece seems to have a combination of *Homo erectus* and early *Homo sapiens* features.

Ramapithecus jaw from Potwar, in Pakistan.

Part of the skull of an *Australopithecus robustus*, from Olduvai Gorge, Tanzania.

Part of the skull of a *Homo habilis* from Olduvai Gorge, Tanzania.

Key (mya = millions of years ago)
- *Ramapithecus* (14-8 mya)
- *Australopithicus* (4-1.5 mya)
- *Homo habilis* (2-1.5 mya)
- *Homo erectus* (1.5-0.5 mya)
- *Homo sapiens neanderthalensis* (100,000-40,000 years ago)

Example of a *Homo sapiens* skull.

27

The theory of evolution

The theory of evolution is made up of many ideas, as you have seen in this book. These two pages summarize the ideas, to help you understand how they all fit together.

There are many questions in the story of evolution which scientists have not yet been able to answer definitely, although there are plenty of possible answers. You can read about two of these puzzling questions here. Why are there so many gaps in the fossil record? Why have many different creatures sometimes become extinct at the same time?

The fossil gaps

Darwin's theory of natural selection suggests that, mostly, new species have evolved slowly and gradually. But in the fossil record there are usually jumps between species. Here are some of the theories to explain the gaps.

● Not all the fossils have been found.

● No fossils were formed, because the conditions at the time were not right for the preservation of plant and animal remains.

● New species evolved in isolated groups on the edges of a main group. When the new species eventually took over from the main group – which had stayed the same – the new species seemed to have evolved suddenly.

● New species evolved so rapidly, that the intermediate stages were unlikely to be preserved.

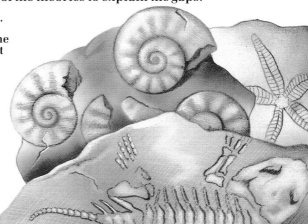

1 All living things are controlled by the same chemical code – DNA – which spells out the genetic instructions for each species. This suggests that all life arose from the same beginning.

Mistakes to the code, which can alter the characteristics of living things, can sometimes be passed on from parents to offspring. This is how life on Earth could have changed over time.

3 The species are classified, by sorting them into larger and larger groups which share some common features. Every species is classified into one of the main groupings: the phyla.

Being able to group species together in this way, supports the idea that all life forms evolved over time from a common ancestor.

These two species look similar, and can be grouped together.

2

A male blue bird of paradise displays his feathers to attract a mate.

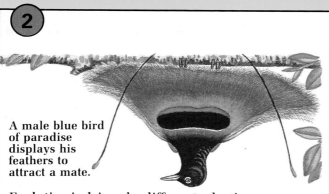

Evolution is driven by different selection processes. Under natural selection, the fittest survive and pass on their genes. In sexual and social selection, this takes the form of competing for and choosing a mate, and how animals behave towards each other.

4 Evidence for many of the species which have existed can be seen from the fossilized remains of plants and animals, which have been trapped during the process of rock formation. This also suggests that life on Earth has evolved over time, as the rock strata, and therefore the fossils inside them, can be dated and arranged in sequence.

Fossil remains of an ammonite and a trilobite.

Mass extinctions

Throughout time, many individual species have become extinct, as a natural process of evolution. Occasionally, however, there have been mass extinctions, when many kinds of plants and animals have died out at the same time.

At the end of the Cretaceous Period, for example, 65 million years ago, all the dinosaurs suddenly died out, and many other life forms as well, especially those living in the seas. Scientists argue about what caused this, particularly as the extinctions happened to marine as well as land-living creatures. Here are some of their theories.

●Meteorites showered the Earth, causing tidal waves, volcanic eruptions, and clouds of dust and gas which blotted out the Sun's rays.

●The lethal rays from the collapse of a supernova (exploding star) caused a long-term drop in temperature.

●Continental drift may have caused a gradual change in the climate, thus destroying sources of food and shelter.

●The extinctions were not "sudden"; they happened over as long as 500,000 years. Many creatures may already have been in decline, and died out naturally, not as a result of sudden changes.

5 The building blocks of life, that is, organic compounds, first appeared about 3,000 million years ago. This probably resulted from chance reaction between various gases in the atmosphere, ultra-violet radiation and electric storms.

Prokaryote cell.▶ Similar life forms still exist today, such as bacteria.

◀Eukaryote cell. Most life forms – extinct and living – are made up of this type of cell.

About 3,000 million years ago, the compounds came together to create simple forms of life – the prokaryotes, in which DNA is not enclosed inside a nucleus. About 1,500 million years ago, more complex forms of life appeared – the eukaryotes, made up of DNA enclosed inside a nucleus and various organelles.

6 Not all species have either evolved or become extinct – some have continued to stay the same for millions of years, often whilst new species have branched off from them. This may be because they are so well-adapted to their habitat, which has also not changed greatly over time.

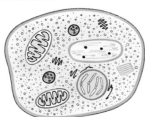

Limulus, the horseshoe crab. Modern species look the same as those which lived 400 million years ago.

7 The fossil record shows that millions of species have become extinct during the evolution of life on Earth. They mostly died out due to natural causes, but humans have killed off many species. Humans have also been responsible for the evolution of new kinds of living things. For example, in artificial selection, people have changed plants and animals, by breeding chosen individuals together.

The 110 breeds of dog are the result of artificial selection.

8 The process of evolution took many thousands of millions of years, as shown on the life clock. And the scientific theory of evolution, as described in this book, shows how the amazing variety of life forms on Earth – extinct and living species – could all have evolved from a common origin.

570 million years ago

3,000 million years ago

Who's who

On this page, you can read about a few of the people who have contributed scientific ideas, which have helped towards working out the theory of evolution.

Carl Linnaeus (1707-78), Swedish naturalist. He was the first to try and sort out living things and look for relationships between them. He devised a system for classifying and naming plants and animals.

James Hutton (1726-97), Scottish geologist. He worked out the process of rock formation, and argued that each stratum took many millions of years to form.

Jean Baptiste de Lamarck (1744-1829), French naturalist. One of the first people to suggest that species changed over time and were not fixed, and to suggest evolution as a reason why. However, he is better known for believing that plants and animals could change their characteristics in their own lifetime, and pass these changes on to the next generation.

Sir Charles Lyell (1797-1875), British geologist. He saw that "the present is the key to the past", that is, that the natural forces responsible for creating the world, such as erosion, are still at work now, and that change is a slow, unending process. He called his idea uniformitarianism, and it greatly influenced Charles Darwin.

Charles Darwin (1809-82), British naturalist. As a result of his voyage on HMS *Beagle* (1831-6), and his studies of living and extinct species, he put forward his idea of natural selection to explain evolution. He published his theory in 1859 in his book, *On the Origin of Species*.

Alfred Russel Wallace (1823-1913), British traveller and naturalist. Like Darwin, Wallace also arrived at the theory of natural selection as an explanation of evolution. He sent a copy of his work to Darwin and they published joint details of the theory in 1858. This encouraged Darwin into finally publishing the book he had been working on for 26 years.

Thomas Henry Huxley (1825-95), British zoologist. He defended Darwin's theory of natural selection, and that humans had evolved from apes (both of which were very controversial ideas at the time).

Gregor Mendel (1822-84), a monk born in Silesia in Austria, in what is now part of Czechoslovakia. He experimented with pea plants and worked out that parents can pass on characteristics to their offspring – the theory of inheritance. The importance of his work was not recognized until the beginning of the 20th century.

George Gaylord Simpson (1902-84), American palaeontologist. He studied and classified the evolution of mammals, especially those of S. America. He also showed that the fossil record is compatible with Darwin's theory of natural selection.

Sir Ronald Fisher (1890-1962), British geneticist, **J.B.S. Haldane** (1892-1964), British geneticist and **Sewall Wright** (1889-), American geneticist. In the 1920s, they worked out the "synthetic" theory of evolution, by showing how Darwin's theory of natural selection and Mendel's theory of inheritance work together, through the genes passed on from parents to offspring.

Ernst Mayr (1904-), German-American zoologist. He defended the "geographic" theory of the formation of species, according to which new species are more likely to arise in a group which has been cut off from the main species group.

Francis Crick (1916-), British molecular biologist and **James Watson** (1928-), American biochemist. In 1953, they worked out that the DNA molecule has the form of a double helix, the two spirals of which can unzip, so that the genetic code can be copied.

Stanley Miller (1930-), American chemist. In 1953, he experimented with a mixture of gases which were probably present in the early atmosphere, and showed that intense heat and electric storms could have created a variety of organic compounds, the building blocks of life. (Earlier, in 1924, the Russian, **A.I. Oparin**, had first put forward the idea that life on Earth was formed from non-living matter, that is, from the gases in the early atmosphere.)

Motoo Kimura (1924-), Japanese geneticist. He has argued that evolutionary changes in molecules usually take place by chance rather than by natural selection.

Louis Leakey (1903-72), British anthropologist and his wife **Mary Leakey** (1913-), British palaeoanthropologist, discovered the fossils of early humans at Olduvai Gorge in Tanzania. Their finds showed that early humans had first evolved in Africa (not in Asia, as had previously been thought). Their son, **Richard Leakey** (1943-) has continued their work of looking for evidence of early humans.

William Hamilton (1936-), British biologist. He has developed the theory of "kin selection" to explain why social animals sometimes help one another.

Stephen Jay Gould (1941-), American evolutionary biologist and **Niles Eldredge** (1943-), American palaeobiologist. They think the jumps in the fossil record show long periods with little or no change, interrupted by shorter period when new species arise – usually in small groups living in isolation, and in which favourable mutations can spread more quickly than in a larger group.

Glossary

Amphibians. Vertebrate animals, most of which have to return to water in order to breed; for example, frogs.

Angiosperms. Flowering plants, with seeds enclosed inside a casing, such as a pod.

Annelids. Aquatic or land animals, with soft bodies that are divided into rings or segments; for example, earthworms.

Characteristics. The way an individual looks and behaves, and how its body works.

Chromosomes. Thread-like structures, found in plant and animal cells, which are made of DNA.

Classification. The system of grouping plants and animals, according to features they have in common.

Creationism. The belief that God created the Earth and every living thing, and in particular that He separately created each species, which never change.

DNA. (deoxyribonucleic acid). The DNA molecule carries the genetic code of instructions that controls the characteristics of living things.

Environment. The surroundings in which a plant or animal lives.

Eukaryote cells. Cells which have a nucleus enclosing the DNA.

Evolution. The gradual change in the characteristics of a group of plants or animals over time, which produces new species.

Extinction. The complete loss of a species, that is, all the members of the species die out.

Fertilization. The fusion of an egg cell and a sperm cell to create a new individual.

Fossils. The preserved remains of plants and animals.

Genes. Portions of DNA, each of which carries part of the chemical code of instructions.

Genotype. The genetic make-up of a plant or animal.

Gymnosperms. Non-flowering plants, the seeds of which are not enclosed inside a casing.

Habitat. The particular place in the environment where a plant or animal is usually found; for example, seashore, desert, etc.

Hybrid. The offspring produced when a male and female of different species mate together. Hybrids are mostly sterile, which means that they are usually unable to reproduce.

Invertebrates. Animals without a backbone.

Mammals. Warm-blooded, vertebrate animals, the young of which are fed on their mother's milk.

Marsupials. Pouched mammals; for example, kangaroos.

Meiosis. Cell division to produce sperm and egg cells in animals and pollen and ovules in plants, each with half the number of chromosomes as in the original cell.

Mitosis. Cell division which results in two new cells, each identical to the original cell.

Molecule. The smallest particle of any substance (such as an organic compound), that could exist on its own in nature.

Molluscs. Soft-bodied and unsegmented creatures that are usually covered by a shell; for example, snail.

Mutation. A change in the DNA code, which can sometimes be passed on from parents to offspring.

Natural selection. Theory according to which, the individuals who are best adapted to the environment survive to reproduce and pass on their helpful characteristics to their offspring.

Phyla. The largest groups of the plant and animal kingdoms.

Placentals. Mammals which are nourished (fed) before birth through the placenta in the mother's womb.

Polyploid. An organism (usually a plant) with more than the usual two sets of chromosomes. In hybrids, polyploidy may enable successful reproduction.

Prokaryote cells. Cells in which the DNA is not enclosed inside a nucleus.

Reptiles. Cold-blooded, egg-laying vertebrate animals with scaly skins; for example, crocodiles.

Species. A group of individuals that can successfully breed together.

Vertebrates. Animals with a backbone.

Books to read

The Age of the Earth by John Thackray (Geological Museum, HMSO)

Dinosaurs by Anne McCord (Usborne)

Discovering Genetics by Norman Cohen (Longman)

Discovering the Origins of Mankind by Leslie Aiello (Longman)

Early Man by Anne McCord (Usborne)

Evolution by Colin Patterson (British Museum, Natural History)

Fossils by Mark Lambert (Ward Lock)

Human Origins by Richard Leakey (Hamish Hamilton)

The NatureTrail Book of Rocks & Fossils by M. Bramwell (Usborne)

Man's Place in Evolution (British Museum, Natural History)

Hunting the Past by L.B. Halstead (Hamish Hamilton)

Origin of Species (British Museum, Natural History)

The Prehistoric Age (GBR Educational)

Prehistoric Mammals by Anne McCord (Usborne)

The Problems of Evolution by Mark Ridley (Oxford University Press)

Spotter's Guide to Dinosaurs & other prehistoric animals by D. Norman (Usborne)

Spotter's Guide to Rocks & Minerals by A. Woolley (Usborne)

The Story of Evolution by Ron Taylor (Ward Lock)

The Story of the Earth (Geological Museum, HMSO)

The Theory of Evolution by J. Maynard Smith (Penguin)

Young Scientist Book of Archaeology by B. Cork & S. Reid (Usborne)

Index

First published in 1985 by
Usborne Publishing Ltd
Usborne House
83-85 Saffron Hill, London
EC1N 8RT, England
© 1991, 1985 Usborne
Publishing Ltd.

Printed in Belgium

THE USBORNE YOUNG SCIENTIST
UNDERSEA

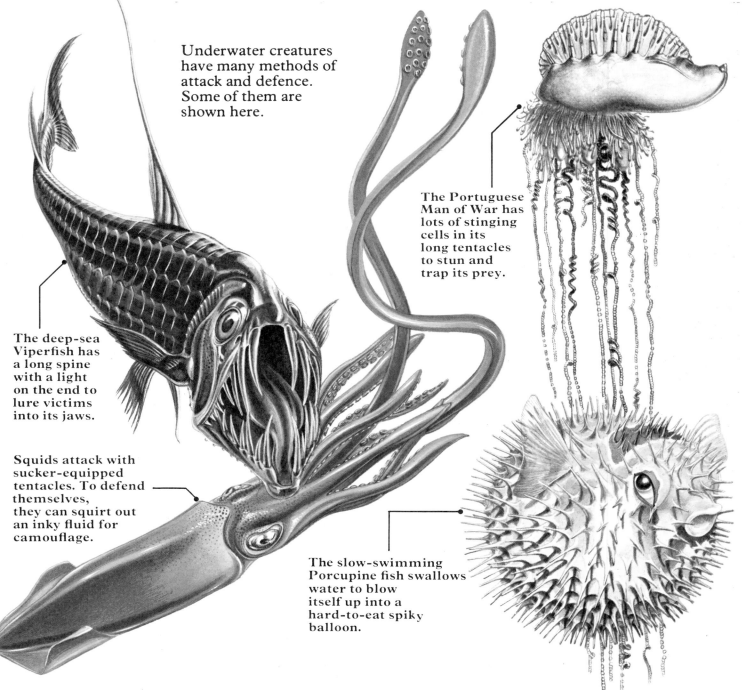

Underwater creatures have many methods of attack and defence. Some of them are shown here.

The Portuguese Man of War has lots of stinging cells in its long tentacles to stun and trap its prey.

The deep-sea Viperfish has a long spine with a light on the end to lure victims into its jaws.

Squids attack with sucker-equipped tentacles. To defend themselves, they can squirt out an inky fluid for camouflage.

The slow-swimming Porcupine fish swallows water to blow itself up into a hard-to-eat spiky balloon.

Credits

Written by
Christopher Pick
Art and Editorial direction
David Jefferis
Design Assistant
Iain Ashman

Illustrated by
Malcolm English
Christine Howes
Malcolm McGregor
Michael Roffe
Phil Weare
John Brettoner
Cover illustration by
Philip Hood

Acknowledgements
We wish to thank the following
for their assistance and for
making available material in
their collections.
Alwyne Wheeler
Robin Eccles
British Sub-Aqua Club
DHB Construction Ltd
DG Swales
Grumman Aerospace
Jerry Hazzard
Royal Navy

Buoyancy meter devised by Heather
Amery.

The experiments

Here is a checklist of the equipment you will need for the
experiments and things to do included in this book.

General equipment

Notebook and pencil
Rule or tape-measure
Sticky tape
Glue
Scissors
Salt
Paperclips
Rubber bands

For special experiments

Light and heavy water (p.5):
Glass bowl
Jug
Bottle of coloured ink

Salts in the seas (p.5):
Shallow bowl or saucer
Table salt

Water buoyancy meter (p.17):
Bowl
250 g plasticine
Sheet of thick card 250 mm
  30 mm
Used match
Three paperclips
Rubber band
Table salt

Underwater corrosion (p.17):
Two baked-bean tin lids
Two iron nails
Bowl
Table salt
Cotton thread

Make your own periscope (p. 20):
Two small hand mirrors
Balsa cement
Sheet of 6 mm thick balsa wood
700 mm × 76 mm
Allow another sheet of 6 mm thick
balsa wood 250 mm × 76 mm
to make the other components
Transparent acetate

The weight of water (p.24):
Two empty ballpoint pen cases
Plasticine
Waterproof sticky tape
Milk bottle
Balloon
Plastic or rubber tubing

Weights and measures

All the weights and measures used in this book are Metric.
This list gives some equivalents in Imperial measures.

mm = millimetre
(1 inch = 25.4 mm)

cm = centimetre
(1 inch = 2.54 cm)

m = metre
(1 yard = 0.91 m)

km = kilometre
(1 mile = 1.6 km)

kph = kilometres per hour
(100 mph = 160 kph)

g = gram
(10 g = 0.353 oz)

kg = kilogram
(1 pound = 0.45 kg)

A tonne is 1,000 kg
(1 ton = 1.02 tonnes)

kg/sq cm = kilograms per
square centimetre
(1 pound per square inch =
0.07 kg/sq cm)

1 litre is 1.76 pints

C = degrees Centigrade

On the cover: A great white shark

**On this page: a diving saucer
cruises over the sea bed**

THE USBORNE YOUNG SCIENTIST
UNDERSEA

About this book

What is a food pyramid? Why do fish have lateral lines? How do submarines dive, steer and surface?

The Undersea answers these questions and many more. It shows the reader how deep-diving machines are now opening up the Earth's last frontier—the world of inner space. It covers developments such as fish farming, mining the ocean floors and new ways to control pollution.

The Undersea also contains safe and simple experiments that can be done at home with ordinary household equipment. They range from projects like building a periscope to demonstrations of the principles of water pressure and buoyancy.

Contents

Planet Earth, the water world

The planet we live on, the Earth, has really been misnamed, as you can see from these three views of it—no less than 70.8 per cent of the world is covered in water!

The different parts of the sea have different names, but they are all connected and water flows continually around the world.

Life started in the sea, and although many forms of life live on land, the majority still live in the cradle of life—the sea.

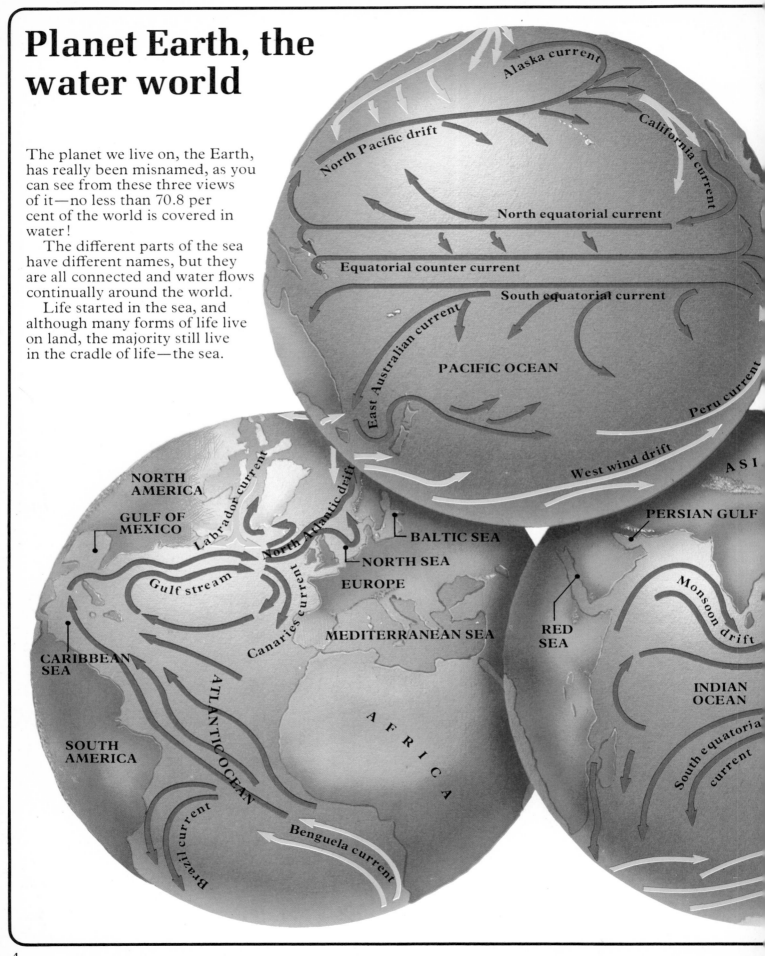

Alaska current

North Pacific drift

California current

North equatorial current

Equatorial counter current

South equatorial current

East Australian current

PACIFIC OCEAN

Peru current

West wind drift

ASIA

NORTH AMERICA

GULF OF MEXICO

Labrador current

North Atlantic drift

BALTIC SEA

NORTH SEA

EUROPE

Gulf stream

Canaries current

MEDITERRANEAN SEA

CARIBBEAN SEA

ATLANTIC OCEAN

SOUTH AMERICA

AFRICA

Brazil current

Benguela current

PERSIAN GULF

RED SEA

Monsoon drift

INDIAN OCEAN

South equatorial current

Highways of the Seas

Cold water currents

Warm water currents

Key to currents on globes at left

Ocean currents are the highways of the seas. Cold currents, produced by melting ice, start in the Arctic and Antarctic. Cold water is heavier than warm, so they flow at a great depth. The faster-flowing warm currents, usually starting around the equator, move nearer the surface.

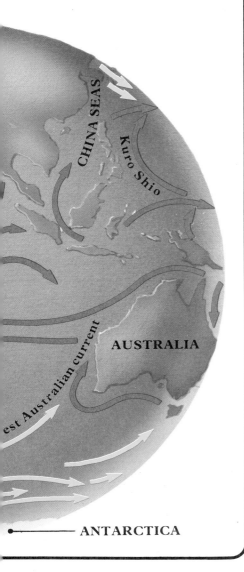

CHINA SEAS

Kuro Shio

AUSTRALIA

est Australian current

ANTARCTICA

Light and heavy water

1

HOT WATER

GLASS BOWL

▲ This simple experiment shows you why cold and warm water currents flow at the bottom and top of the seas. You need a glass bowl, a small jug and a bottle of ink. Fill the bowl three-quarters full of cold water.

2

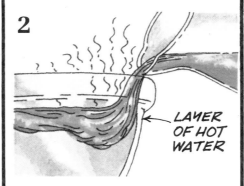

LAYER OF HOT WATER

▲ Fill the jug up with hot (but not boiling) water, and drop some ink in to colour it. Gently pour the hot water into the bowl. You will see that the hot water stays on the surface, forming a definite top layer.

3

WATER MIXES AS IT COOLS

HOT WATER COOLING DOWN

▲ After a while the hot water will cool off and mix with the rest. The reason why hot water stays on top is because water expands when it is heated—this makes it lighter, so it floats on top of the heavier, denser cold water.

Salts in the seas

1

RAIN FALLS ON LAND

MINERALS WASHED INTO SEA

MINERALS FORCED OUT OF CRACKS

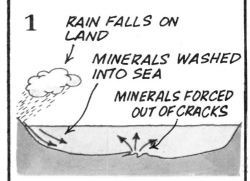

▲ Most salts and minerals are washed off the land by rain and carried into the sea by streams and rivers. The salts remain in the sea even when the water evaporates. This experiment shows how the process of evaporation works.

2

SAUCER OR SHALLOW TIN LID

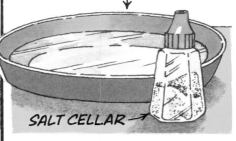

SALT CELLAR

▲ Fill the saucer with water, and put in as much salt as will dissolve—stir with a teaspoon to help if necessary. Put the saucer in a warm, dry place and leave it for a few days. Keep a daily note of the water level.

3

SALT CRYSTALS

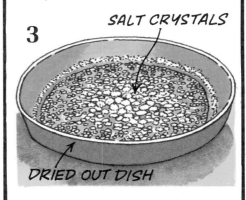

DRIED OUT DISH

▲ You will find the level sinking. The water is gradually turning into vapour—evaporating—and escaping into the atmosphere. It leaves the salt behind (like the salts in the oceans) to leave nothing but large salt crystals.

The living oceans

The sea is not just a flat expanse of water, the same from top to bottom. It varies a lot from place to place. The creatures in the sea, like those on land, have adapted in different ways to the kind of environment in which they live. Deep-sea fish, for example, are equipped with organs to lure prey and big jaws to swallow with.

Studying the undersea, the science of oceanography, is fairly new—the first detailed studies were not made until the 19th century.

▲ The first scientific expedition to explore the undersea sailed in *HMS Challenger* (shown above) in 1872. The scientists on board mapped the ocean floors and collected many specimens of ocean life during the voyage.

A habitat four kilometres deep

The sea is divided into two main parts. The Benthic area is the sea bottom, together with the creatures that live on it. The rest of the ocean is called the Pelagic area and is divided into three zones.

The photic, sunlit, zone at the top receives a lot of sunlight. Many creatures live there, in contrast with the euphotic, twilight zone, where there is little plant life.

Deeper down, there is no light at all, and little food. The inhabitants of the abyss, the sunless zone, are mainly small and well equipped to trap any prey that may come their way.

Sea level

20 C

16 C

1,000 m

8 C

4 C

2,000 m

3.5 C

3 C

3,000 m

3 C

2.5 C

4,000 m

2.5 C

Plankton live very near the surface.

Whales dive as deep as 1,200 m.

Gulper eel

Tripod fish

Starfish live even in the deepest parts of the oceans.

Landscape under the sea

The bottom of the sea has a 'landscape' of its own. Off most coasts the land gently slopes out across the continental shelf before falling steeply to the seabed. Nor is the seabed itself flat. There are trenches, canyons and mountain ranges—the tiniest islands are often merely the tips of enormous underwater peaks.

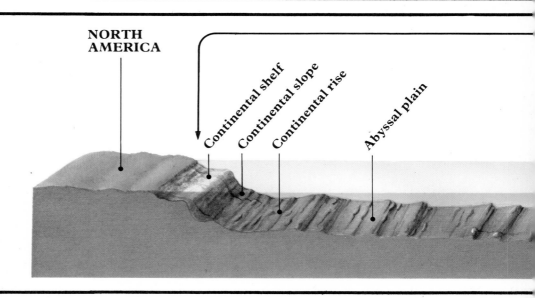

NORTH AMERICA

Continental shelf

Continental slope

Continental rise

Abyssal plain

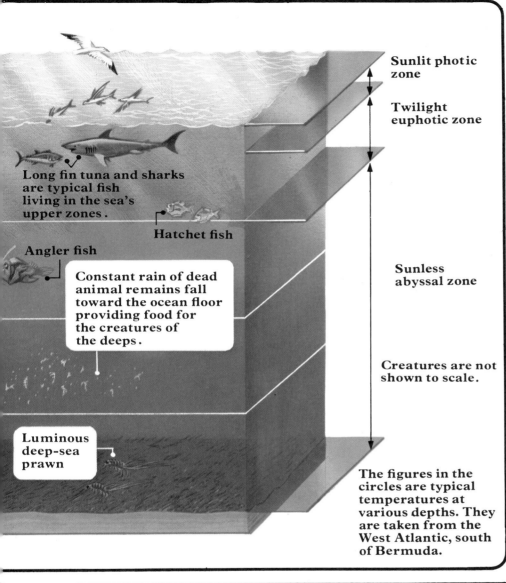

Sunlit photic zone

Twilight euphotic zone

Long fin tuna and sharks are typical fish living in the sea's upper zones.

Hatchet fish

Angler fish

Constant rain of dead animal remains fall toward the ocean floor providing food for the creatures of the deeps.

Sunless abyssal zone

Creatures are not shown to scale.

Luminous deep-sea prawn

The figures in the circles are typical temperatures at various depths. They are taken from the West Atlantic, south of Bermuda.

Food pyramids

The diagram below shows just one example of a food pyramid. 1,000 kg of phytoplankton, tiny plants, will feed 100 kg of zooplankton, animals. These zooplankton will in turn provide enough food for 10 kg of fish such as mackerel, which will sustain 1 kg of killer whale. Because so many small creatures are needed to feed larger ones there are always fewer large animals in the oceans than small ones.

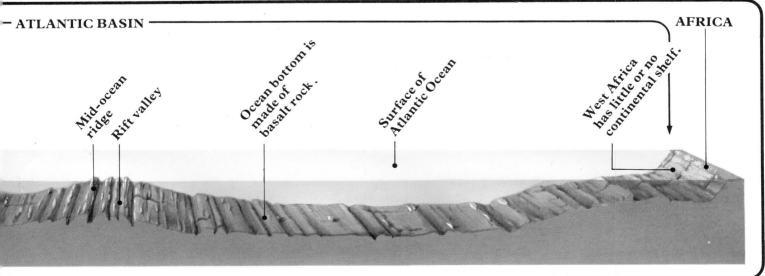

ATLANTIC BASIN

AFRICA

Mid-ocean ridge

Rift valley

Ocean bottom is made of basalt rock.

Surface of Atlantic Ocean

West Africa has little or no continental shelf.

Creatures of the sea

About 20,000 kinds of fish live in the sea. Most have bony skeletons. They are called teleosts after the Greek words which mean 'made of bone'. Others, like rays and sharks have skeletons of gristle. Octopuses and squids (which are not fish, but molluscs) have skeletons of chalky calcium carbonate.

Water

▲ Like people, fish need oxygen, but they get it from water, not air. As a fish swallows, water passes through its gills which 'strain' the oxygen from it. The de-oxygenated water is expelled through the gill covers.

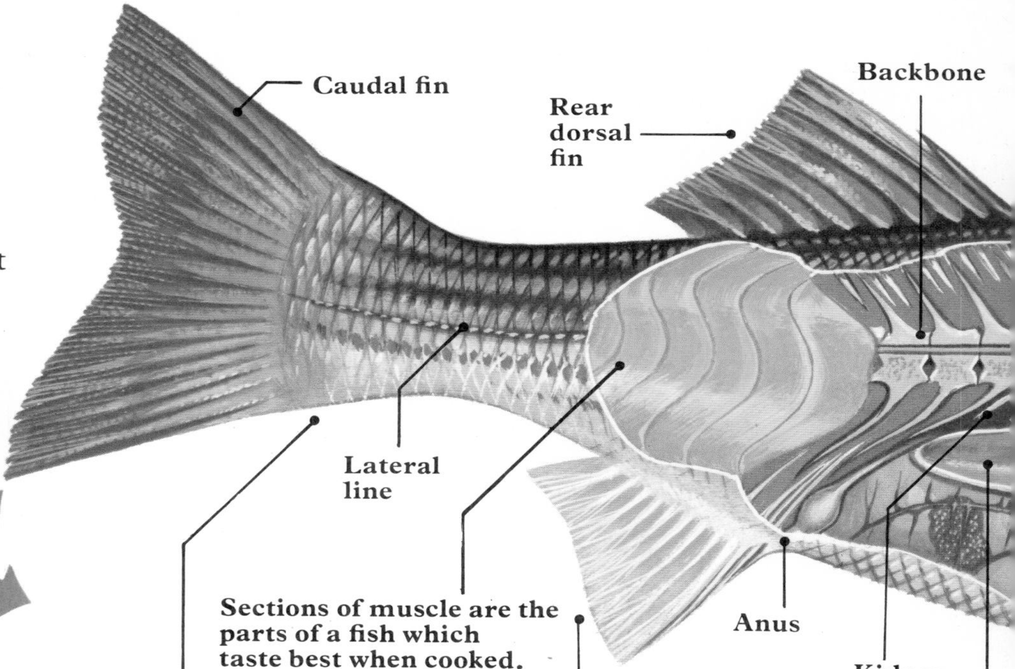

Caudal fin

Rear dorsal fin

Backbone

Lateral line

Sections of muscle are the parts of a fish which taste best when cooked.

Smooth slimy skin helps the fish swim quickly and easily.

Anal fin

Anus

Kidney

Gas bladder lets fish adjust its depth in the water. The more gas in the bladder, the more buoyant the fish.

Colour and camouflage

Camouflage is a fish's main protection against attack by a larger fish. Some fish also use camouflage when attacking and blend into the background until they are ready to strike.

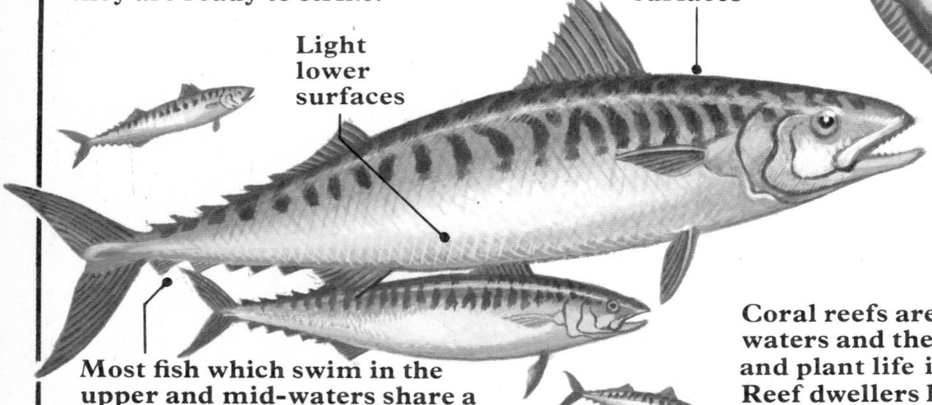

Light lower surfaces

Dark upper surfaces

Most fish which swim in the upper and mid-waters share a basic camouflage. They are light coloured on their lower bodies to blend in with the bright water surface above. Their upper parts are darker to blend in with the dark depths below.

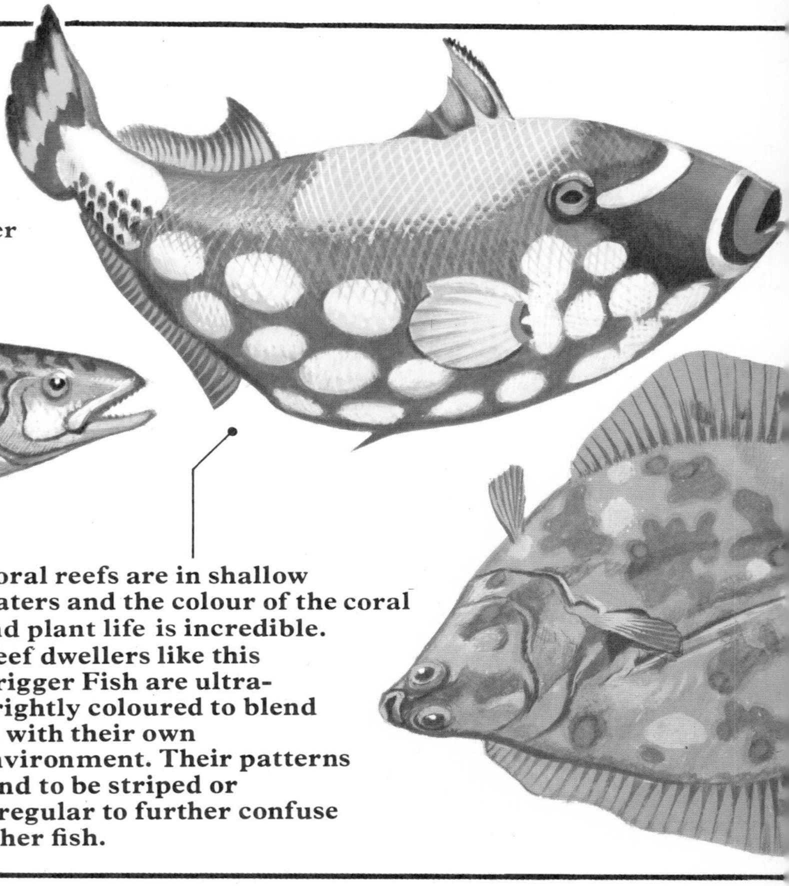

Coral reefs are in shallow waters and the colour of the coral and plant life is incredible. Reef dwellers like this Trigger Fish are ultra-brightly coloured to blend in with their own environment. Their patterns tend to be striped or irregular to further confuse other fish.

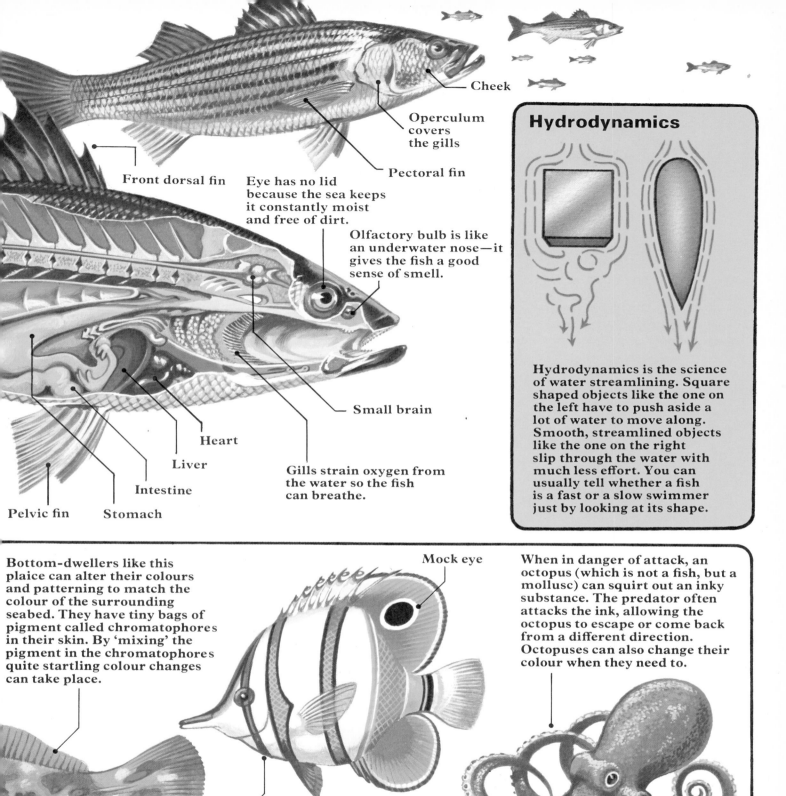

Cheek

Operculum covers the gills

Pectoral fin

Front dorsal fin

Eye has no lid because the sea keeps it constantly moist and free of dirt.

Olfactory bulb is like an underwater nose—it gives the fish a good sense of smell.

Small brain

Heart

Liver

Intestine

Gills strain oxygen from the water so the fish can breathe.

Pelvic fin

Stomach

Hydrodynamics

Hydrodynamics is the science of water streamlining. Square shaped objects like the one on the left have to push aside a lot of water to move along. Smooth, streamlined objects like the one on the right slip through the water with much less effort. You can usually tell whether a fish is a fast or a slow swimmer just by looking at its shape.

Bottom-dwellers like this plaice can alter their colours and patterning to match the colour of the surrounding seabed. They have tiny bags of pigment called chromatophores in their skin. By 'mixing' the pigment in the chromatophores quite startling colour changes can take place.

Mock eye

When in danger of attack, an octopus (which is not a fish, but a mollusc) can squirt out an inky substance. The predator often attacks the ink, allowing the octopus to escape or come back from a different direction. Octopuses can also change their colour when they need to.

Some fish use markings to deceive their enemy. This butterfly fish has a mock eye on its dorsal fin which confuses an attacker as to the position of its head. The dark lines on an angel fish look like the weeds and plants among which it lives.

Underwater diving

People have explored underwater for many centuries. They used to hold their breath and come up frequently for air. It was not until the invention of SCUBA gear that they had the freedom to swim underwater like fish.

SCUBA – which stands for Self Contained Underwater Breathing Apparatus – was invented by two Frenchmen, Emile Gagnan and Jacques Cousteau. They used the equipment for the first time in June 1943.

Since then, SCUBA, also known as the aqualung, has become popular world-wide.

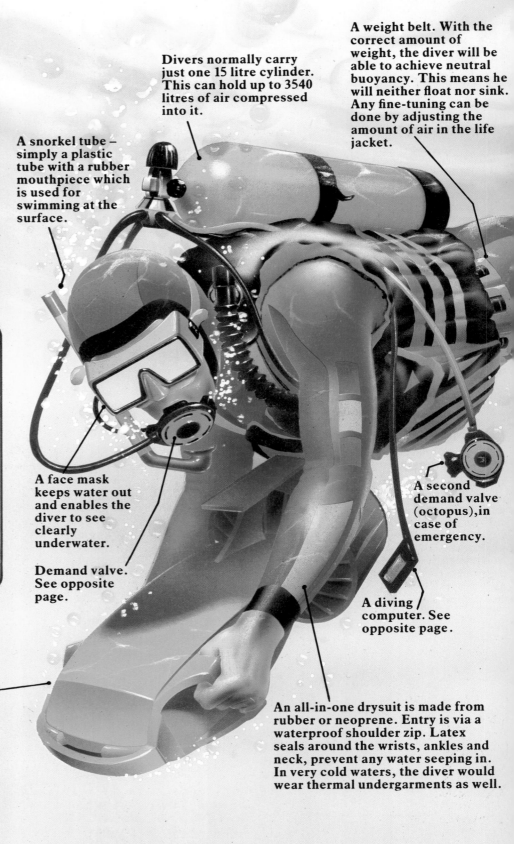

Water creatures

Humans are very watery creatures. Believe it or not, 73% of your body is made of ordinary water.

Divers normally carry just one 15 litre cylinder. This can hold up to 3540 litres of air compressed into it.

A weight belt. With the correct amount of weight, the diver will be able to achieve neutral buoyancy. This means he will neither float nor sink. Any fine-tuning can be done by adjusting the amount of air in the life jacket.

A snorkel tube – simply a plastic tube with a rubber mouthpiece which is used for swimming at the surface.

A face mask keeps water out and enables the diver to see clearly underwater.

Demand valve. See opposite page.

A second demand valve (octopus), in case of emergency.

A diving computer. See opposite page.

Swimming underwater for long distances can be very tiring and some divers choose to use a diver propulsion vehicle like the one shown here. It is electrically powered and can tow a diver through the water at about three to four kph. It will work down to a depth of 75m.

An all-in-one drysuit is made from rubber or neoprene. Entry is via a waterproof shoulder zip. Latex seals around the wrists, ankles and neck, prevent any water seeping in. In very cold waters, the diver would wear thermal undergarments as well.

Fins are made of plastic and rubber. They improve the diver's swimming ability.

Knife

Flash gun

Waterproof housing

Underwater cameras are both waterproof and robust. Divers can use an ordinary camera protected by a waterproof housing. They need a powerful flash gun to illuminate the picture.

How SCUBA gear works

Demand valve

▲ Divers need a regular supply of air – neither too much nor too little. It must also be at exactly the same pressure as the water in which they are swimming. The demand valve controls both these things.

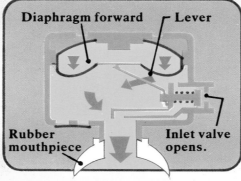

Diaphragm forward — Lever

Rubber mouthpiece

Inlet valve opens.

▲ The diagrams above show how the demand valve works. By breathing in, the diaphragm is sucked forward operating the lever and opening the inlet valve. The air flow is then directed to the diver's mouth via the mouthpiece.

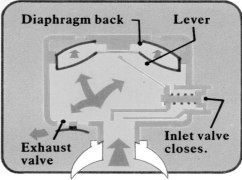

Diaphragm back — Lever

Exhaust valve

Inlet valve closes.

When the diver breathes out, the diaphragm is allowed to fall back into position and the lever pushes the inlet valve closed. Exhaled air passes out into the water via the small one-way exhaust valve.

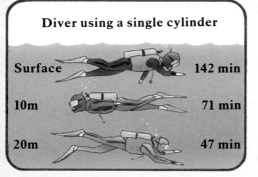

Diver using a single cylinder

Surface	142 min
10m	71 min
20m	47 min

▲ The deeper a diver goes, the more air is needed to counter-balance the increasing pressure from the surrounding water. The diagram above shows how long a 15 litre cylinder will last at various depths.

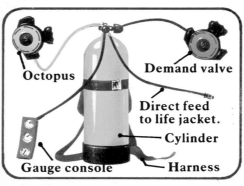

Octopus

Demand valve

Direct feed to life jacket.

Cylinder

Gauge console

Harness

▲ A complete aqua-lung assembly as shown here, is fitted with a 15 litre cylinder, a harness and a number of hoses. The hoses are needed to feed air to the demand valve, octopus, life jacket and gauge console.

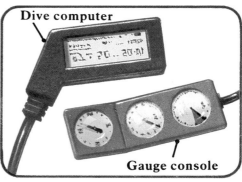

Dive computer

Gauge console

▲ The console may hold such things as a contents gauge, depth gauge, compass, thermometer or timer. Some divers prefer a diving computer which offers all of the above facilities but is often smaller and lighter.

11

Wrecks and treasures

There have been wrecks for as long as there have been ships, and thousands of vessels and their cargoes lie scattered on the seabed. In fact, the oceans are one of the world's greatest treasure hoards and are an important source of information about how people lived in the past.

Serious underwater investigations by trained archaeologists only started in the 1950s. Before then, many wrecks had been looted and spoiled by treasure-seekers interested not in the past but only in the cash they could get for their finds.

► **This picture shows some of the ways in which underwater archaeologists record and retrieve remains from ocean wrecks. These remains are from an ancient Greek trading boat.**

This bag catches any valuable items sucked up by the air lift.

This diver is letting air from his aqualung into an ancient wine jug. Once filled with air, it will rise up to the surface.

Air-filled balloons lift heavy loads from the seabed to the surface. This odd-shaped lump is made of lots of iron fragments rusted together.

Metal detectors like the one this diver is carrying help to locate objects such as coins and jewellery.

Undersea air lift, used to suck up the sand and mud that the current continually deposits on the wreck.

Danger in the deeps

1

▲ The invention of SCUBA gear meant that divers were able to explore freely in the depths, like the camera-equipped diver above. One danger remained though—the bends—agonizing pains which can cause paralysis or death.

2

▲ Water pressure will crush a diver's lungs unless the force of his air supply equals it. Under high pressure, the diver breathes more air than normal and the extra nitrogen in the air is absorbed into the diver's body.

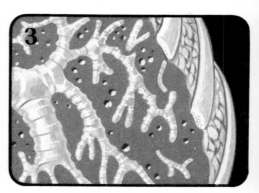

3

▲ As the diver surfaces, the pressure from the surrounding water decreases. If he comes up too quickly the nitrogen absorbed into his body (lungs are shown in close-up above) will not escape, but will bubble like fizzy lemonade.

This two-man submarine, specially built for underwater archaeology, is the easy way to map out a wreck. Equipped with two cameras, it can go down as deep as 180 m and can photograph a whole site in only a few hours.

Scaffolding divides up remains into small areas.

A sketch book and pencil is one way of recording a find—but because the artist is underwater, the 'pencil' has to be a graphite crayon and the 'paper' a sheet of plastic.

Two centuries under the sea

Not all wrecks are as well preserved as the Vasa, a ship which was raised intact more than 300 years after she sank in Stockholm harbour in Sweden. Ships usually broke up, either against rocks or as a result of the pounding action of the sea. In these cases, marine archaeologists have to turn detective and scour the seabed over wide areas looking for finds just as they would on land, their work being even more difficult.

▲ The pictures above and right show what could happen to a wreck. Above, the contents are strewn over rocks as the hull is torn open. Right, currents and sand spread and cover the ship's remains.

Hull after sinking

1

100 years later 2

150 years later 3

200 years later 4

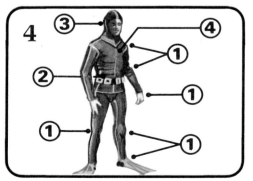

▲ Nitrogen bubbles in the body can have effects like this. In nerves (1), they cause pains in bones, joints and muscles. In the spine (2), they cause paralysis. In the brain (3), dizzyness and convulsions. In the blood (4), asphyxia and choking.

Recompression chamber

▲ To overcome an attack of the bends, the victim is put into a recompression chamber. Air is pumped in at high pressure and then very slowly released. The diver is brought slowly back to the correct pressure, giving the nitrogen time to escape without forming bubbles. The diagram above shows how long a diver can spend underwater at different depths without risking an attack of the bends and without slowing down his ascent to the surface.

6

Depth of dive	Length of dive
10m	232mins
20m	46mins
30m	20mins
40m	11mins
50m	7mins

Sharks and rays

Sharks, rays and skate are fish which have no bony skeletons—they are made of gristly cartilage—so they are called cartilaginous fish.

Sharks have no gill covers, so they cannot retain water in their gills. So that they can strain enough oxygen from the water to breathe, they have to keep swimming all the time, so that water is flowing continuously over their gills.

Though only 12 species of shark are classed as man-eaters, the behaviour of all except the harmless whale and basking sharks is utterly unpredictable.

▼ ▶ **Sharks are the biggest group of cartilaginous fish and are among the oldest creatures in the ocean. The first sharks lived 350 million years ago and their modern descendants have hardly changed in appearance.**

The thresher shark's strongpoint is its tail, which it uses to round-up and stun smaller fish such as mackerel and herring before it devours them.

The whale shark is the gentle giant of the oceans. Though it grows up to 17 m long, it lives off plankton, swims very slowly and is quite harmless. It is the largest fish in the sea.

The hammerhead shark gets its name because of the shape of its head. Its eyes and nostrils are at each end of the hammer.

▲ The manta ray does not live on the bottom like most rays but swims close to the surface. The horns on either side of its mouth guide in water from which it can filter plankton to eat. If it is ever chased, the manta ray can leap out of the water to safety.

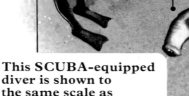

This SCUBA-equipped diver is shown to the same scale as the sharks.

Detecting prey

Lateral line

Seawater
Shark's skin
Opening
Fluid-filled channel
Sensitive hairs
Nerves

▲ Like other fish, sharks have a special system for locating prey called the lateral line. Underneath the lateral line are lots of openings, each at the head of a channel filled with fluid. If a fish moves nearby, the movement of the water presses on the fluid. In turn, this presses on to sensitive hairs at the end of the channel. These are attached to nerve endings linked to the shark's brain. The system is so sensitive that the shark knows the exact position of its prey and can attack. It even knows, within limits, the health of its prey—wounded fish thrash about, dying fish move much more gently. Both movements are sensed by the lateral line system.

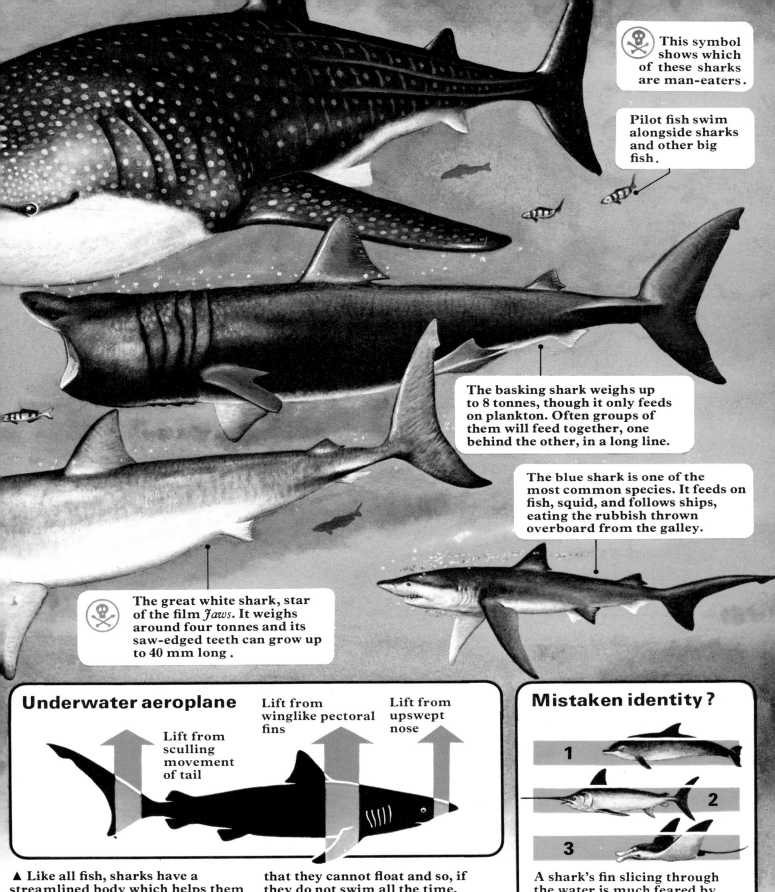

This symbol shows which of these sharks are man-eaters.

Pilot fish swim alongside sharks and other big fish.

The basking shark weighs up to 8 tonnes, though it only feeds on plankton. Often groups of them will feed together, one behind the other, in a long line.

The blue shark is one of the most common species. It feeds on fish, squid, and follows ships, eating the rubbish thrown overboard from the galley.

The great white shark, star of the film *Jaws*. It weighs around four tonnes and its saw-edged teeth can grow up to 40 mm long.

Underwater aeroplane

Lift from sculling movement of tail

Lift from winglike pectoral fins

Lift from upswept nose

▲ Like all fish, sharks have a streamlined body which helps them to move through the water with as little effort as possible. But for sharks this is especially important, because they do not have a swimbladder. This means that they cannot float and so, if they do not swim all the time, they will sink.

Their nose, pectoral fins and tail all help to give them lift like an aeroplane's wings while they move through the water.

Mistaken identity?

1

2

3

A shark's fin slicing through the water is much feared by swimmers and divers. Other, friendlier, fins can belong to Dolphins (1), Swordfish (2) and harmless Manta rays (3).

15

Underwater armour

JIM is the nickname for a type of armoured diving suit developed in the 1970s. The air pressure inside it is the same as that of the Earth's atmosphere. This means that most of the problems of working at considerable depths are avoided. Divers can explore down to about 610m and can return to the surface without having to decompress.

Also, there is an example below of a submersible machine in which divers can work at these depths with similar protection.

The JIM in this picture is the Type II model which has four circular windows in front and two behind. In the newer Type IV JIM, vision is improved by a completely clear plastic dome over the head.

Diver breathes through close fitting mask

JIM is lifted to and from the surface by this heavy cable. It also doubles as a telephone line.

JIM Type II's hull is made of hardened magnesium alloy. Glass reinforced plastic has replaced this for the Type IV.

JIM's mechanical hands, called manipulators, can pick up quite small objects.

The limb joints on JIM's arms and legs contain fluid which prevents them seizing up.

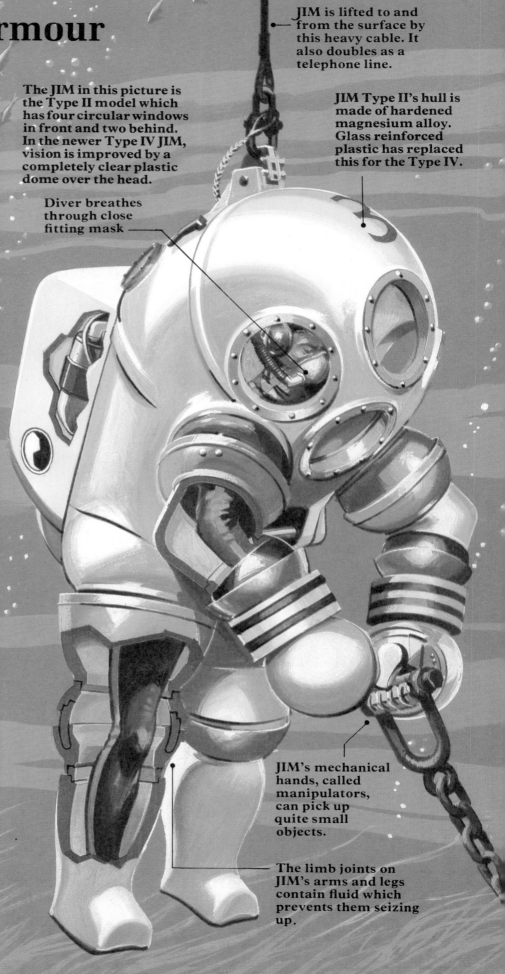

▲ Shown here is one of JIM's ancestors, made in 1715 by John Lethbridge. He reached a depth of 20 m during a dive in his wood and iron invention. The diver lay flat on his front looking out of a window, his arms poking out of two holes.

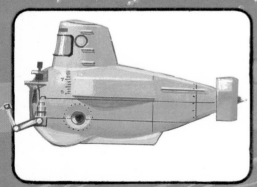

▲ Shown here is Alvin, a three-man submersible in which divers can work at great depths. The Alvin was one of the underwater vehicles used to film the *SS Titanic* when it was discovered in 1988.

Testing water buoyancy

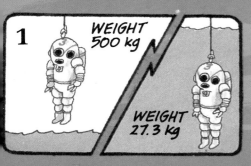

1 WEIGHT 500 kg WEIGHT 27.3 kg

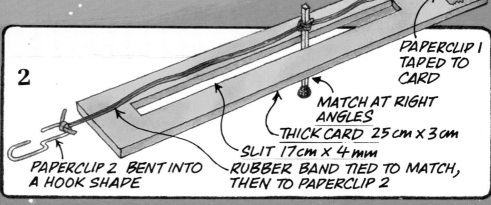

2 PAPERCLIP 1 TAPED TO CARD

MATCH AT RIGHT ANGLES

THICK CARD 25 cm × 3 cm

SLIT 17 cm × 4 mm

PAPERCLIP 2 BENT INTO A HOOK SHAPE

RUBBER BAND TIED TO MATCH, THEN TO PAPERCLIP 2

▲ When JIM is on land, it weighs 500 kg. Underwater however, its weight drops to a more manageable 27.3 kg. This effect is called buoyancy. Any object will weigh less when it is in water than it will out of it.

▲ This water buoyancy meter will let you measure the weight drop of objects in water. You need a bowl, plasticine, a used match, some thick card, three paperclips and a rubber band. Cut the rubber band in half to get a single length.

Cut out the card and assemble the meter as shown in the picture above. Make sure that the match pointer moves smoothly in the central slit. To add the weighing scale, first mark on the position at which the match points.

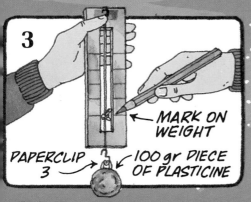

3 MARK ON WEIGHT

PAPERCLIP 3

100 gr PIECE OF PLASTICINE

4 DO NOT DROP METER IN !

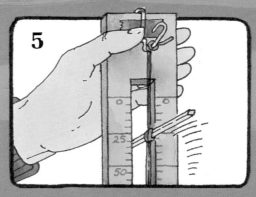

5

▲ Using kitchen scales, cut four pieces of plasticine weighing 25, 50, 75, and 100 g each. Hang them in turn from the meter's hook. Mark on the scale where the match points to with each different piece of plasticine.

▲ Hook the 100 gr piece of plasticine onto the meter. Check that the match pointer is against the 100 g mark on the scale. Fill the bowl with water, and lower the plasticine gently in. Its weight will drop to about 45 g.

▲ Salty water is even more buoyant than fresh. Try dissolving lots of salt in the bowl. The plasticine's weight will drop even more. When you have finished with the weight experiments, use the salty water for the corrosion experiment below.

Corrosion underwater

1 SALTY WATER

TIN LIDS

NAILS

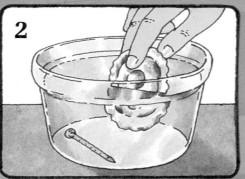

2

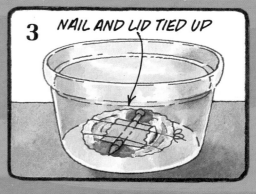

3 NAIL AND LID TIED UP

▲ JIM's magnesium hull is hardened to resist corrosion from the sea, which acts just like a weak acid. Try this experiment using two baked-bean tin lids, two iron nails and the bowl of salty water from the buoyancy experiment

▲ Metals rust at different rates. Test this by putting a tin lid and a nail into the bowl of salt water. Make sure they do not touch. You will see that the nail starts to rust in a few hours, whereas the tin lid takes much longer.

▲ Galvanic corrosion is caused when different metals touch one another. Bind the other tin lid and nail together with cotton thread and put them in the water. You will see that the touching parts rust quicker than the rest.

Development of the submarine

The first submarine was invented in 1578 by an Englishman, William Bourne, but it had no means of propulsion. The Turtle, launched in 1776, was little better, using muscle powered propellers. The German U (Unterseeboote—undersea boat) boats used in World War I were the first major use of submarine power at war.

Since then, submarines have developed into the most important weapon in modern military arsenals. The picture on the right is typical of a present-day missile-carrying atomic-powered submarine. The details may change from type to type, but the general features are similar the world over. The whale-shaped hull is designed to operate most efficiently underwater.

David Bushnell's *Turtle* **was armed with a 68 kg gunpowder bomb and cruised underwater for about 30 minutes before the pilot had to open the hatch for fresh air.**

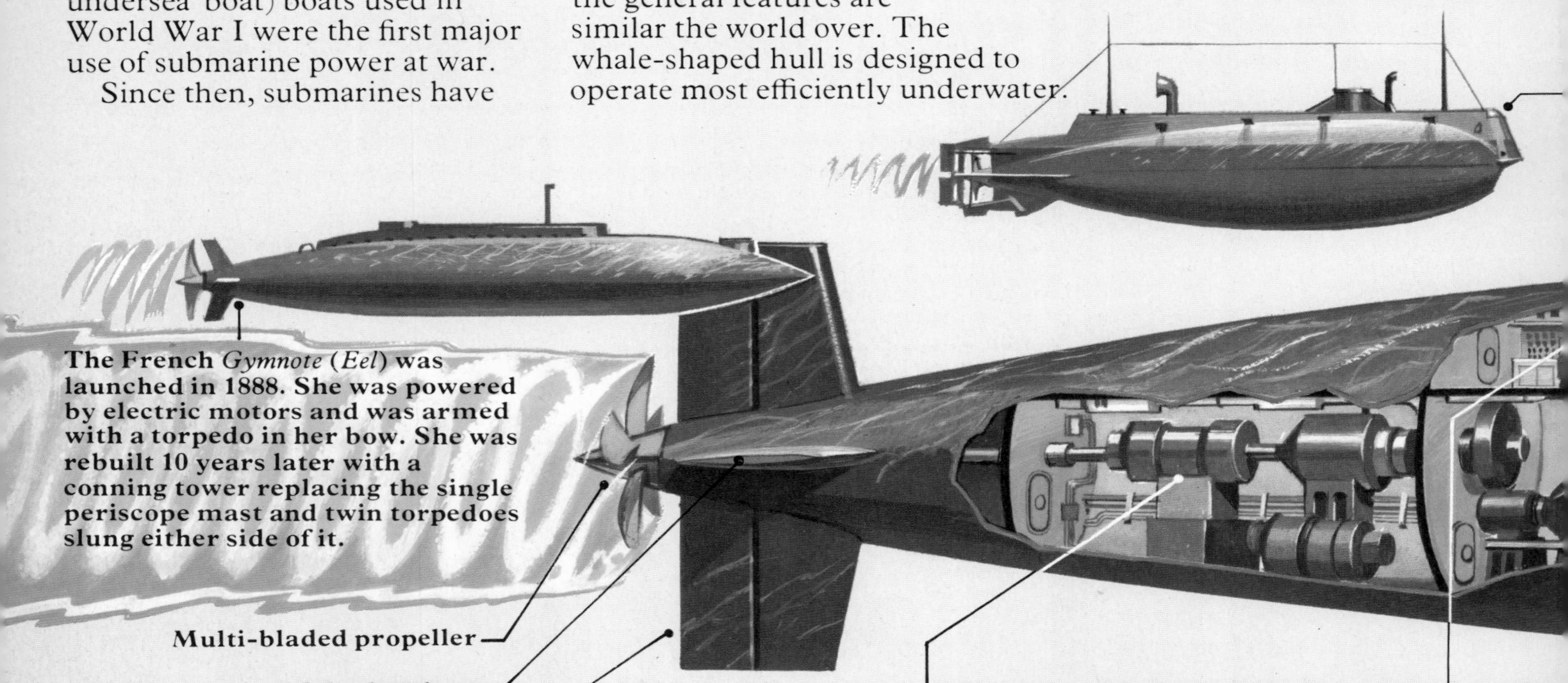

The French *Gymnote* (*Eel*) **was launched in 1888. She was powered by electric motors and was armed with a torpedo in her bow. She was rebuilt 10 years later with a conning tower replacing the single periscope mast and twin torpedoes slung either side of it.**

Multi-bladed propeller

Aft hydroplane

Rudder

Main motor room housing the propulsion turbines, which turn the propeller, and the turbo-generators, which supply electricity.

Aft escape tower. Four men at a time can escape through the aft and forward escape towers. If a diver needs to examine the outside of the hull, he leaves and returns by the escape tower.

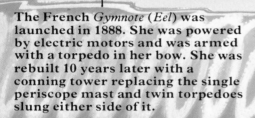

1 Keeping control of a submarine

If a submarine is too buoyant it will stay on the surface like a ship. If its weight is increased it becomes less buoyant. At a certain weight it will submerge. To stay submerged without sinking or rising—to be neutrally buoyant—the submarine must weigh the same as the amount of water that it displaces. So, as fuel and stores (up to 2,500 tonnes of them) are used up, water is let into compensating tanks to make up the weight difference.

2

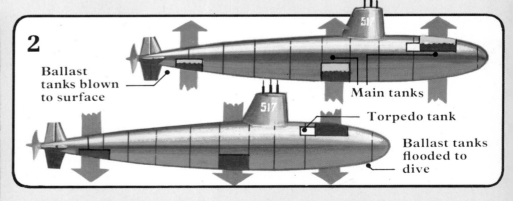

Ballast tanks blown to surface

Main tanks

Torpedo tank

Ballast tanks flooded to dive

▲ **The main ballast tanks are the key to submerging and surfacing. On the surface, these tanks are filled with air. To submerge, they are both completely filled with water. To return to the surface, compressed air is forced** into the tanks. This forces the water out, and the submarine rises to the surface.

After missiles or torpedoes have been fired, water is let into small torpedo tanks to compensate for the weight loss.

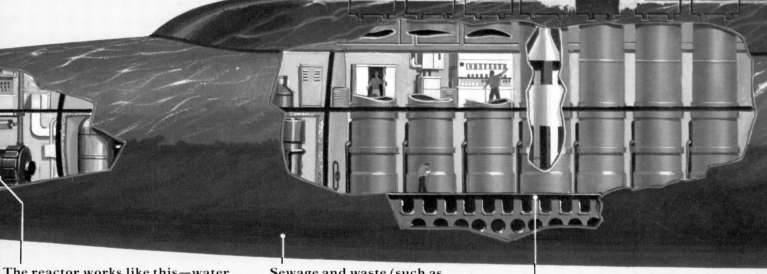

Speed at sea is usually measured in knots. One knot is equivalent to 1.85kph (1.15mph).

The cigar-shaped Holland submarine was built for the US Navy and the British Royal Navy. The Number 8 design, shown here, was bought by the US Navy in 1900. She was equipped with a single torpedo and could cruise underwater at 9 kph.

Typical cruise speed is around 45 kph underwater, 36 kph on the surface.

A typical warload is 16 Polaris missiles. Each has three separate H-bomb warheads which can be directed to different targets far apart. The missiles are blown out of their launch tubes by compressed air. The missiles' engines fire when they are clear of the tube.

The missile hatches are opened just before the missiles are fired.

The reactor works like this—water is pumped around the radio-active hot core and is turned into steam. The steam spins turbines which turn the propeller and generate electricity.

Sewage and waste (such as potato peelings) are a problem as disposal is difficult at depth. They are normally stored and pumped out back at base.

Missile decks where the missiles are prepared for firing, and minor servicing undertaken.

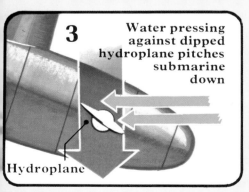

3 Water pressing against dipped hydroplane pitches submarine down

Hydroplane

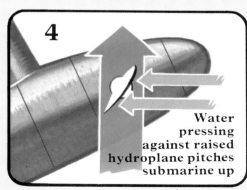

4 Water pressing against raised hydroplane pitches submarine up

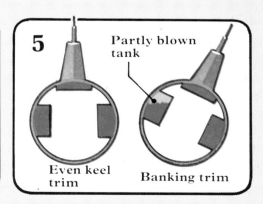

5 Partly blown tank

Even keel trim   Banking trim

▲ Underwater, hydroplanes control the angle of the submarine. To dive, the forward hydroplanes are dipped, the aft pair raised. As the submarine moves along, water pressing against the tops of the forward hydroplanes forces the bows down (above left), water pressing against the bottoms of the aft hydroplanes forces the stern up. The submarine then cruises down at the dipped angle, its tanks flooded to make it sink. To surface, this sequence is reversed (above right).

▲ Special trimming tanks help to keep the submarine stable as it changes course. If the craft turns to starboard (to the right), water is blown from the port (left) tank to bank the submarine into the 'corner'.

On top of the fin (called the sail in the US Navy) are the search and attack periscopes, radio antennae, and the snort induction mast. This sucks in air if the submarine is not running on its reactor and has come close to the surface to recharge its batteries.

In the missile control centre the missiles are given their target instructions and, if necessary, fired.

The control room is the nerve centre of the ship.

Wardroom where the submarine's officers eat and relax.

The wireless office receives messages and orders. It never transmits—to do so would give the submarine's position away.

The navigation centre where the submarine's course is plotted and checked.

The sound room. The sonar team can locate nearby ships and submarines using a sound analysing system.

Make your own periscope

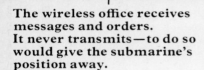

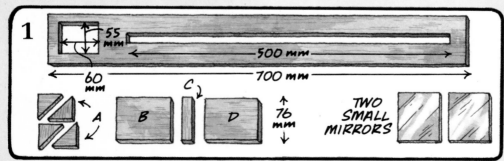

1

55 mm

500 mm

60 mm

700 mm

C

A

B

D

76 mm

TWO SMALL MIRRORS

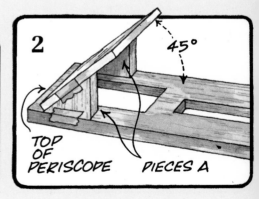

2

45°

TOP OF PERISCOPE

PIECES A

▲ This periscope, though not designed for underwater work, will enable you to spy over walls and see around corners. You need two small hand mirrors, which you can get from the cosmetics department of a large store. You also need sticky tape, balsa glue, 6 mm thick balsa wood, and some transparent acetate. Cut out the balsa wood to the sizes and shapes shown in the plans above. An easy way to cut a 45° triangle is to cut a square in half from corner to corner.

▲ The square hole for the top mirror should be a little smaller than the mirror itself, so its size will vary depending on the size of your mirror. Tape a mirror to two triangle struts, then tape the assembly in place as shown.

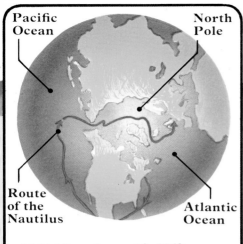

At 11.15 on August 3, 1958 Commander Anderson took the atomic submarine _USS Nautilus_ under the North Pole.

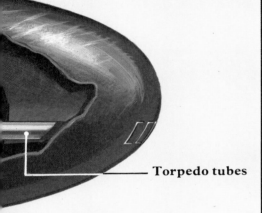

Torpedo tubes

— Each torpedo is powered by its own electric motor and can be guided onto its target after it has been fired. It creates neither wake nor noise, either of which might reveal the submarine's position.

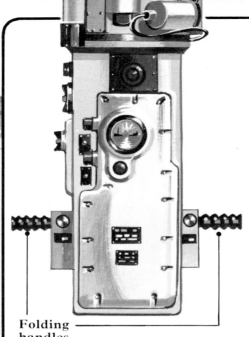

Folding handles

A periscope is one of the ways a submarine can discover what is happening on the surface and in the sky while remaining submerged. Most submarines have two—the search and the attack periscopes. The search periscope is for normal use. It can easily be seen, so the attack periscope, which is slim and difficult to spot, is used if the submarine is attacking enemy craft.

Most periscopes have an image-intensifier. This aids visibility in poor weather, by amplifying the picture, rather like turning up the brightness on a television screen. Periscopes also have range-finders to calculate how far away a target is.

Commander's eye-view of the sea

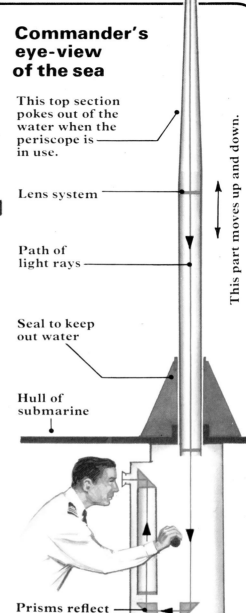

This top section pokes out of the water when the periscope is in use.

This part moves up and down.

Lens system

Path of light rays

Seal to keep out water

Hull of submarine

Prisms reflect light to eyepiece

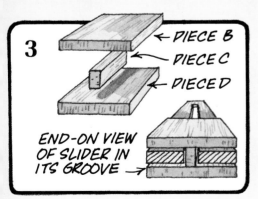

3

PIECE B
PIECE C
PIECE D

END-ON VIEW OF SLIDER IN ITS GROOVE →

▲ The H-shaped slider moves in the central slot. Assemble the three parts of it together with glue, making sure they can move freely up and down. Hold the parts together with pins until they have dried thoroughly.

4

SLIDER MOVES UP & DOWN

PATH OF LIGHT RAYS TO YOUR EYE

▲ Glue and tape the other two triangle struts onto the slider, then tape the mirror in place as the picture above shows. The dotted red line shows the path light rays take on their way from the target to your eye.

5

TAPE

▲ Draw sights on a piece of acetate (or any clear plastic) and tape it in front of the square hole. To use, hold the slider to your eye with your left hand. Move the main body of the periscope up and down with your right hand.

Mammals of the sea

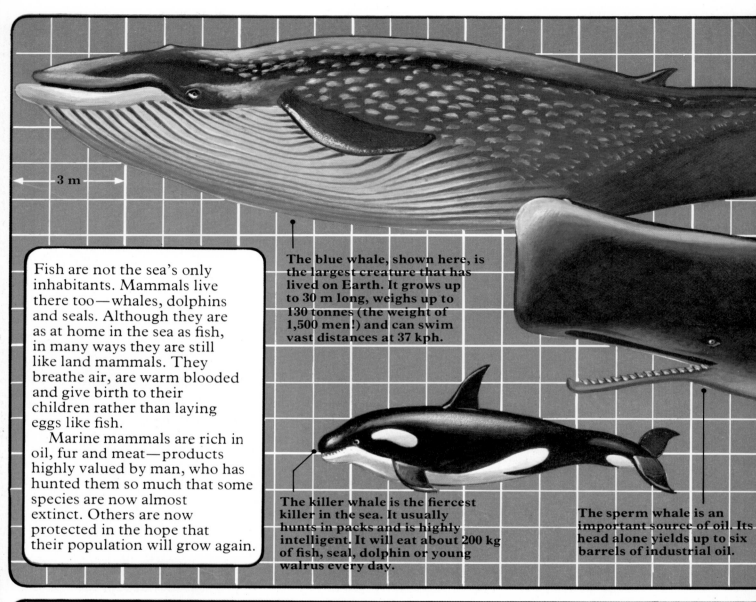

Fish are not the sea's only inhabitants. Mammals live there too—whales, dolphins and seals. Although they are as at home in the sea as fish, in many ways they are still like land mammals. They breathe air, are warm blooded and give birth to their children rather than laying eggs like fish.

Marine mammals are rich in oil, fur and meat—products highly valued by man, who has hunted them so much that some species are now almost extinct. Others are now protected in the hope that their population will grow again.

The blue whale, shown here, is the largest creature that has lived on Earth. It grows up to 30 m long, weighs up to 130 tonnes (the weight of 1,500 men!) and can swim vast distances at 37 kph.

The killer whale is the fiercest killer in the sea. It usually hunts in packs and is highly intelligent. It will eat about 200 kg of fish, seal, dolphin or young walrus every day.

The sperm whale is an important source of oil. Its head alone yields up to six barrels of industrial oil.

Two types of whale . . .

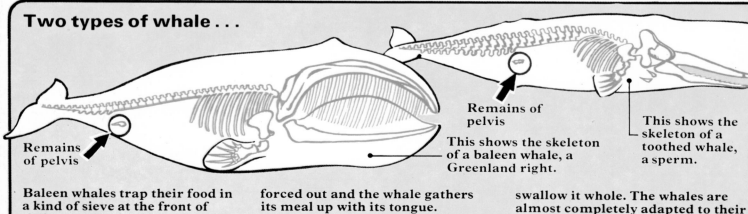

Remains of pelvis

Remains of pelvis

This shows the skeleton of a baleen whale, a Greenland right.

This shows the skeleton of a toothed whale, a sperm.

Baleen whales trap their food in a kind of sieve at the front of their mouths. As they swim along openmouthed, water flows in and food is caught in the strands of baleen. The water is then forced out and the whale gathers its meal up with its tongue. Toothed whales are equipped with 60 teeth, each one about 200 mm long and weighing around 3 kg. They do not chew their food, but swallow it whole. The whales are almost completely adapted to their life at sea—the only remains of their pelvis for example, is the tiny bone structure arrowed in the skeletons shown above.

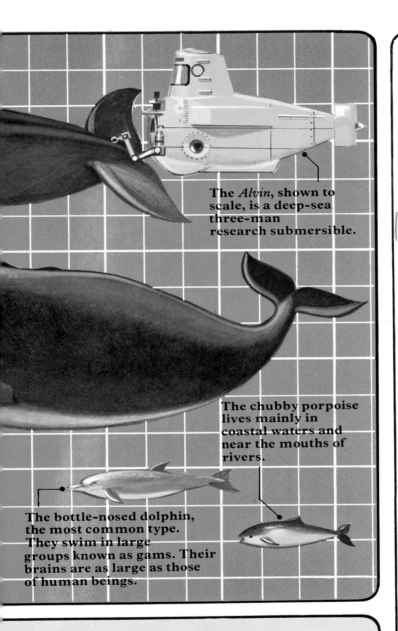

The *Alvin,* shown to scale, is a deep-sea three-man research submersible.

The chubby porpoise lives mainly in coastal waters and near the mouths of rivers.

The bottle-nosed dolphin, the most common type. They swim in large groups known as gams. Their brains are as large as those of human beings.

. . . and their menu for lunch

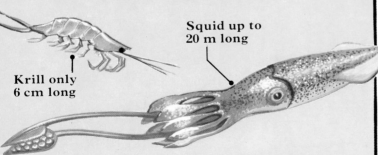

Squid up to 20 m long

Krill only 6 cm long

Baleen whales live on krill, a small shrimp-like plankton creature. Sperm whales live mainly on squid, which are more difficult to capture than krill. Sucker-scars have been found on whales showing that they have fought giant squids up to 20 m long.

Dolphins—marvels of nature's engineering

Hungry dolphins use an echo-reflecting system to find their prey. They make very high pitched clicks in their nose passages, sending them out as concentrated beams of sound waves. The sound waves reflect off anything in their way, the dolphin hears the echoes and 'homes-in' on the unfortunate fish.

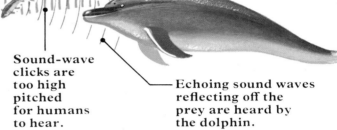

Sound-wave clicks are too high pitched for humans to hear.

Echoing sound waves reflecting off the prey are heard by the dolphin.

▼ Dolphin skin is fixed into long internal grooves, like inside-out fingerprints. They keep the skin taut and firm, cutting down the drag—the slowing down effect—of the water. The skin wobbles as it speeds along, constantly adjusting to eddies and turbulence, cutting down drag even more.

The underskin grooves exactly follow the line water takes as it flows around the body.

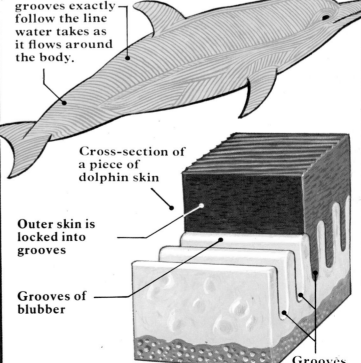

Cross-section of a piece of dolphin skin

Outer skin is locked into grooves

Grooves of blubber

Grooves

In the abyss

The struggle to survive in the cold and pitch black abyss is intense. Few fish live there because food is so short. Those that do tend to be small and their bodies are built to hunt for food. Many have tiny lights which shine out to lure their prey. Their mouths and stomachs are very flexible too, so they can attack and swallow up other fish that are sometimes bigger than themselves.

▲ The first deep-sea explorations were made by Barton and Beebe, two American scientists. In 1934 they went down to 923 m in their bathysphere, shown above, a record depth that was only exceeded 15 years later.

Ugly faces of the deep

Large-mouthed and ugly tends to be the general rule in the deeps. Here are just five examples of deep-sea dwellers.

0   50mm

As her name implies, this female angler fish goes fishing for food. Her bait is the lighted tip of an extended ray that grows from her head.

0   50mm

The gulper eel is quite capable of eating a fish as big as itself. Having lured its victim by the reddish light at the end of its tail, it extends its jaws and gulps. There's no capacity problem— its stomach can stretch to twice its normal size.

The weight of water

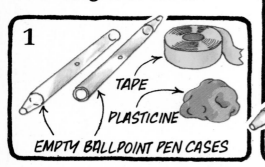

1 TAPE / PLASTICINE / EMPTY BALLPOINT PEN CASES

▲ This experiment shows you how water pressure works at a depth, even though you only need to dive to the bottom of a bottle. You need two empty ballpoint pen cases, some plasticine and a roll of waterproof sticky tape.

2 PLASTICINE SEAL / TAPE PEN CASES TOGETHER / SEAL BREATHER HOLES

▲ Tape the two pen cases together ends-on as shown above. Make sure you tape up the small 'breather' holes half-way up each case. Use the plasticine to seal one end of the long tube you have made. Blow down the tube to check the seals.

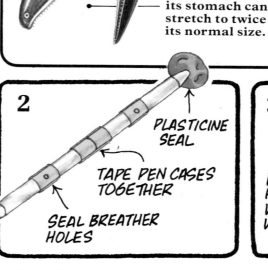

3 BOTTLE FILLED WITH WATER

▲ Fill up a milk bottle (or any other tall glass jar) with water. Plunge the tube, open end down, to the bottom of the jar. You should see the surrounding water press a little way, about 10 mm, up into the tube.

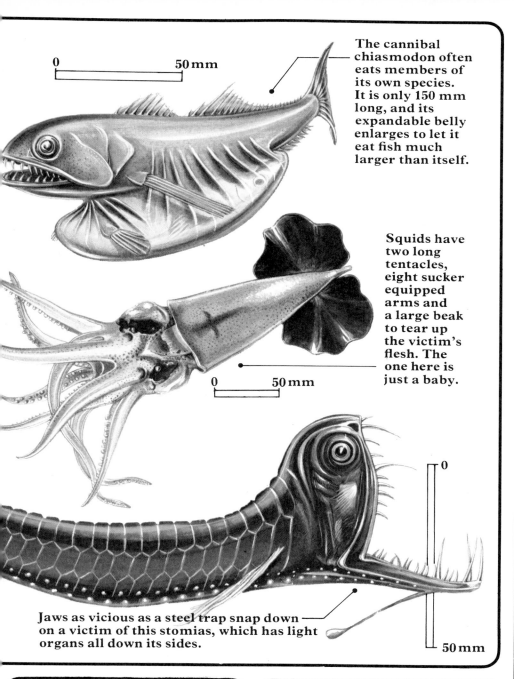

0　　　　　50 mm

The cannibal chiasmodon often eats members of its own species. It is only 150 mm long, and its expandable belly enlarges to let it eat fish much larger than itself.

Squids have two long tentacles, eight sucker equipped arms and a large beak to tear up the victim's flesh. The one here is just a baby.

0　　　50 mm

0

50 mm

Jaws as vicious as a steel trap snap down on a victim of this stomias, which has light organs all down its sides.

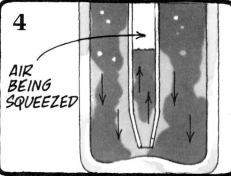

4

AIR BEING SQUEEZED

▲ The water is squeezing the air in the tube. The deeper you go, the more the increasing water pressure will squash the trapped air. Move the tube quickly up and down to see how the effect of the water pressure varies with depth.

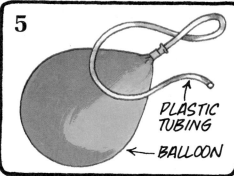

5

PLASTIC TUBING

BALLOON

▲ Try blowing up a balloon tied to a plastic or rubber tube. It is quite easy to do in air, but with the balloon at the bottom of a water-filled sink, it is next to impossible because of the water pressing in on the balloon.

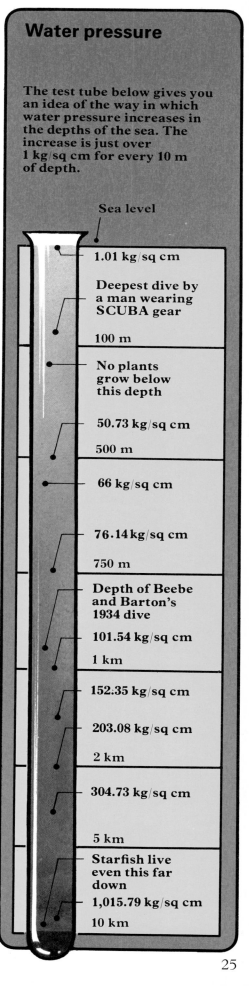

Water pressure

The test tube below gives you an idea of the way in which water pressure increases in the depths of the sea. The increase is just over 1 kg/sq cm for every 10 m of depth.

Sea level

1.01 kg/sq cm

Deepest dive by a man wearing SCUBA gear

100 m

No plants grow below this depth

50.73 kg/sq cm

500 m

66 kg/sq cm

76.14 kg/sq cm

750 m

Depth of Beebe and Barton's 1934 dive

101.54 kg/sq cm

1 km

152.35 kg/sq cm

203.08 kg/sq cm

2 km

304.73 kg/sq cm

5 km

Starfish live even this far down

1,015.79 kg/sq cm

10 km

Ocean harvest

For thousands of years the oceans have been a rich source of food. Now they are also an important source of energy, since oil and gas have been discovered under the seabed.

Many of the resources of the seas are in danger of being spoilt by man. Pollution not only directly harms seabirds and fish but also enters the food pyramid, causing enormous damage to the whole of ocean life.

Overfishing has reduced the size of fish stocks in some areas because too many young fish have been caught before they can breed.

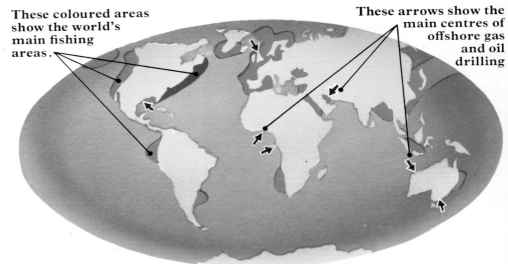

These coloured areas show the world's main fishing areas.

These arrows show the main centres of offshore gas and oil drilling

Purse seine and Otter trawl

The purse seine is used to encircle schools of fish such as tuna. Once the fish are surrounded, the net is drawn together and hauled up. Trawls are dragged along the seabed, frightening bottom-dwelling fish such as sole into the net.

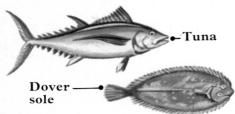

Tuna

Dover sole

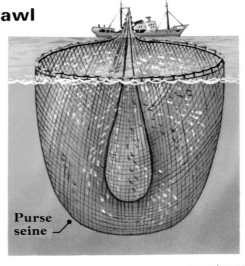

Purse seine

Otter trawl

Drift net

Drift nets trap herring and mackerel when they come to the surface at night to feed on plankton. The nets are stretched across the water, suspended from air-filled floats, and trap the fish as they try to swim through.

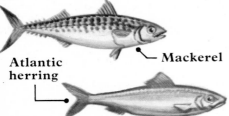

Atlantic herring

Mackerel

Shoal of fish

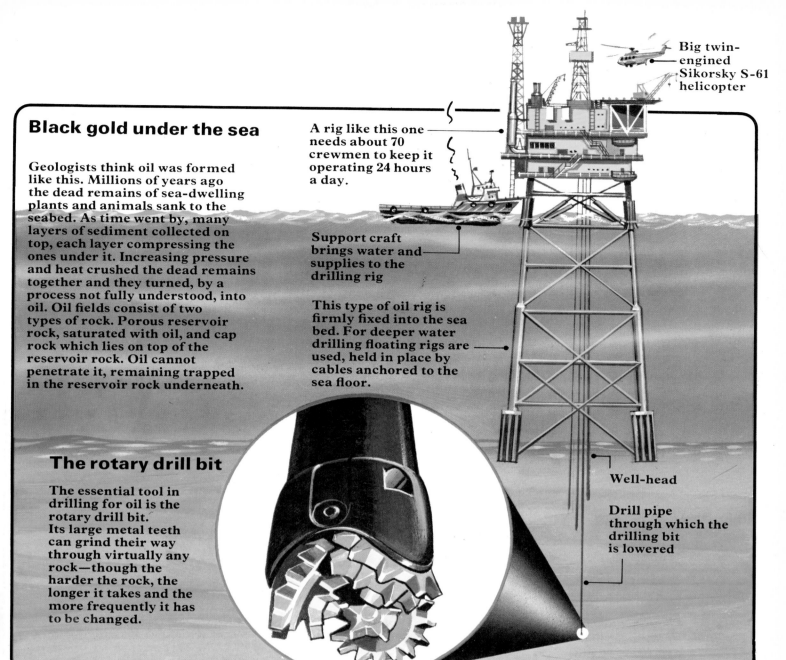

Black gold under the sea

Geologists think oil was formed like this. Millions of years ago the dead remains of sea-dwelling plants and animals sank to the seabed. As time went by, many layers of sediment collected on top, each layer compressing the ones under it. Increasing pressure and heat crushed the dead remains together and they turned, by a process not fully understood, into oil. Oil fields consist of two types of rock. Porous reservoir rock, saturated with oil, and cap rock which lies on top of the reservoir rock. Oil cannot penetrate it, remaining trapped in the reservoir rock underneath.

A rig like this one needs about 70 crewmen to keep it operating 24 hours a day.

Big twin-engined Sikorsky S-61 helicopter

Support craft brings water and supplies to the drilling rig

This type of oil rig is firmly fixed into the sea bed. For deeper water drilling floating rigs are used, held in place by cables anchored to the sea floor.

Well-head

Drill pipe through which the drilling bit is lowered

The rotary drill bit

The essential tool in drilling for oil is the rotary drill bit. Its large metal teeth can grind their way through virtually any rock—though the harder the rock, the longer it takes and the more frequently it has to be changed.

Oil traps

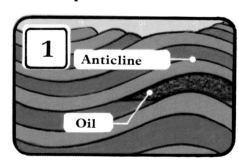

1 Anticline
Oil

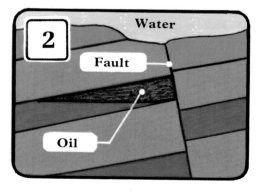

2 Water
Fault
Oil

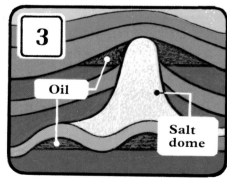

3 Oil
Salt dome

▲ When geologists hunt for oil, they try to find special rock formations where oil deposits are likely to be trapped. Three of these formations are shown in the diagrams above. An anticline (1), is a fold of rock. Oil can be

trapped at the top of the fold. In a fault (2), oil can be trapped behind a wedge of cap rock which has slipped down into the reservoir rock. Another trap occurs when a rock salt dome (3), forces its way upwards, bending the reservoir

rock into arches and sealing it off with a layer of salt. Oil is trapped in the reservoir rock rather like water in a wet sponge. Have a look at one next time you have a bath to see the effect.

27

Inner space

Inner space is the name given to the new frontier under the sea. More people and more demand for raw materials for industry mean that the sea is growing in importance as a source of supply for food and minerals.

The difficult problem is to devise ways of using the seas' resources, whilst controlling pollution and conserving fish stocks.

A few ideas of the scenes you might see if you went on an underwater trip in the future are shown on these two pages.

▲ This picture shows the sort of undersea city that may be built in the future, perched right on the edge of a continental shelf. The globular 'people-pods' shown in this design are built on steel legs with entry hatches on their undersides. They are pressurized and provide the diving community with all the comforts of life on land. Schools, libraries and theatres are just a few of the things inside the warm air-conditioned spheres.

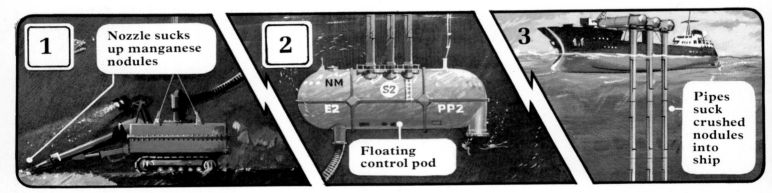

1 Nozzle sucks up manganese nodules

2 Floating control pod

3 Pipes suck crushed nodules into ship

▲ Mineral mining will be one of the most important developments in the future. The pictures above show a design for harvesting manganese nodules, which lie scattered over the world's seabeds. Manganese nodules look like jagged lumps 2–30 cm across and contain other minerals as well, such as nickel, copper, cobalt and lead. The picture sequence shows a robot crawler (1) sucking up nodules with its vacuum cleaner nose-probe. They are piped to a floating control pod (2) where they are ground up into a fine powder. The powder is sucked up by powerful pumps into the hold of a waiting cargo ship (3) on the ocean surface far above.

Underwater fish farm

This picture shows a two-seat sea scooter (1) nearing a fish farm cage (2). The cage 'walls' are made of bubbles leaked from a compressed-air pipe system on the sea-bed. Fish can be kept like this because they do not like passing through the bubble walls. Trained dolphins (3) help the fish farmers tend the cages. On the right, divers poke the suction hose of a fishing boat (4) into a cage. Fish are then simply sucked up and into the ship's hold to be fresh-frozen.

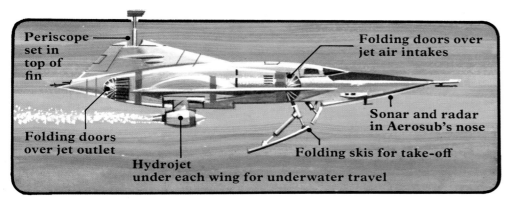

Periscope set in top of fin

Folding doors over jet air intakes

Folding doors over jet outlet

Hydrojet under each wing for underwater travel

Folding skis for take-off

Sonar and radar in Aerosub's nose

▲ Military developments will be an important part of tomorrow's world. One new idea is shown above—the flying submarine. The Aerosub would fly to within a few hundred miles of its target, then dive down into the water to hide from the enemy's radar. It would carry on underwater, only emerging when near the target. It would then accelerate to supersonic speeds for the final part of its mission.

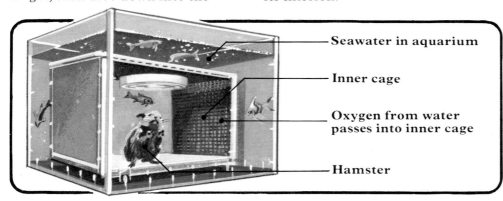

Seawater in aquarium

Inner cage

Oxygen from water passes into inner cage

Hamster

▲ Scientists are already trying to develop artificial gills and the picture above shows one type they are experimenting with. The hamster is in a rubber-walled cage. The rubber, called neoprene, allows the oxygen of the water in the outer cage to pass through it. Enough oxygen percolates through for the hamster to breathe easily. Miniaturized versions of this system would be ideal for the 21st century diver.

Water power

The core of this design for a pollution-free power station is a tank of ammonia. Ammonia only needs a very small temperature difference to change from liquid to gas and back again.

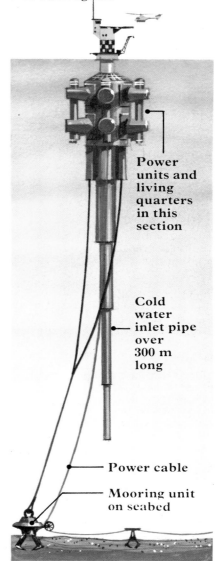

Power units and living quarters in this section

Cold water inlet pipe over 300 m long

Power cable

Mooring unit on seabed

Warm, surface water is pumped around the ammonia tank. The ammonia turns into gas and is used to spin turbines which generate electricity. Cold, bottom water is pumped up the inlet pipe to turn the gas back into a liquid again. The cycle continues indefinitely, generating electricity 24 hours a day.

Undersea firsts

Stories of men's exploits undersea go back to ancient legends. The first account that seems reasonably certain is of a father and daughter team of divers, Scyllias and Cyana, who successfully recovered valuables from a sunken ship for King Xerxes of Persia in about 450 BC.

These are some of the other firsts in the history of the undersea.

323 BC
A diving bell was used by Alexander the Great to examine the underwater defences of Tyre, a stronghold on the shores of what is now the Lebanon.

1624
Cornelius van Drebbel, a Dutchman living in England, launched the first 'submarine' on the Thames. In fact, it was more like a half-submerged rowing boat.

1819
The first standard 'open' diving suit was perfected by a German, Augustus Siebe, but water could leak in if the diver bent over or moved too quickly.

1837
Siebe produced the first totally sealed 'closed' diving suit, far safer than the open version. Its basic design is still in use today.

1896
The first off-shore oil well was drilled off the coast of California, USA.

1930
Barton and Beebe made the first test-dive in their bathysphere.

1955
The first nuclear submarine, *USS Nautilus*, was completed.

1962
As an experiment in living under the sea, Jacques Cousteau began the first of his Continental Shelf Station (Conshelf) projects. In it, two men spent just over a week 10m down off Marseilles in Southern France.

1981
An Anglo-Russian expedition located the wreck of *HMS Edinburgh* which sank in the Second World War. They salvaged hundreds of gold bars which had been part of her cargo.

1982
Henry VIII's flagship, the *Mary Rose* which sank in the Solent was lifted to the surface following an underwater archaeological dig. This was led by the diver and archaeologist, Margaret Rule.

1988
An expedition led by Russ Ballard located and filmed the *SS Titanic* which sank in 1911. It lies on the seabed two miles down in the Atlantic.

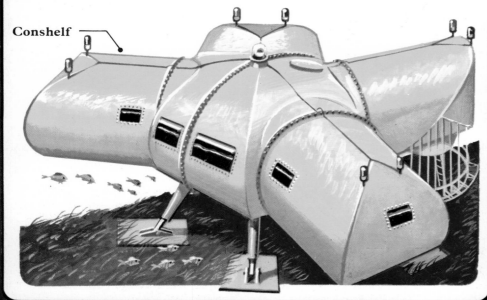

Conshelf

Undersea facts

Water makes life possible. Without it, neither people nor animals could live, and the Earth would be uninhabitable. This is the most important fact of all about the sea – that it gives us life and that life started there. But there are lots of other fascinating facts about the oceans and the creatures that live there. Here are just a few of them.

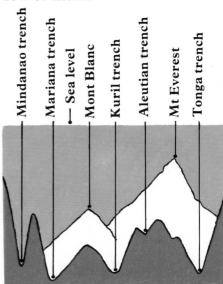

Mindanao trench · Mariana trench · Sea level · Mont Blanc · Kuril trench · Aleutian trench · Mt Everest · Tonga trench

The diagram above shows some of the deepest trenches in the oceans. The world's highest mountain, Mount Everest (8,848 m) and the highest peak in the Alps, Mont Blanc (4,800 m) are quite small in comparison.

Over 97 per cent of all the world's water is stored in the oceans. They hold 1,373 million cubic km of water spread out over 356 million square km.

The fastest swimmers in the ocean are marlin and sailfish, both of which can reach speeds of 80 kph. Flying fish move at 56 kph as they take off.

Tuna fish rarely stop swimming and usually move along at a steady 15 kph. By the time it is fifteen years old, a tuna will have travelled more than 1.6 million km.

The record for an undersea stay is held by four scientists who took part in Operation Tektite off the Virgin Islands in 1968. They spent 60 days in a pressurized laboratory at a depth of 15 m.

The most endangered dolphin is the Chinese river dolphin. There may be as few as 200 left. This is because the river in which they live is constantly being fished and is polluted with sewerage.

The manganese nodules scattered on the floor of the Pacific Ocean contain enough aluminium to supply man's needs for about 20,000 years, enough copper for 6,000 years and enough manganese for no less than 400,000 years.

The wobbegong is the 'black sheep' of the shark family. First, it doesn't have to keep moving in order to breathe, unlike other sharks. Second, it uses cunning, not speed, to trap its food. Since it looks rather like a rock overgrown with seaweed, all it needs to do is to lie on the ocean bottom and snap up its victims as they swim unsuspectingly by.

The coelacanth, shown below, is a living fossil of the sea. Its appearance has hardly changed for over 350 million years. It was thought to have become extinct more than 70 million years ago, but in 1938 one was caught by fishermen off the mouth of the Chalumna River in South East Africa.

Coelacanth

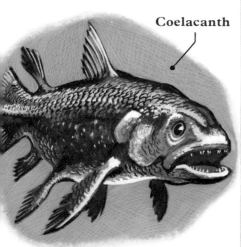

Undersea words

This list of words only covers terms not fully explained elsewhere in this book. You will find some of the words to do with fishes explained on pages 8 and 9.

Continental slope

Continental shelf

Abyssal plain

Bathysphere
Kind of diving bell, shaped like a globe, used for observing the undersea. Winched down on a cable from its support ship.

Bends
Pains suffered by a diver in his joints and muscles as a result of surfacing too quickly. So-called because divers tend to twist and bend their bodies in an attempt to relieve the pain. Its scientific name is caisson sickness.

Continental shelf
The relatively shallow area of the seabed that surrounds most land masses. It is usually no more than 200 m deep but extends for widely varying distances from the coast.

Continental slope
The steeper slope down from the end of the continental shelf towards the ocean bed.

Decompression
The reduction of pressure in the body as a diver goes up toward the surface. Usually carried out by stopping from time to time on the way up or in an underwater decompression chamber.

Habitat
The place in which a plant or animal lives.

Lateral line
Pressure sensitive line running along a fish's body, from just behind the gills to the base of the tail fin. It can detect other fish or object nearby

Mollusc
Soft-bodied creature with no backbone. Most molluscs have hard shells, such as oysters. They all have a single foot, but that of, for example, the octopus is divided into eight tentacles.

Plankton
Small organisms drifting in the upper parts of the oceans. Phyto-plankton are plants, zooplankton are animals.

Snort
The snort mast enables a conventional submarine to recharge its batteries and to renew its air supply by running its engines while still submerged. Only the top of the snort induction mast—down which the engines suck air— appears above the surface of the sea.

Sonar
Detection device in ships and submarines. It sends out a sound beam and receives the echo which bounces off other objects in the sea. The distance of the object is worked out by the time gap between the sound pulse sent out and the echo received. Sound travels at 3,600 kph underwater, so a two second delay between the beam being sent out and its echo being received, means that the object is about 1 km away.

Index

Going further

Places to visit

There are a number of ways in which you can follow up your interest in the Undersea.

If you are keen on studying underwater technology, visit science, naval and maritime museums.

If the animal life of the sea is your main interest, an aquarium is the place to see it at first hand. Some seaside towns have sealife centres which house a range of aquariums showing examples of local sealife.

If you can swim well, the most exciting way to get to know the Undersea is to go diving. Try to find a club where you can learn to snorkel dive and move on to SCUBA diving when you are fourteen. But – diving is dangerous. Don't attempt it except under the supervision of a qualified adult.

Books to read

Encyclopaedia of Underwater Life
by Banister and Campbell
Allen and Unwin, 1985

Usborne Mysteries and Marvels of Ocean Life
by Rick Morris
Usborne, 1983

Guide to the Seashore and Shallow Seas
by A C Campbell
Hamlyn, 1989

The Living Sea
by Jacques Cousteau
Hamish Hamilton, 1988

THE USBORNE YOUNG SCIENTIST
ELECTRICITY

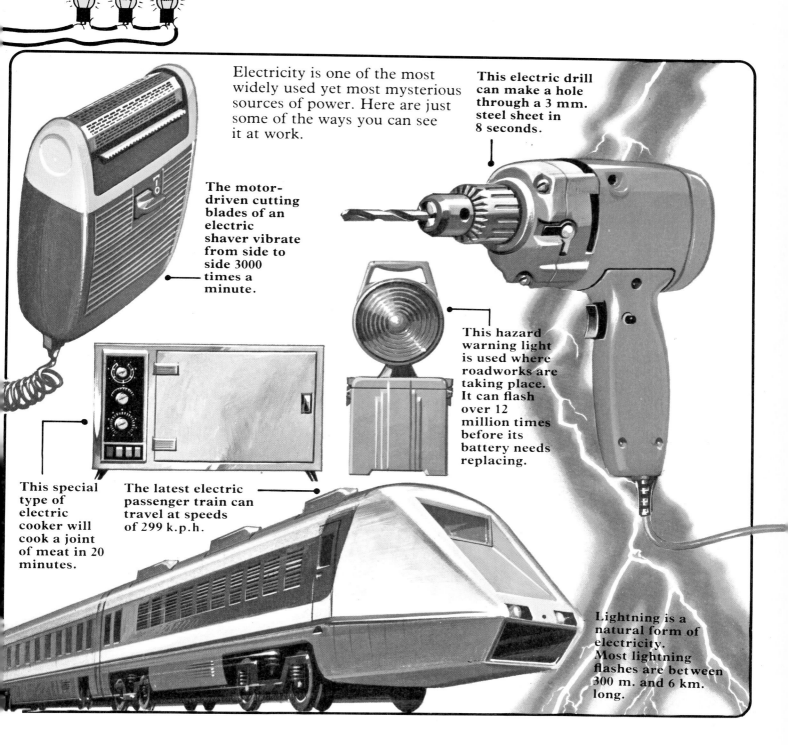

Electricity is one of the most widely used yet most mysterious sources of power. Here are just some of the ways you can see it at work.

This electric drill can make a hole through a 3 mm. steel sheet in 8 seconds.

The motor-driven cutting blades of an electric shaver vibrate from side to side 3000 times a minute.

This hazard warning light is used where roadworks are taking place. It can flash over 12 million times before its battery needs replacing.

This special type of electric cooker will cook a joint of meat in 20 minutes.

The latest electric passenger train can travel at speeds of 299 k.p.h.

Lightning is a natural form of electricity. Most lightning flashes are between 300 m. and 6 km. long.

Credits

Written by
Philip Chapman
Revised by
David Crawley
Art and editorial direction
David Jefferis
Educational adviser
Frank Blackwell

Illustrators
Roland Berry
Sydney Cornford
Malcolm English
Phil Green
John Hutchinson
Malcolm McGregor
Michael Roffe

Acknowledgments
We wish to thank the following
individuals and organizations for
their assistance and for making
available material in their
collections: British Post Office,
Brook Motors Ltd , Central
Electricity Generating Board .

First published in 1976 by
Usborne Publishing Ltd,
Usborne House,
83-85 Saffron Hill,
London,
EC1N 8RT
© 1991, 1976 Usborne
Publishing Ltd.
The name Usborne and the
device ⚛ are Trade Marks of
Usborne Publishing Ltd.

On the cover: a generator makes
million-volt sparks

Opposite page: the transformer
in a power station

The experiments

All the experiments in this
book are absolutely safe
if you always use a 4.5 volt
battery.
NEVER play with electricity
from the mains.

Here is a list of equipment
you will need.

General equipment

Four 6 volt bulbs in bulbholders
Two 4.5 volt batteries with
screw-down connections
About 5 m. of connecting wire
Sticky tape
Scissors
Glue
Compass
15 m. of fine insulated wire
Paper clips
12 cm. long nail
Wire cutters
Two magnets
Plasticine

For special experiments

Current detector (p. 13):
Saucer
Water
Small cork
Needle

Motor (p. 15):
15 × 17 cm. sheet of balsa wood
50 cm. of 5 × 5 mm. balsa wood
strip
Balsa cement
Ten 3 cm. long pins
15 cm. long knitting needle
Two drawing pins

The battery we have chosen for
all the experiments in this
book supplies electricity at
4.5 volts. Not all batteries
supplying this voltage look
the same, so get ones looking
like either of the two
shown below.
　　The battery with screw-on
terminals is best because
you can fix the wires very
easily. You can use the
battery with springy
terminals but you will have to
wind the wires onto them.

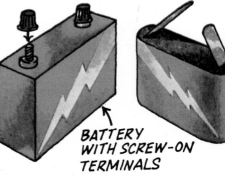

BATTERY
WITH SCREW-ON
TERMINALS

Large cork
Two horseshoe magnets
Two aluminium milk bottle tops

Turbine (p.21):
15cm. long knitting needle
Card or thick aluminium foil
about 10 × 10 cm.

Telegraph set (p. 26):
Sheet of cooking foil
Length of 3-core cable
Large sheet of cardboard

Weights and measures

All the weights and measures used in this book are metric. This
list gives some equivalents in Imperial measures.

mm. = millimetre
(1 inch = 25.4 mm.)

cm. = centimetre
(1 inch = 2.54 cm.)

m. = metre
(1 yard = 0.91 m.)

km. = kilometre
(1 mile = 1.6 km.)

k.p.h. = kilometres per hour
(100 m.p.h. = 160 k.p.h.)

sq. km. = square kilometre
(1 square mile = 2.59 sq. km.)

kg. = kilogram
(1 pound = 0.45 kg.)

A tonne is 1000 kg.
(1 ton = 1.02 tonnes)

1 litre is 1.76 pints

M means one million
(1 MW = one million watts)

k means 1000
(1 kW. = 1000 watts)

C. = degrees Centigrade
(Water freezes at 0°C. and boils
at 100°C.)

THE USBORNE YOUNG SCIENTIST
ELECTRICITY

About this book

Do you know why an electric light bulb shines or how a battery works? Have you ever wondered how electricity is made in a power station or how an electric motor works?

This book explains in simple terms what electricity is, how it works and how we use it. It tells the story of how electricity is made, transmitted around the country, and finally reaches our homes, offices and factories.

A series of safe and simple experiments, easily carried out on the kitchen table, shows you how to construct simple circuits, including working models of an electromagnet, an electric motor and a two-way telegraph system.

Contents

Inside the atom

Everything is made up of atoms. The air you breathe, the pages of this book, your own body—all are built up from millions of invisibly small atoms. They are so small that ten million of them lined up side by side would measure only one millimetre!

At the centre of each atom is a nucleus containing tiny particles called protons. Even smaller particles called electrons move round the nucleus. They orbit round the nucleus like planets round the Sun, and there are always as many electrons as protons.

Each electron has a negative electric charge; each proton has a positive electric charge.

This ⊖ sign means negative and this ⊕ sign means positive.

► Hydrogen is the simplest atom. It has only one proton and one electron. All the other atoms are more complicated. They have other particles called neutrons, but these have no electric charge at all. The big picture shows you the important parts of an atom.

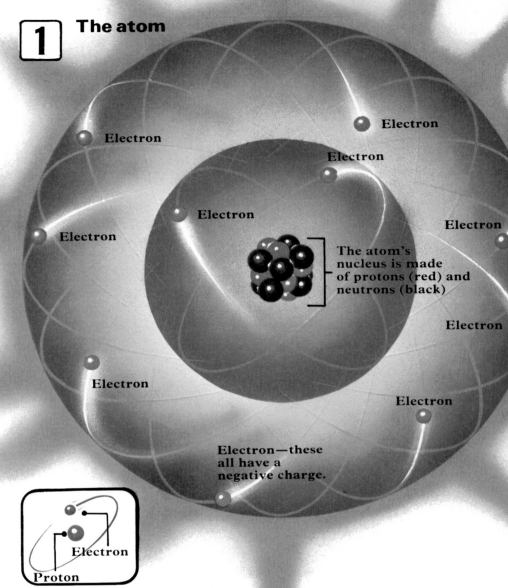

1 The atom

Electron

Electron

Electron

Electron

Electron

Electron

Electron

The atom's nucleus is made of protons (red) and neutrons (black)

Electron

Electron

Electron—these all have a negative charge.

Electron
Proton

Electric circuits

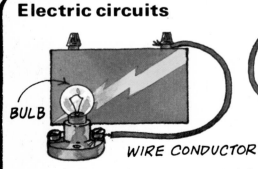

BULB

WIRE CONDUCTOR

▲ To light a bulb using a supply of electricity from a battery, the bulb must be connected to the battery. An electrical conductor such as a wire provides an easy path for the electrons to follow.

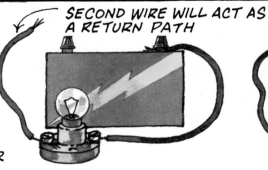

SECOND WIRE WILL ACT AS A RETURN PATH

▲ But simply connecting a single wire from the battery to the bulb will not light it. A second wire must be connected to the battery's other terminal. This makes a path for the electrons to flow back to the battery.

BULB GLOWS

▲ This unbroken path is called a circuit. The second wire has completed the circuit, and the bulb lights up. The electrons flow through the bulb but are not used up in it. They pass through and return to the battery.

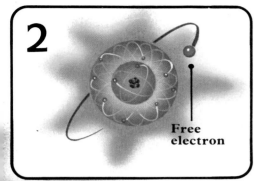

2

Free electron

▲ An electrical conductor is something that allows electricity to pass through it easily. A good conductor has one 'free' electron orbiting outside the others. It can be separated from its atom.

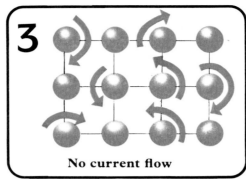

3

No current flow

▲ In metals, the atoms form a regular pattern. This gives metals their strength. The free electrons do not orbit round their own atoms, but can wander from atom to atom through the metal. The red arrows above show them moving.

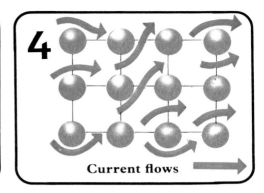

4

Current flows

▲ When a metal wire is connected to a battery, the free electrons in the wire start to drift from one end to the other, passing from atom to atom. This drift of electrons is called an electric current.

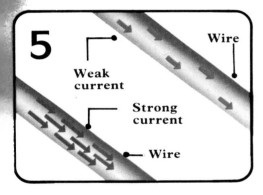

5

Wire

Weak current

Strong current

Wire

▲ The strength of an electric current flowing in a wire depends on the number of free electrons passing along it. Lots of free electrons mean a strong current, a few mean a weak current is flowing.

6

Filament

▲ When you switch on a light in your home, this lets the electric current flow through the bulb. About 3 million million million free electrons are passing through the filament in the bulb every second!

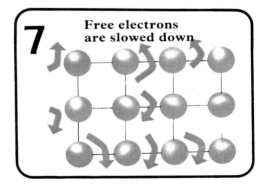

7

Free electrons are slowed down

▲ Free electrons do not pass along a wire smoothly. They bump into the atoms of the wire and their progress is slowed down. This slowing-down effect is called resistance. The better the conductor, the lower its resistance.

Instant electricity

The free electrons drifting along a wire move quite slowly—only a few millimetres a second. This mini-experiment shows you why you do not have to wait when you turn on an electricity supply.

Get some marbles and line them up between two books. Push the left-hand marble a little way to the right. See how all the other marbles move as well, even at the far end. Like marbles, electrons all begin to move at the same time, but they do so only when their circuit is completed—so they have a return path back to the battery.

ALL THE OTHER MARBLES MOVE AS WELL

PUSH THIS MARBLE

Nature's electricity

A lightning storm is one of nature's most dramatic shows of strength. Flashes of electricity leap down from thunderclouds in the sky.

Although people have known about thunderstorms for thousands of years, exactly what causes them is still not very clear.

Scientists say that lightning is the releasing of electricity that has built up inside the clouds. It is probably like the electricity that is built up when you comb your hair on a warm dry day. You can sometimes hear a crackling noise as the teeth of the comb pass the strands of hair.

Lightning conductors are strips of metal running down the side of a building. They provide an easy path for the electricity to follow and so keep the lightning away from the building itself.

Lightning will strike a tree rather than go direct to the ground because the tree gives the lightning an easier path to earth. Why? Because the tree-top is nearer to the cloud than the ground.

1 Making electricity with a comb

Things sometimes get charged with electricity just by rubbing. Have you ever felt a small shock when you touch a door knob after walking across a thick pile carpet? This is because electrons have been rubbed off the carpet and onto your body. This 'static' charge then escapes suddenly as you touch the door knob, and you feel a tingling shock.

Here are two experiments you can do to show the effects of static electricity.

▲ Comb your hair with a plastic comb. As the comb's teeth pass the strands of your hair, electrons are transferred across, and the comb becomes charged with static electricity. Make sure you comb your hair vigorously.

▲ Hold the comb a little way from some small scraps of paper. You will see the pieces of paper jump up to the comb and stick to it. The static electricity in the comb is attracting the pieces of paper.

Electricity may flash across between two clouds. This is the most common type of lightning. It appears as a bright flash across the sky.

Lightning strikes direct to the ground are quite rare. The lightning normally strikes a tree or building as these provide an easier path for the electricity to follow.

▲ The skin of an electric eel conceals hundreds of tiny cells all acting like miniature batteries. The cells charge up to a voltage of more than 600 volts which the eel then uses to stun its victim.

▲ Glow worms are light-producing beetles. Their pale yellowish-green glow is made by a chemical process in the rear part of their bodies. They can flash their lights in special rhythms to attract each other.

▲ Your own body is one of the most complicated electrical systems. All information from the senses—sight, sound, touch, taste and smell—is passed to the brain along nerve fibres. The information is passed along as an electric signal. This footballer's brain receives all the information needed for him to aim and kick the ball. His brain then sends out electric signals along nerve fibres to tell his muscles when and where to kick the ball.

4 PIECES OF PAPER FALL

▲ After a minute or two, the electricity in the comb leaks away through your body, and the scraps of paper will fall off. You can repeat the experiment if you comb your hair again to recharge it with static electricity.

5 SLOW AND STEADY FLOW

▲ Another static electricity trick is bending water. Turn on a water tap and adjust it carefully until a slow, steady stream of water is flowing. Comb your hair again and hold the comb near the stream of flowing water.

6 TILT COMB WATER BENDS TOWARDS COMB

▲ You will see the water bend towards the tip of the comb. The static electricity in the comb is attracting the water towards it. Again the charge leaks away through your body. As it does so, the water flows normally again.

How batteries work

Electric current is the movement of electrons through a wire. They won't travel along the wire by themselves, so a force is needed to push them along. This force is produced by a battery and is called the electromotive force.

The strength of the force is measured in volts, named after Alessandro Volta, the inventor of the first battery.

Batteries are not as powerful as the electricity supplied to our homes, but they can be carried about from place to place or used as an emergency supply during a power cut.

▲ In 1800, Count Volta, an Italian scientist, made the first battery. A supply of electric current was now available to experimenters who until then had used static electricity which lasts for only a few seconds at a time.

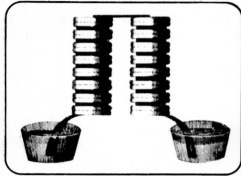

▲ The voltaic pile, as Volta's battery came to be known, was made of lots of silver and zinc discs separated by damp fabric pads. The electric current made by the voltaic pile could be used for lots of long-lasting experiments.

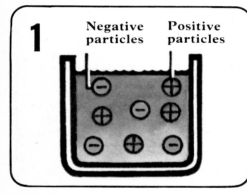

1 Negative particles · Positive particles

▲ This is how a battery works. It is made of lots of cells and one of them is shown above. In the cell is a liquid called the electrolyte. It is made of billions of positive and negative particles.

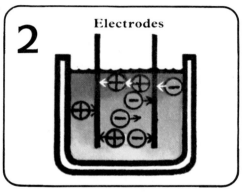

2 Electrodes

▲ Two rods made of different materials are submerged in the electrolyte in each cell. These are called electrodes. A chemical reaction in the electrolyte sends positive particles to one electrode, negative particles to the other.

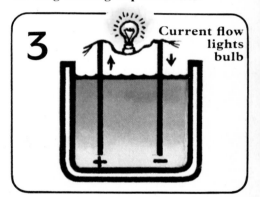

3 Current flow lights bulb

▲ When a wire is connected to the two electrodes, current flows along the wire. This can be used to light a bulb like the one shown above. When the chemicals in the cell are used up, the current stops flowing.

Dry cells

Liquids can easily spill out so special dry batteries are made for things like torches. There are still two electrodes, the carbon rod and the zinc case, but the cell has a paste electrolyte sealed into its leakproof case.

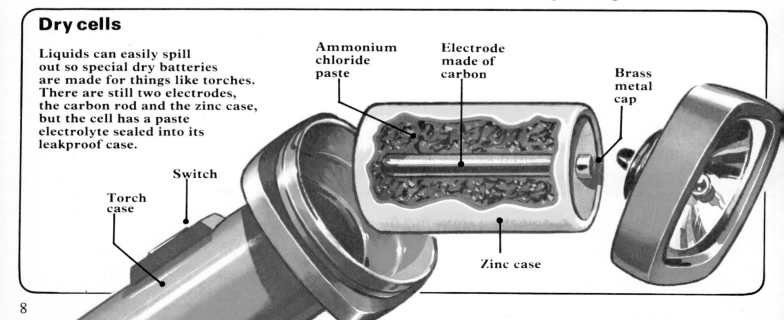

Ammonium chloride paste

Electrode made of carbon

Brass metal cap

Switch

Torch case

Zinc case

Rechargeable power for the motor car

A modern car uses many small electrical machines: starter motor, heater motor and fan. They would soon wear out an ordinary battery so special car batteries are made. These are designed so that they can be recharged with electricity.

A small electric generator is driven by the car engine. The power it produces when the engine is running is fed back into the battery to replace that used by the starter motor in starting the car.

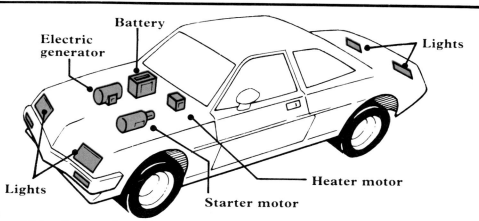

Battery

Electric generator

Lights

Lights

Heater motor

Starter motor

This picture shows just some of the things in a car which use up the battery's electricity supply. You can also see the generator which recharges the battery. Almost all car batteries provide a 12 volt power supply.

Non-polluting power of the future

Two electric cars draw up at a future version of our filling station. The driver on the right has just inserted his credit card (1). Robot machinery underground slots in a newly charged battery module (2) under the driving compartment. The old battery is pushed out of the other side of the car by the new module. It passes into the automatic receiving bay (3) to go for recharging. Once recharged, (4) it glides along a conveyor belt to be used again (5). A 30 second 'fill-up' gives another 1000 km. driving.

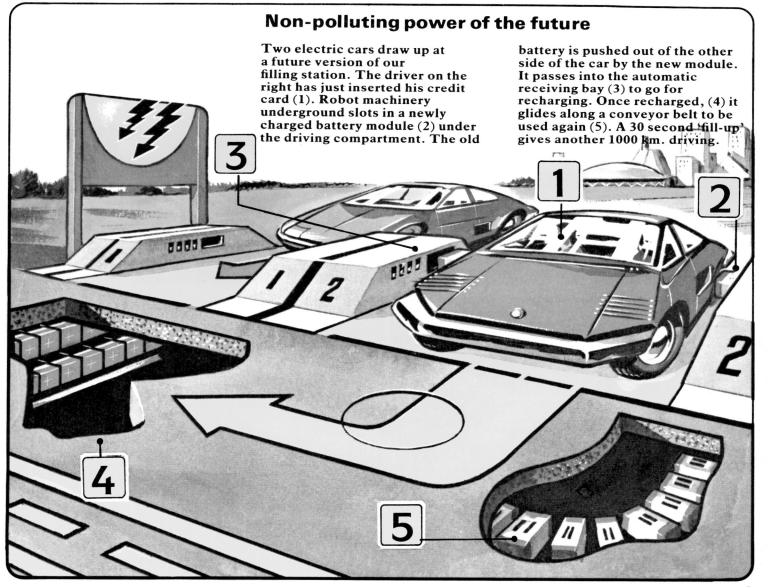

Turning power into light

American inventor Thomas Edison

Thomas Edison produced the first electric light bulb in 1879. He sealed a fine cotton thread into a glass bulb. After pumping out the air he saw that the thread glowed brightly when a current was passed through it.

The thread had a high resistance because it was so fine. The electrons passing through it kept bumping into the atoms of the thread. This heated it up so much that it glowed white hot.

If you look at a new light bulb in its cardboard packet, you will see a number—60W or 100W. This tells you how much power the bulb uses and how brightly it glows. The bigger the number the brighter the glow. The W stands for watt, the unit of power named after James Watt the Scottish inventor.

Length and resistance

Current flow

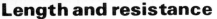

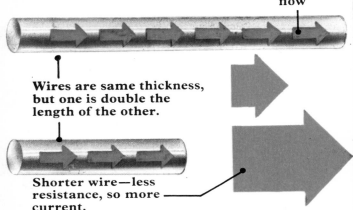

Wires are same thickness, but one is double the length of the other.

Shorter wire—less resistance, so more current.

Good conductors of electricity allow electrons to flow easily. Sometimes they bump into atoms in the wire. This slows them down. The braking effect is called the wire's resistance. Halving the length of the wire halves the resistance.

Width and resistance

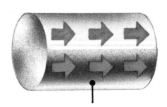

Wires are the same length, but one is twice as thick as the other.

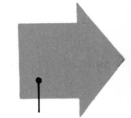

Thick wire—less resistance, so more current.

A thick wire has a lower resistance than a thin wire. There is a greater area of wire for the electrons to pass through. It is like a wide three-lane motorway that can carry far more traffic than a narrow single-lane country road.

Current and resistance

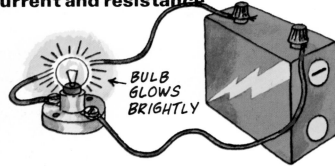

BULB GLOWS BRIGHTLY

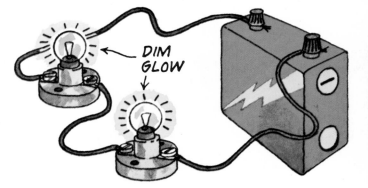

DIM GLOW

▲ Connect a wire from the ⊕ terminal of a battery to a bulbholder terminal. Then wire the other bulbholder terminal to the ⊖ of the battery. The battery forces current round the wire and through the bulb.

▲ Now connect up the second bulb to the first and complete the circuit to the battery. The bulbs glow less brightly now. By connecting up the second bulb you have doubled the resistance so less current flows.

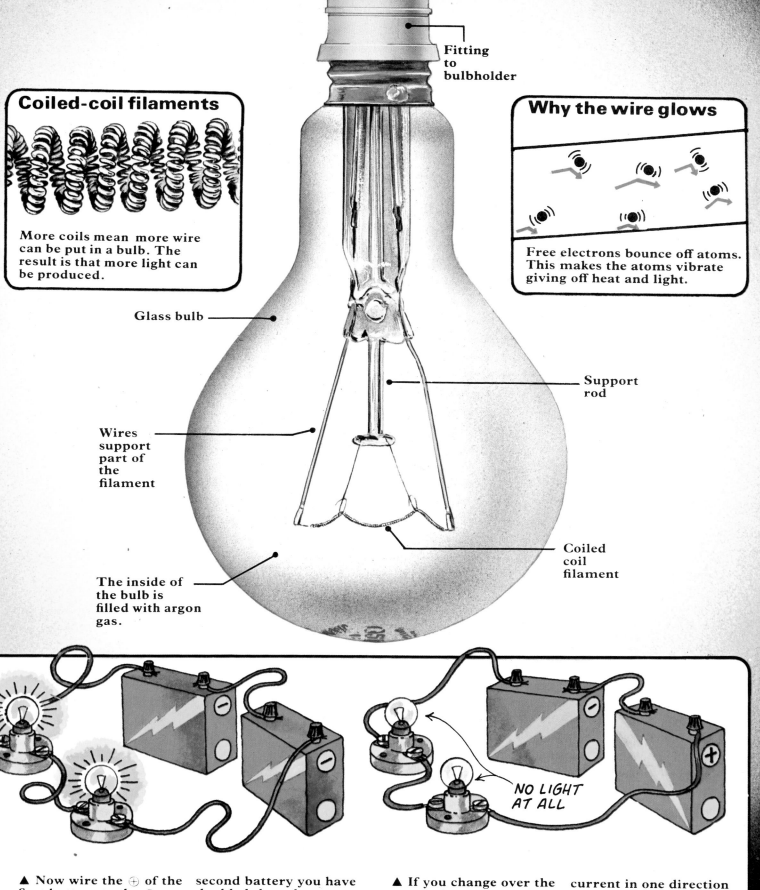

Coiled-coil filaments

More coils mean more wire can be put in a bulb. The result is that more light can be produced.

Fitting to bulbholder

Why the wire glows

Free electrons bounce off atoms. This makes the atoms vibrate giving off heat and light.

Glass bulb

Wires support part of the filament

The inside of the bulb is filled with argon gas.

Support rod

Coiled coil filament

NO LIGHT AT ALL

▲ Now wire the ⊕ of the first battery to the ⊖ of a second battery. The bulbs glow brightly again. By connecting the second battery you have doubled the voltage. Twice the current flows and the bulbs shine brightly again.

▲ If you change over the connections to one of the batteries, the bulbs will not light up. The first battery tries to send current in one direction and the other tries to send it the other way. The result is no current flow at all.

Magnetism and electricity

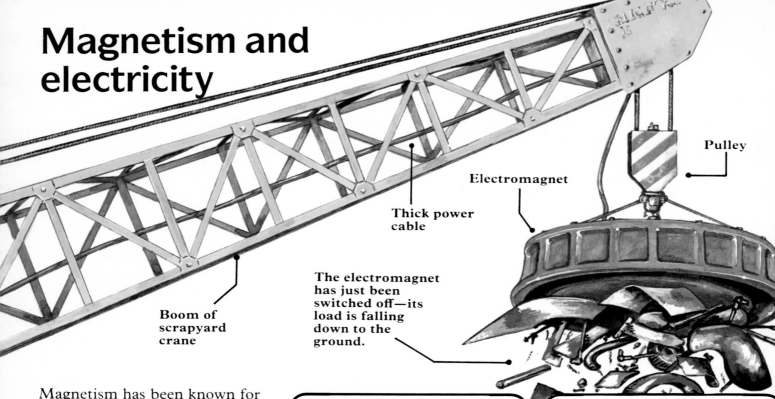

Pulley

Electromagnet

Thick power cable

Boom of scrapyard crane

The electromagnet has just been switched off—its load is falling down to the ground.

Magnetism has been known for thousands of years, and scientists have puzzled over it for just as long. The strange invisible force that attracts pieces of iron and steel to a magnet is still not fully understood.

A magnet affects only certain materials, and then only when they are close to it. They must be within its magnetic field.

Magnetism has been put to good use. Giant electromagnets like the one above lift very heavy loads, and for centuries sailors have used the compass for navigation.

Needle points north

▲ A compass needle is a small magnet, and it always points to the Earth's north pole. All magnets are therefore said to have magnetic poles. The north-seeking pole is the north pole and the other is the south pole.

Unlike poles attract

Like poles repel

▲ When a pair of magnets are placed close together, they attract one another if a north pole faces a south pole. Two north poles or two south poles face to face repel one another.

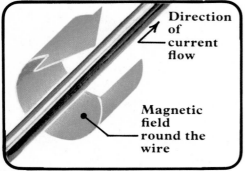

Direction of current flow

Magnetic field round the wire

▲ When a wire carries an electric current, a magnetic field is produced round the wire. The field is present along the whole length of the wire, and if the current is increased the field gets stronger.

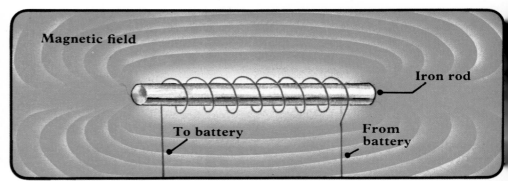

Magnetic field

Iron rod

To battery

From battery

▲ Simple and small magnets like horseshoe-shaped ones are not very powerful. A stronger magnet is produced when a coil of wire is wound round an iron bar. As soon as the current is switched on the bar becomes a very powerful magnet that can be switched off simply by stopping the current flow. Giant electromagnets like the one above are used in scrap metal yards and lift huge loads of metal at a time.

Make an electromagnet

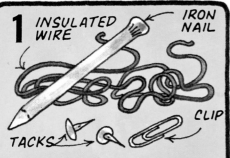

1 INSULATED WIRE — IRON NAIL — CLIP — TACKS

To make an electromagnet you need a nail about 12 cm. long, 3 m. of wire and a battery. Wind 60 turns of wire around the nail. Put sticky tape on to stop it unwinding.

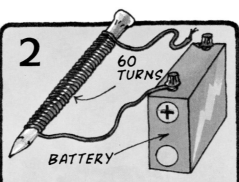

2 60 TURNS — BATTERY

Remove about 2 cm. of the plastic insulation from each loose end of the wire. Wind one end of the bare wire around the $\oplus$ terminal of the battery. Make sure that the wire will not slip.

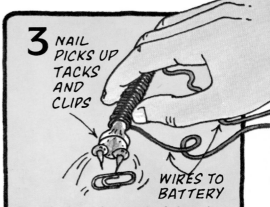

3 NAIL PICKS UP TACKS AND CLIPS — WIRES TO BATTERY

Touch the other end of the wire onto the $\ominus$ terminal of the battery. The electromagnet will now pick up nails, paperclips and other small objects with iron in them.

Detect electric currents

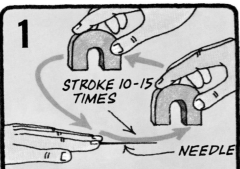

1 STROKE 10-15 TIMES — NEEDLE

Magnetise a needle by stroking it with a magnet. Make sure the return path of the magnet is well away from the needle, otherwise the needle will be very poorly magnetised.

2 THIN SLICE OF CORK — MAGNETISED NEEDLE PUSH NEEDLE THROUGH MIDDLE

Cut a slice of cork about 1 cm. thick. Push the needle through the cork, making sure it passes through the centre so that it will float properly when you put it into a dish of water.

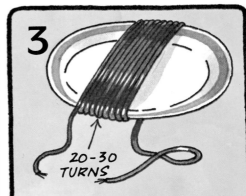

3 20-30 TURNS

Now wind 20 to 30 turns of wire around the dish. Keep the wire in place with sticky tape. Place the dish well away from electrical appliances, and pour in enough water to float the cork.

4 WATER — NEEDLE AND COIL SHOULD POINT THE SAME WAY

Float the cork gently on the surface of the water and let it come to rest. It will settle with one end pointing northwards. The needle must be able to float without scraping against the wire.

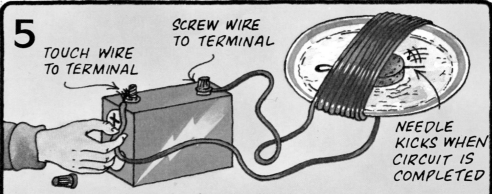

5 TOUCH WIRE TO TERMINAL — SCREW WIRE TO TERMINAL — NEEDLE KICKS WHEN CIRCUIT IS COMPLETED

Remove 2 cm. of insulation from the ends of the wire. Connect one end to the $\ominus$ terminal of the battery. Touch the other wire to the $\oplus$ terminal. The needle will give a 'kick' and spin round.

This is because the coil round the dish produces a magnetic field when a current flows through it. The needle then turns round to line itself up with this field.

The electric motor

English scientist Michael Faraday invented the first electric motor in 1831. He could hardly have known at the time just how revolutionary this discovery would turn out to be.

Now industry all over the world uses electric motors to make everything from pins to spacecraft.

Motors drive inter-city and underground trains, and kitchens throughout the world would come to a halt without motors to drive food mixers, refrigerators, washing machines and other gadgets.

Inside an electric motor

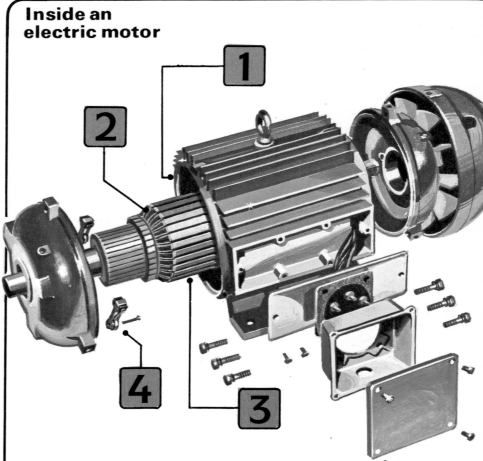

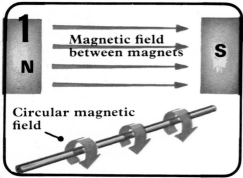

▲ The force that makes an electric motor turn round is produced when two magnetic fields meet. The first is the field between two magnetic poles and the second is the one round a wire carrying an electric current.

In the motor shown here, the magnetic field is produced by electromagnets (1), the coils carrying the current (2) are wound round the armature (3). The current goes to the coils through brushes (4).

In the model opposite, the magnetic field is produced by two horseshoe magnets, the armature is made from coils wound round a cork, and the current is passed to them using milk bottle tops as brushes.

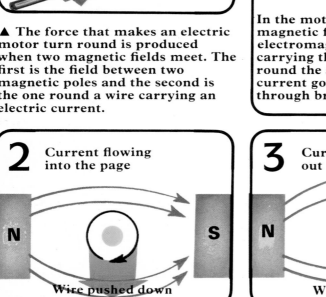

▲ In an electric motor, a wire is put between two magnets. (The circle in the picture above is an end-on view of the wire.) When the current is flowing along the wire, into the page, the wire is pushed downwards.

3 Current flowing out of the page

▲ If the current in the wire is travelling the other way—out of the page in this picture—the push on the wire changes as well. The wire is now pushed upwards instead of downwards.

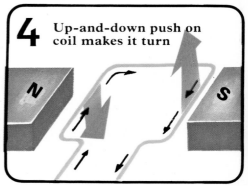

▲ Using a coil of wire means that the current flows first into, then out of, the page. So one part of the wire is pushed downwards and the other pushed upwards. Putting the coil on a shaft lets it spin round.

1 Make your own electric motor

You can make an electric motor that works just like the real one shown opposite. You will need the following pieces of equipment:

Sheet of balsa wood 15 cm. × 17 cm.
50 cm. of 5 mm. × 5 mm. balsa strip
Balsa cement
Two horseshoe magnets
Large cork
15 cm. knitting needle
15 m. of fine insulated wire
Three 30 cm. lengths of wire
Two drawing pins
A milk bottle top
Two 4.5 volt batteries
Ten 3 cm. long pins
Sharp knife
Sticky tape

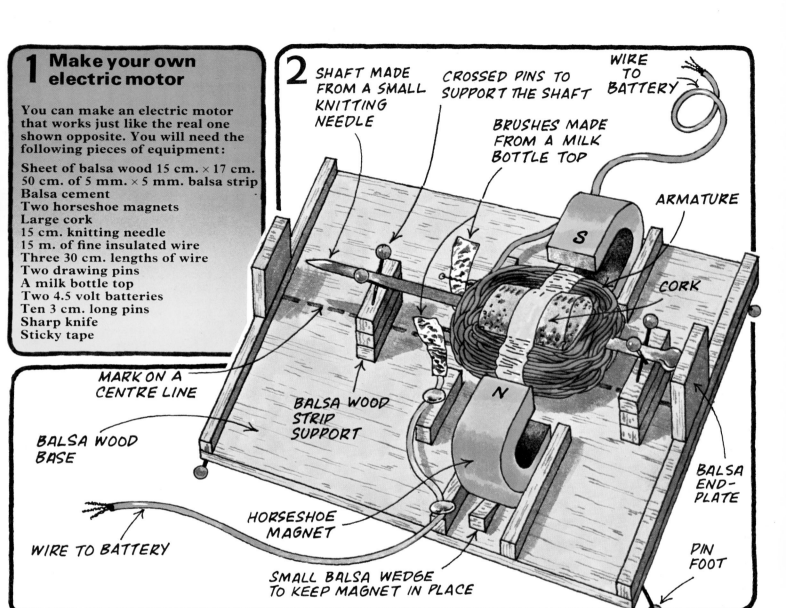

2

SHAFT MADE FROM A SMALL KNITTING NEEDLE

CROSSED PINS TO SUPPORT THE SHAFT

WIRE TO BATTERY

BRUSHES MADE FROM A MILK BOTTLE TOP

ARMATURE

S

CORK

N

BALSA WOOD STRIP SUPPORT

BALSA END-PLATE

PIN FOOT

MARK ON A CENTRE LINE

BALSA WOOD BASE

WIRE TO BATTERY

HORSESHOE MAGNET

SMALL BALSA WEDGE TO KEEP MAGNET IN PLACE

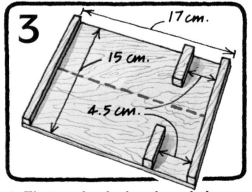

▲ First make the baseboard. A 15 cm. × 17 cm. sheet of balsa is about the right size. Draw in the centre line as shown above. Glue down the end strips and the first two magnet guides 4.5 cm. from one end of the baseboard.

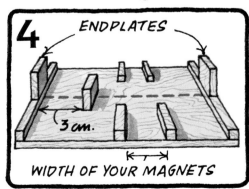

ENDPLATES

3 cm.

WIDTH OF YOUR MAGNETS

▲ Glue the next pair of magnet guides. The magnets should slide smoothly in the channel you have made. Stick down the endplates across the centre line. These will keep the motor in place when it goes round.

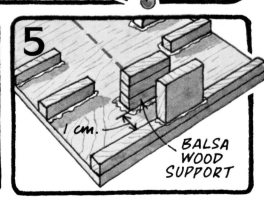

1 cm.

BALSA WOOD SUPPORT

▲ The supports for the bearings should be made from three layers of the balsa wood strip.

Continued next page ⟶

Make your own electric motor
continued from p.15

6 CROSSED PINS

▲ Use crossed pins to support the armature shaft. They do not need plastic ends like the ones shown, but they should be at least 3 cm. long. Push them very firmly into the wood, so they will not come loose when the motor is working.

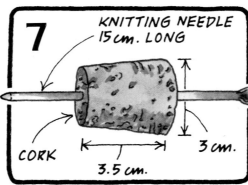

7 KNITTING NEEDLE 15 cm. LONG

CORK

3.5 cm.

3 cm.

▲ Push the knitting needle into the centre of the cork. If there is already a hole in the cork, fill up the space with plasticine to make a tight fit. Make sure there are about 5 cm. of knitting needle sticking out of each side.

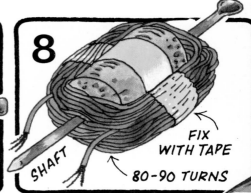

8 FIX WITH TAPE

SHAFT

80-90 TURNS

▲ Wind 80-90 turns of fine wire round the cork. Stick in two pins (see 9 below) which should be the same distance from the shaft. If you find this difficult, stick the pins into the cork before winding on the wire.

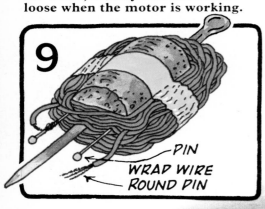

9 PIN

WRAP WIRE ROUND PIN

▲ Remove 4 cm. of insulation from the loose ends of the wire. Wind one of the bare wires round a pin. Repeat for the other wire and pin. Make sure they are firmly in place. Place the shaft on its crossed-pin supports.

10 FOLD OVER

5 cm.

▲ Take two 30 cm. lengths of the thicker wire. Remove the insulation from one end of each wire for a distance of about 5 cm. Place half a milk bottle top over the end and fold it over to make a 5 cm. long strip.

11 PINS

BRUSHES SHOULD TOUCH PINS LIKE THIS

DRAWING PIN

▲ Pin the thicker wires to the baseboard so that the flexible bottle top brushes touch the pins at the same instant when the shaft turns. These wires will be connected to the batteries when the motor is ready to run.

12 MAKE SURE POLES OF MAGNETS ARE LIKE THIS

N   S

▲ Place the magnets in position. Make sure that the two poles facing each other are opposite poles (test this by seeing that they attract one another). The armature should lie directly between the two poles.

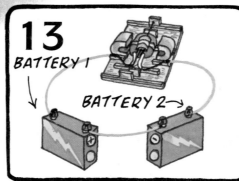

13 BATTERY 1

BATTERY 2

Connect the ⊕ of battery 1 to the ⊖ of battery 2 with the third length of wire. Then connect the brush wires to the ⊖ of battery 1 and the ⊕ of battery 2. A gentle push should start the motor spinning round.

14 Troubleshooting!

No matter how much care you take, your motor might not work first time. Points to check are:

1 Make sure the armature is free to turn.
2 Keep the magnets as close as possible to, but not touching, the armature.
3 When the armature is horizontal it should lie between the poles of the magnets.
4 Make sure the brushes touch the pins at exactly the same instant.
5 The brushes should just stroke the pins as they pass.

How electric motors are used

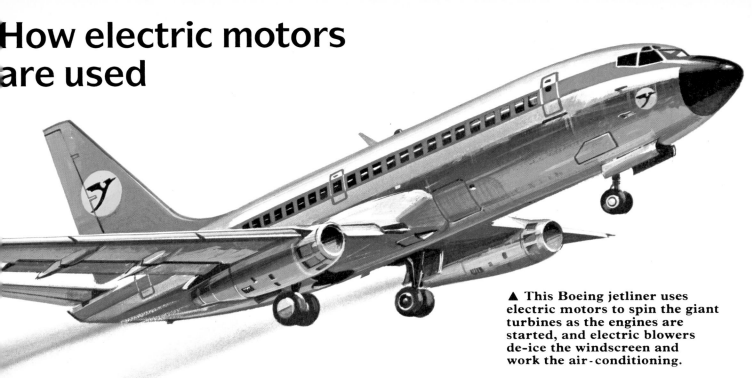

▲ This Boeing jetliner uses electric motors to spin the giant turbines as the engines are started, and electric blowers de-ice the windscreen and work the air-conditioning.

Electricity is used to drive all sorts of things—from huge locomotives to electric clocks.

The combination of great power and high precision has led to the widespread use of electric motors in the home as well as in factories.

You will probably be surprised at the number of gadgets in your home that use motors. Try making a check list of all the things in your house that have one.

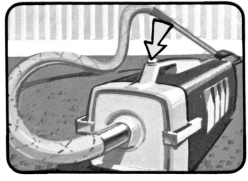

▲ The vacuum cleaner is a useful tool in the home. The motor turns a high speed fan which produces a suction effect in the flexible pipe. Dust and dirt sucked in are trapped in a disposable paper bag.

▲ The motor shown here is lifting sweets from a conveyor belt into a container that weighs out the right quantity and packs them automatically. The motor lifts over 100,000 sweets every day. That's a lot of sweets!

▲ As motor-cycles get bigger, the old-fashioned kick starter is being replaced by an electric starter motor like those used in motor cars. The rider simply presses a button on the handlebars to set the engine going.

▲ Manufacturers have to use more and more motors to speed up production in factories. In this picture cans of beans are passed along a motor-driven belt ready to have their labels stuck on.

▲ Motor-driven machines can do many jobs much better and faster than people. All the pages in this book were stitched together by machines like the one above. If you look carefully, you can see this page in the picture above.

17

Alternating current

The electricity supplied by a battery flows in one direction and is called direct current.

The other sort of electricity, made in power stations, is called alternating current. The electrons move to and fro in the wire instead of in one direction. But they produce the same effect as electrons drifting only one way.

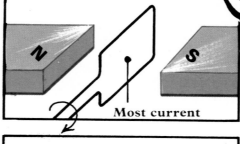

Most current

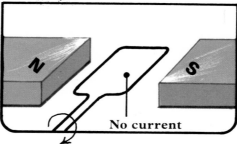

No current

► To make alternating current, power stations use generators that have coils like an electric motor. As each coil is turned between the two magnets, current is made—the exact opposite of an electric motor. But the amount of current varies as the coil turns round.

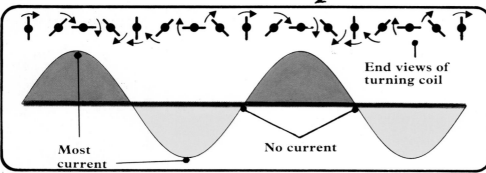

End views of turning coil

Most current

No current

▲ The picture above shows you how the amount of current varies as the coil turns. The turning coil is shown end-on along the top of the picture. You can see that when the coil is upright, no current is made at all. As it turns the current flow begins to increase, but soon the flow gets smaller again. After the coil has turned half a circle, the current starts to flow the other way. Power stations produce 50 of these two-way cycles every second.

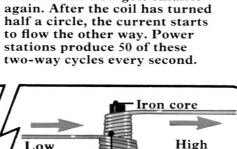

Iron core

High voltage

Low voltage

Only a few turns of wire

Iron core

Low voltage

High voltage

Lots of turns of wire

▲ Alternating current is useful because its voltage can be changed by using a transformer, which is simply two coils of insulated wire wound round an iron core. Although there is no electrical connection between the two coils, any voltage in the first coil sets up a voltage in the second coil. This effect is called induction. Larger or smaller voltages—whatever is needed—can be set up by varying the number of turns in the two coils.

Transformers like this one are used in power stations all over the world.

These insulators are several metres long. They keep the very high voltages away from the metal tank.

The transformer coils and core are kept in this thick metal tank.

Increasing the voltage is called stepping up. Making it smaller is called stepping down.

High voltage power lines enter and leave the transformer through large insulators.

Oil flows round the coils keeping them cool.

1 How induction works

The current flow in a transformer's second coil is set up by a magnetic effect called induction. Induction only works when a current is getting bigger or smaller, not when it is a steady flow. This is why power stations use alternating current which varies all the time as the coils in a generator spin round. Turn your battery on and off to provide the varying current you need.

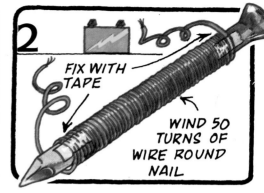

FIX WITH TAPE

WIND 50 TURNS OF WIRE ROUND NAIL

▲ You will need a large nail and enough wire to make 100 turns of wire round it. Cut the wire in half and wind 50 turns round the nail. Use sticky tape to stop it unwinding. Leave 10 cm. of wire free at each end.

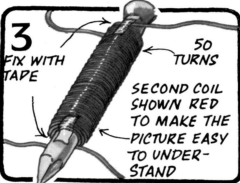

FIX WITH TAPE

50 TURNS

SECOND COIL SHOWN RED TO MAKE THE PICTURE EASY TO UNDERSTAND

NORTH

30 TURNS

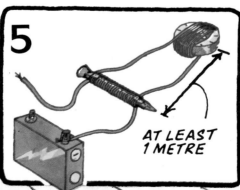

AT LEAST 1 METRE

▲ Connect the compass wires to the second coil wires. Make sure the compass is 1 m. away from the coil. This is because the compass might point towards the nail when you switch the current from the battery on.

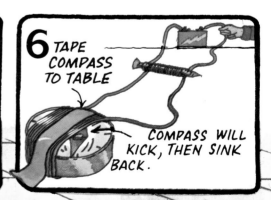

TAPE COMPASS TO TABLE

COMPASS WILL KICK, THEN SINK BACK.

▲ Connect a wire to one of the battery terminals. Touch the other wire to the other terminal. The needle will kick, then sink back. Switch off and the needle will kick again in the other direction.

Inside a power station

Although electricity appears naturally as lightning, it is impossible to turn this to our own use. Even if the power of lightning could be used there is no way to know when or where it would strike.

The electricity used for lighting, warming homes and running industry is completely man-made.

It is difficult to store large amounts of electricity, so power stations are designed to produce electricity at the time that it is needed.

▲ Power stations use turbine wheels (which are rather like propellers on a ship) to turn the coils in their generators. One way to spin turbines is to use fast flowing water, so rivers are dammed to provide the water.

▲ Most power stations use coal or oil. The fuel burns and boils water. The steam from the boiling water is passed through pipes to spin turbines which turn the generator coils. Most modern power stations are very clean.

A giant turbine generator

Power stations burn coal or oil, or use nuclear fuel, to heat water up to make high pressure steam. The steam spins turbines, and a generator attached to the turbine shaft produces hundreds of megawatts of electricity. A megawatt is a million watts— enough to light 10,000 powerful light bulbs.

 1 Steam produced by the boiler is fed into cylinders containing the turbines.

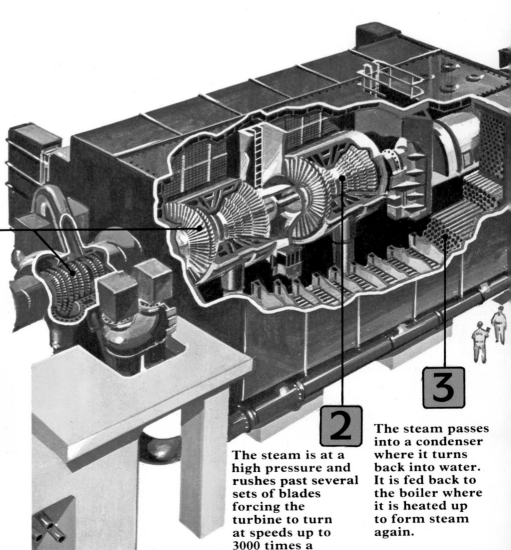

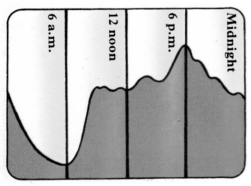

▲ This chart shows when power is most needed. There is a steep increase in the morning as people wake up and put on the kettle at breakfast time. There is another peak at 6 p.m. when they return from work.

2 The steam is at a high pressure and rushes past several sets of blades forcing the turbine to turn at speeds up to 3000 times a minute.

3 The steam passes into a condenser where it turns back into water. It is fed back to the boiler where it is heated up to form steam again.

▲ The power behind the atom bomb can be used peacefully, and nuclear power stations are producing more and more of the world's electricity. But one problem is the dangerous radioactive waste produced.

4 An electrical generator attached to the end of the turbine shaft turns round with it and produces power.

1 Make a spinning turbine wheel

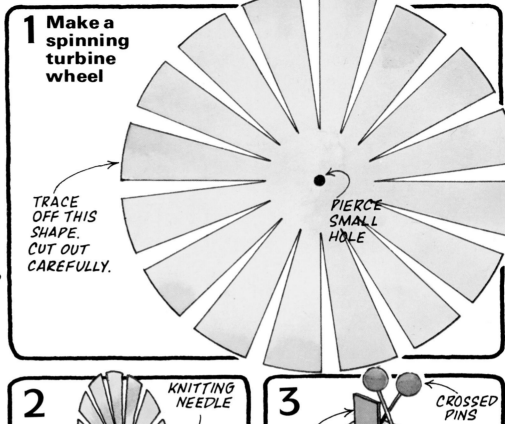

TRACE OFF THIS SHAPE. CUT OUT CAREFULLY.

PIERCE SMALL HOLE

2

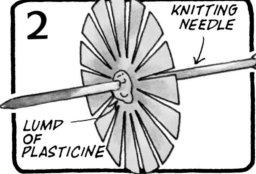

KNITTING NEEDLE

LUMP OF PLASTICINE

▲ Trace the wheel shown in 1 above onto card or thick aluminium foil. Cut it out, and pierce the middle with a knitting needle. Fix a lump of plasticine on each side to keep it steady, otherwise it will not work.

3

CROSSED PINS

STICK ON A SMALL PIECE OF CARD

6 cm.

▲ Two crossed pins stuck into a block of balsa wood are the bearings. A small piece of card stuck on the back will stop the needle sliding through the crossed pins. Make two sets of bearings.

4

BEND BLADES

▲ Carefully twist each of the blades at a small angle. This will make the turbine spin round when you blow through it. You will have to experiment to find the angle which will spin the wheel round fast.

5

BLOW GENTLY

FIX WITH PLASTICINE

▲ Place the balsa blocks on a table. Place the needle on the crossed-pin bearings. Using your breath just like the steam in a power station, blow along the needle. The turbine will spin round just like the real thing.

21

Power lines across the country

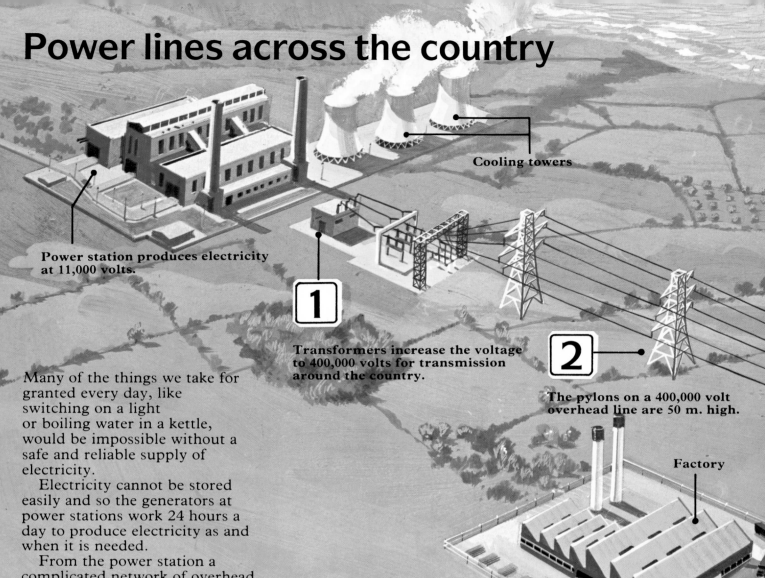

Power station produces electricity at 11,000 volts.

Cooling towers

1 Transformers increase the voltage to 400,000 volts for transmission around the country.

2 The pylons on a 400,000 volt overhead line are 50 m. high.

Factory

Many of the things we take for granted every day, like switching on a light or boiling water in a kettle, would be impossible without a safe and reliable supply of electricity.

Electricity cannot be stored easily and so the generators at power stations work 24 hours a day to produce electricity as and when it is needed.

From the power station a complicated network of overhead lines and underground cables brings the power to your home.

The numbers on this big picture match up with the numbers in the boxes below.

▲ Power station generators make electricity at 11,000 volts. To deliver electricity with as little waste as possible a very high voltage must be used. So transformers at the station step up the voltage to 400,000 volts.

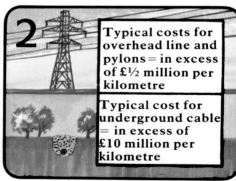

Typical costs for overhead line and pylons = in excess of £½ million per kilometre

Typical cost for underground cable = in excess of £10 million per kilometre

▲ Electricity can be carried over the countryside on overhead lines or underground cables. Pylons over the ground are ugly but they are much cheaper to make and erect than underground cables as you can see above.

▲ When lightning strikes an overhead line, switches called circuit breakers cut off that section of the line. Users on the 'dead' part are left without electricity until the fault is put right.

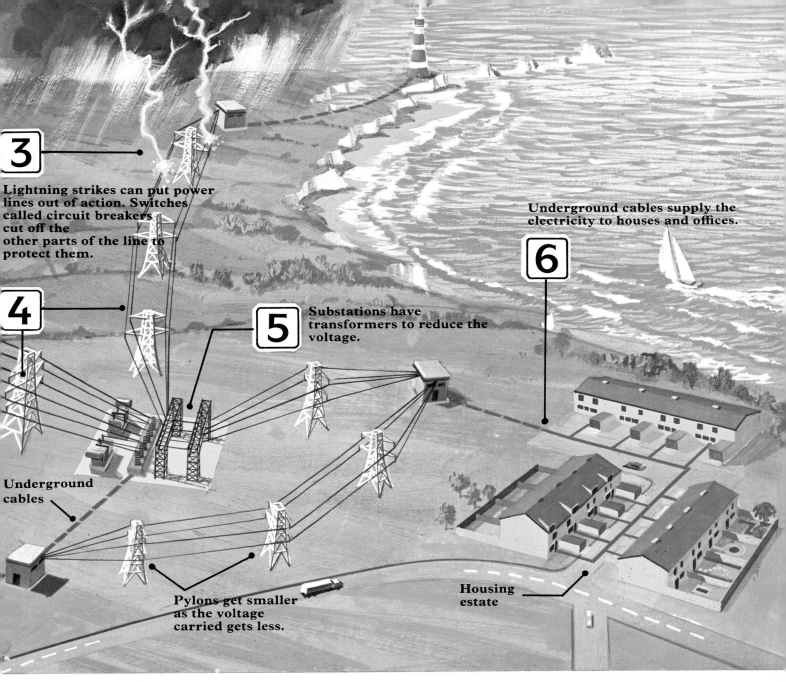

3

Lightning strikes can put power lines out of action. Switches called circuit breakers cut off the other parts of the line to protect them.

4

5

Substations have transformers to reduce the voltage.

Underground cables

6

Underground cables supply the electricity to houses and offices.

Pylons get smaller as the voltage carried gets less.

Housing estate

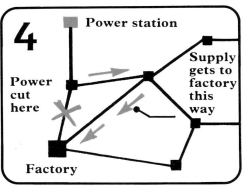

4

Power station

Supply gets to factory this way

Power cut here

Factory

▲ To avoid power cuts caused by lightning, electricity supply lines are arranged in an inter-connecting grid. If one of the supplies to a factory is cut off, it can still get its supply from another line.

5

▲ When the electricity reaches the main substation, it is still at a very high voltage. Step-down transformers in the substation reduce the voltage to a lower level which is carried on smaller, lighter pylons.

6

▲ The final link in the chain from power station to home. Underground cables are used in towns because overhead lines would be dangerous. They pass beneath the pavement and feed the power to your home.

Inside the home

Once the power has come into your home, the many gadgets and appliances are fed by several different circuits. There are usually 5 circuits. One for the downstairs wall sockets, one for those upstairs, one each for the downstairs and upstairs lighting circuits, and one for the electric cooker.

The wires carrying the power are run in metal or plastic tubes hidden in the walls and ceiling, or under the floor, so they can't be touched. This picture shows some of the uses for electricity in your home.

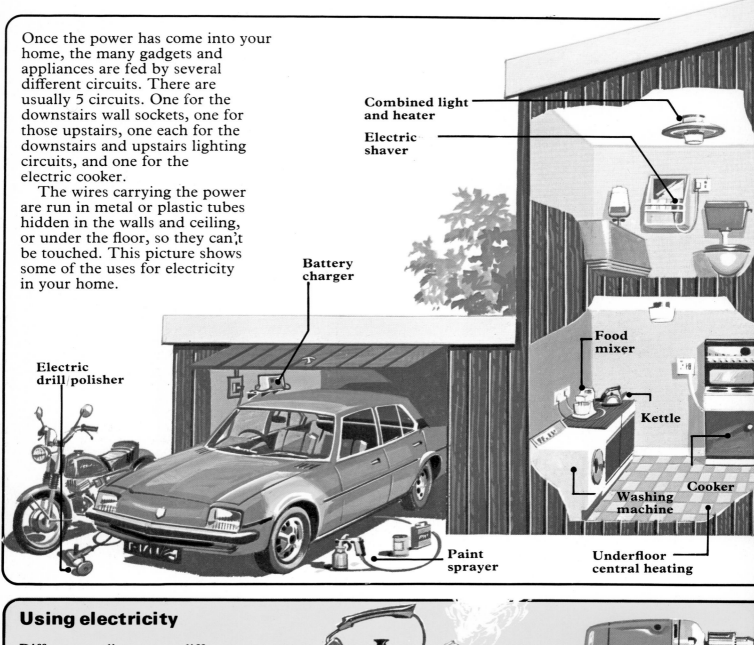

Combined light and heater

Electric shaver

Battery charger

Electric drill/polisher

Food mixer

Kettle

Washing machine

Cooker

Paint sprayer

Underfloor central heating

Using electricity

Different appliances use different amounts of electricity. They all work at mains voltage but use different amounts of current. The same amount of energy provides enough electricity to power the following appliances as shown:

To boil 7 litres of water in a kettle.

To use a drill for 4 hours.

To light a 100W bulb for 10 hours.

To light a 40W strip light for a day.

To run a clock for 3 months

22 14 19

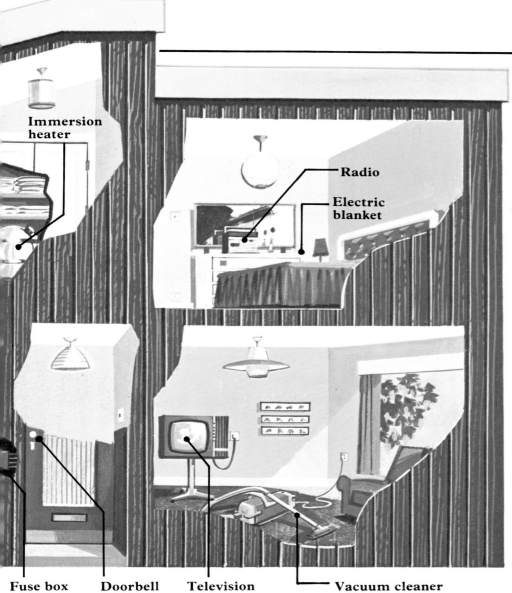

Immersion heater

Radio

Electric blanket

Fuse box **Doorbell** **Television** **Vacuum cleaner**

Fuse protection

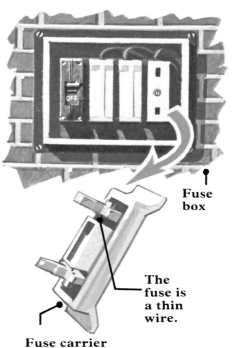

Fuse box

The fuse is a thin wire.

Fuse carrier

▲ The current flow to each circuit in a house passes through a fuse, which is a strand of wire held in a plastic carrier. If a fault in the circuit makes a high current flow, the fuse heats up and breaks, cutting off the power supply.

The fault must then be put right and the fuse replaced.

Some houses have circuit breakers instead of fuses to cut off the power supply.

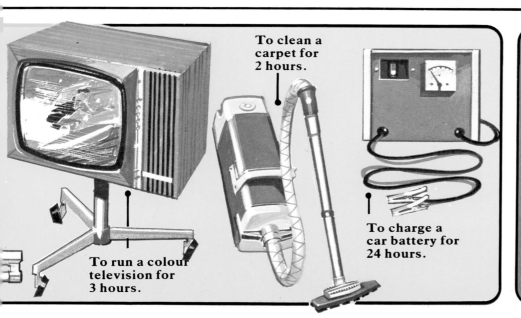

To clean a carpet for 2 hours.

To charge a car battery for 24 hours.

To run a colour television for 3 hours.

MAINS ELECTRICITY IS DANGEROUS

The electricity in your home is at a very high voltage. It can easily KILL people.

This is why all the wiring in a house is built into the walls, ceilings and floors.

NEVER play with plugs, sockets or anything connected to the mains supply.

25

Telegraph and telephone

The invention of the electric telegraph in 1838 enabled people to communicate directly with one another over long distances. The only connection between then was the wire which carried the message.

Before Bell invented the telephone in 1876 it was not possible to talk over a telegraph wire. So the message had to be coded into a series of long and short electrical currents which were passed along the wire and decoded at the receiving station. This is why a telegram is sometimes called a 'wire'.

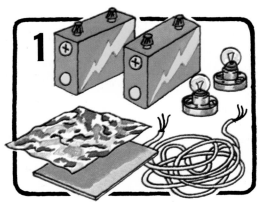

▲ You will need two 4.5 volt batteries, two 6 volt bulbs in holders, a sheet of cardboard and a sheet of cooking foil. Decide where to put the two telegraph stations. Get enough 3-core flex to join the two.

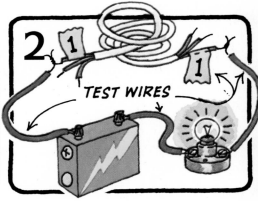

TEST WIRES

▲ To find out which wire is which, wire up a battery and bulb as shown. Connect a test wire to one of the flex wires. Touch the other wires until the bulb glows. Mark the wires and repeat for the others.

4 Station B

ENDS TWISTED TOGETHER

SPARE WIRE

▲ To make station B, wire 3 of the flex's other end is connected to the ⊕ terminal of the other battery. Wire 2 is connected to the other bulbholder. Join the holder's other terminal to wire 1 with a spare wire. Fix the other spare wire to the battery ⊖ terminal. Double-check all the connections you have made so far, to avoid mistakes—the wiring is quite complicated and if you make a mistake, you might have to start all over again!

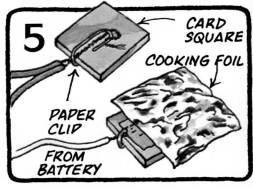

CARD SQUARE

COOKING FOIL

PAPER CLIP

FROM BATTERY

▲ You need four Morse tappers. One on each of the spare wires from a battery, and one on each pair of twisted-together wires. Clip the wires to squares of cardboard with paper clips, and glue cooking foil over the top.

A century of telephones

"Mr. Watson, come here, I want to see you." Alexander Graham Bell's historic call to his assistant in 1876 was the first time speech had been transmitted over a wire.

Bell realised the importance of his new invention and set up ·a telephone company to satisfy the sudden demand for telephones.

Within two years of this first demonstration thousands of telephones had been installed in offices in America, and within five years Bell retired from the business a famous and wealthy man.

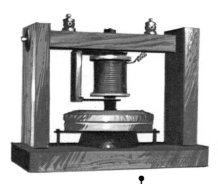

Bell's first telephone, 1875

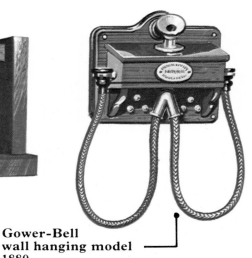

Gower-Bell wall hanging model 1880

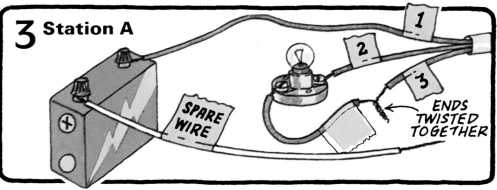

3 Station A

SPARE WIRE

ENDS TWISTED TOGETHER

▲ To make station A, attach wire 1 from the flex to the ⊖ terminal of a battery. Connect wire 2 to a bulbholder. Connect a piece of spare wire to the bulbholder's other terminal, twisting its other end with wire 3.

The second spare wire should be attached to the battery's ⊕ terminal. Remember that these details are to show you how to wire up the telegraph system properly. The wire lengths depend on where you put the stations.

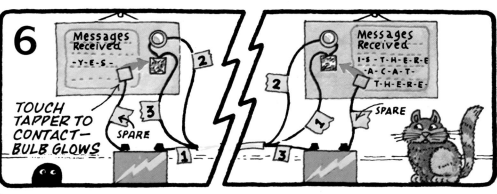

6

Messages Received
- Y - E - S -

TOUCH TAPPER TO CONTACT— BULB GLOWS

SPARE

Messages Received
I - S   T - H - E - R - E
A - C - A - T
T - H - E - R - E

SPARE

▲ Fix each bulbholder and one of the tappers to a sheet of card that will hang on the wall of Station A. Do the same for Station B. It's a good idea to have a pad of paper there too to write down messages as they come

in. Unless you already know the Morse Code, you will need to use the one we have printed here to code any message you want to send, or to decode messages that come in. Once you get the hang of it, see how fast you can decode Morse!

Table model 1920's

Push button model 1970's

Before messages can be sent over a telegraph wire they must be coded into electrical signals at the sending end. In the code invented by Samuel Morse the 26 letters of the alphabet are represented by 26 different combinations of long and short dots and dashes. Remember that to be exact, your dashes should be three times as long as your dots.

A ·—
B —···
C —·—·
D —··
E ·
F ··—·
G ——·
H ····
I ··
J ·———
K —·—
L ·—··
M ——
N —·
O ———
P ·——·
Q ——·—
R ·—·
S ···
T —
U ··—
V ···—
W ·——
X —··—
Y —·——
Z ——··

1 ·————
2 ··———
3 ···——
4 ····—
5 ·····
6 —····
7 ——···
8 ———··
9 ————·
10 —————

21st century electricity

If we go on using coal, oil and gas as fast as we do now, they could be used up in under 100 years. So scientists are looking for other ways of producing electricity.

One idea shown here is for an orbiting solar collector that turns sunlight into electricity and then sends it down to Earth.

Another possibility is a nuclear fusion reactor. The fuels needed for fusion are found in sea water, so the world's oceans could one day produce almost limitless supplies of energy.

The solar collector picks up the sunlight and converts it into electricity using solar cells like the ones which power many of today's satellites. The bigger it is the more electricity it produces. This one measures 8 km. by 8 km. which is as large as 13,000 football pitches.

The Sun

Sun's rays caught by the collector.

The sunlight reaching the Earth's surface has been filtered through the atmosphere, but the solar collector out in space catches all the direct rays of the Sun. It produces far more electricity out in space than it would do on Earth.

The power transmitter is connected to the solar collector, and the pair orbit the Earth. They stay in orbit above the receiving station on the Earth's surface 35,880 km. below.

Superspeed railways

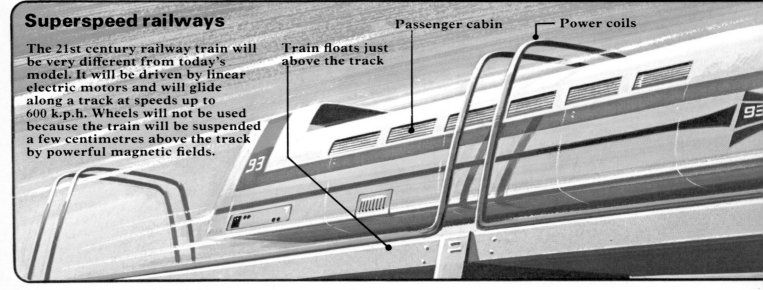

The 21st century railway train will be very different from today's model. It will be driven by linear electric motors and will glide along a track at speeds up to 600 k.p.h. Wheels will not be used because the train will be suspended a few centimetres above the track by powerful magnetic fields.

Train floats just above the track

Passenger cabin

Power coils

Power beam
to Earth

To collect the power
beamed down from the
orbiting collector,
a large collecting
area is needed. Each
receiving station
collects enough
power to supply one
major city with
electricity.

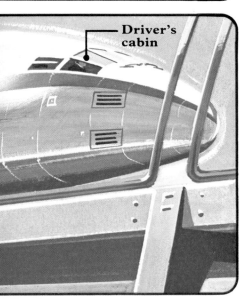

Driver's
cabin

Power from the atom

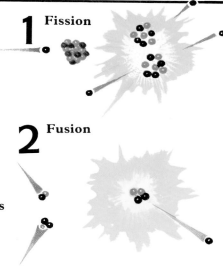

1 Fission

2 Fusion

Today's atomic power stations
are all fission reactors. Atoms
are split in the reactor and
the heat given off is used
to boil water for steam.
Fission reactors have one
major problem—radioactive
waste. So scientists are trying
to make fusion reactors. A
fusion reactor would have little
or no dangerous waste.

▶ Fusion is the combining of atoms
of deuterium and tritium—both
found in sea water. When the two
atoms join they give off a lot of
energy as heat, which can be used
to produce electricity.

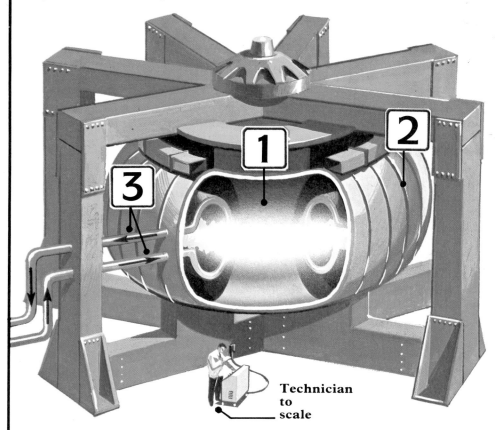

Technician
to
scale

Tomorrow's fusion reactor

▲ Deuterium and tritium atoms
join only at a temperature of
100 million°C. No known material
will withstand such a high
temperature and the only suitable
container for the reaction is a
powerful magnetic field (1).
The field is produced by a
huge electric current flowing
through coils of wire embedded in
the doughnut-shaped concrete wall
(2). Lithium—a metal liquefied by
the heat—is pumped through pipes
(3) to boil water. The steam given
off turns turbines, which turn
the coils in a generator.

29

Electric firsts

1600
English scientist William Gilbert published his theory that the Earth has a magnetic field.

1672
Otto von Guericke invented the first electrical machine. A large sulphur ball, turned by a handle, produced static electricity when a hand was rubbed against it.

1752
Benjamin Franklin showed that thunderclouds are charged with static electricity.

1800
The first electric battery was made by Count Alessandro Volta in Italy.

1831
English scientist Michael Faraday built the first generator of electric current.

1837
The first electric telegraph was built by Samuel Morse in America. The Morse code is still used today.

1858
The first transatlantic telegraph cable was laid.

1876
Scottish born inventor Alexander Graham Bell invented the telephone.

1879
The world's first electric railway was opened in Berlin.

Thomas Edison made the first electric light bulb.

1882
Edison set up the first public electricity supply. His Pearl Street station in New York supplied power to shops and houses over an area of 2 square kilometres.

1956
The first power station to produce electricity from the power of the atom was opened at Calder Hall, England.

1975
The first electric car to be built on a production line was made.

Electric words

Here is a list of some of the technical words used in this book and their explanations.

Armature
The coils in an electric motor that are forced to spin round by the magnetic fields.

Brushes
Conducting pads in an electric motor that pass current to the spinning armature.

Circuit
A path along which electric current travels. Current will not flow until the circuit is complete.

Conductor
A material that allows electric current to flow through it easily.

Condenser
In a power station steam from the turbines is passed into the condenser where it is turned back into water.

Electrodes
The two rods that carry current into and out of the electolyte in a battery.

Electrolyte
The liquid or paste in a battery. Chemical changes in it produce electricity.

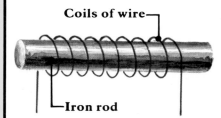

Coils of wire

Iron rod

Electromagnet
An iron rod with many coils of wire wrapped round it. When current is passed through the coils, the iron becomes a very powerful magnet.

Fission
The splitting of uranium atoms by shooting neutrons at them. As the atoms split they release energy that can be turned into electricity.

Fusion
The joining up of two atoms. A lot of energy is given off as they combine.

Tyre

Dynamo

Generator
A machine that produces electric current as it spins round. Generators in power stations produce alternating current. Generators that produce only direct current are called dynamos. Bicycles often have a dynamo on the back wheel to power the front and rear lights.

Insulator
Any material that does not allow electricity to flow through it.

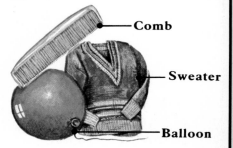

Comb

Sweater

Balloon

Things like this can produce lots of static electricity.

Static electricity
The form of electricity produced when some materials are rubbed together.

Substation
An electricity station where a transformer reduces the voltage of the electricity supply.

Switch
A switch controls the flow of electric current. When the switch is off the circuit is broken and the current flow stops.

Transformer
A device used for increasing or reducing a voltage. Transformers work only with alternating current.

Circuits and switches

The experiments in the book have had pictures of bulbs, batteries and so on to show you how to connect them up. But when complicated circuits are drawn it is easier to use symbols. Connect up the circuits on this page using the list of symbols shown on the right.

See the effect of putting a switch in another part of the circuit; check how brightly bulbs glow when two are used instead of one. When you have done these, you can try designing some circuits of your own.

What the signs and symbols mean

Wire

Connection between wires

Battery

Light bulb

Switch

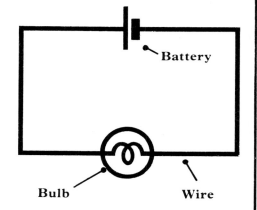

Battery

Bulb   Wire

The simplest circuit is a bulb connected to a battery. There must be a wire to take the current out of the battery to the bulb, and another to return it to the battery.

Making a switch

PAPERCLIP   WOOD BLOCK

To help you use these other circuits, you need to make this switch. You need two drawing pins, a small block of wood and a paperclip. Make it up as shown in the picture.

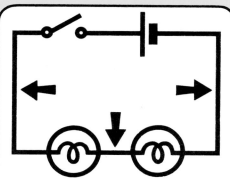

Here the bulbs are connected 'in series'. When the switch is off current will not flow. Try connecting the switch in the other places arrowed. Does it still work?

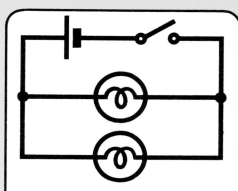

This is a 'parallel' circuit. You can see that when the circuit is completed by turning the switch on, both bulbs are controlled by it.

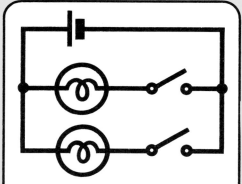

This circuit is very like the one before, but two switches are in the circuit instead of one. How many bulbs does each switch control when you turn it on?

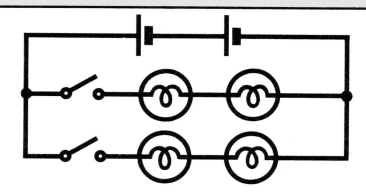

It is possible to connect batteries in series or parallel too—just like the bulbs earlier on. But remember to connect the ⊖ of the first battery to the ⊕ of the second. This means that the voltage in the circuit is twice that of each 4.5 volt battery, making a total of 9 volts. Each switch in this circuit controls two of the four light bulbs.

Index

THE USBORNE YOUNG SCIENTIST
HUMAN BODY

Susan Meredith, Ann Goldman and Tom Lissauer
Designed by Roger Priddy

Contents

Illustrated by Kuo Kang Chen, Dee McLean, Sue Stitt, Penny Simon
and Rob McCaig

 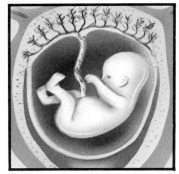 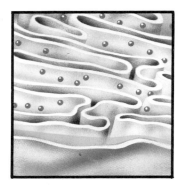 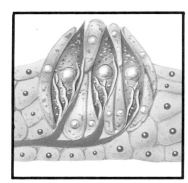

What is your body made of?

Your body is a complex mass of many different parts. All the parts have vital jobs to do and they all have to work properly together to keep you alive and healthy. Your body is made up of more than 50 billion individual living units called cells. All human beings develop from just two cells: an egg cell (ovum*) from their mother and a sperm cell from their father. Egg cells are the largest human cells and can just be seen without a microscope. Most of the other cells can only be seen through very powerful microscopes.**

What is a cell made of?

Although there are differences between the various types of cell, most have the same basic structure and they all need certain substances, such as food and oxygen, to stay alive and to work properly. Here is a cell shown with a section removed so you can see its different parts.

Membrane

This is a fine layer which holds the cell together and separates it from other cells. It is rather like the frontier of a country. It allows certain substances to pass into the cell, while keeping others out. It also allows waste products made in the cell to pass out.

Mitochondria

These are the cell's power stations. Here food and oxygen react together to produce energy so that the cell can live and work.

Ribosomes

Ribosomes are the cell's factories. They manufacture proteins, including those from which the cell itself is made.

*Many words used to describe the body are Latin or Greek. Their plurals are formed differently from those of English words. It may help to remember that most Latin words ending in "um" change the ending to "a" in the plural and those ending in "us" usually change to "i".

**The cells in this book are shown magnified many times. The colours are not true to life.

Types of cell

You have many different types of cell in your body, each with different jobs to do. (The cells shown here are not to scale.)

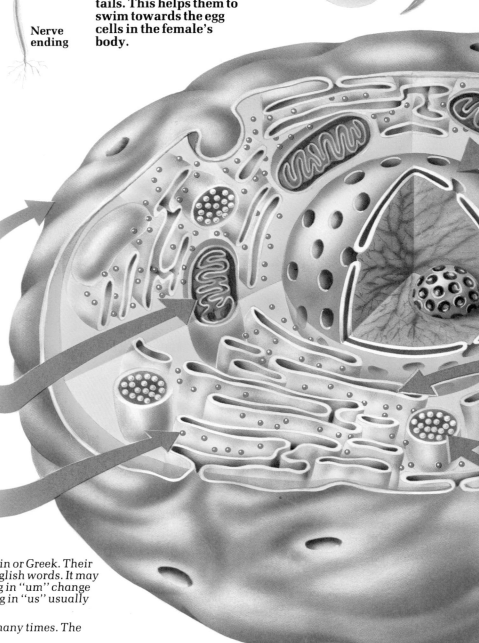

◄ Nerve cells have long fibres which send messages to other parts of the body. Some have special endings for feeling sensations.

Muscle cells are long and thin. They can shorten their length (contract) and then relax, which causes movement. ▶

Nerve fibre

Tail

Nerve ending

Sperm cells, from the male's body, have long tails. This helps them to swim towards the egg cells in the female's body. ▶

Tissues

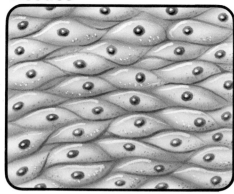

A group of cells of mainly the same type is called a tissue. The minute spaces among the cells are filled with a watery substance called tissue fluid. This picture shows a type of muscle tissue.

Organs

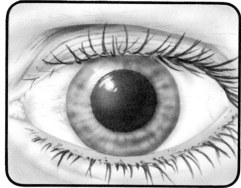

Different types of tissue are grouped together to form organs. An organ has a particular job to do in your body. For instance, your heart pumps blood, your stomach digests food and your eyes enable you to see.

Systems

A group of organs whose jobs are closely related is often referred to as a system. Examples are the circulatory system, which includes your heart and blood vessels, and the skeletal system, shown here.

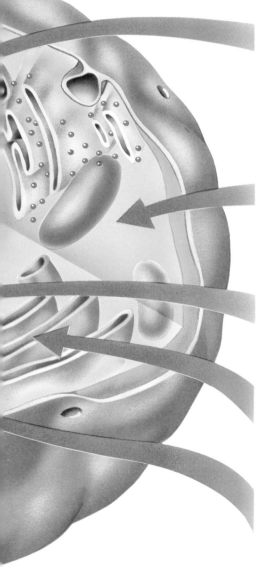

Nucleus

The nucleus acts rather like a government headquarters, controlling and directing all the activities of the cell. It is in the centre of the cell body. (You can see the nucleus in each of the cells on the page opposite.) The nucleus contains special threads called chromosomes. These carry complex coded instructions for the workings of the cell, rather like a computer program. You inherit your chromosomes from your parents.

Cytoplasm

This is a jelly-like substance, which makes up most of the cell, rather like a background landscape. It consists mainly of protein and water, especially water. Your cells are about two-thirds water.

Endoplasmic reticulum

These channels are the cell's industrial estates. They are where the ribosomes are found.

Golgi complex

This acts as a storage depot. Some of the proteins made by the ribosomes are kept here until they are needed.

Lysosomes

These are the cell's secret police. They contain chemicals which destroy harmful foreign substances and any old or diseased parts of the cell.

How cells reproduce

Millions of your cells die every second but new cells are constantly being made to take their place. Some cells live longer than others. The cells lining your intestines get worn away by food and live for only about six days. Red blood cells live for about four months, bone cells for up to 30 years, and nerve and muscle cells, which cannot reproduce, up to a lifetime. A cell reproduces by dividing into two to produce a pair of identical new cells.

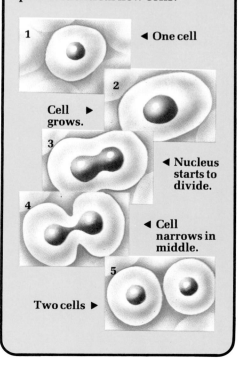

1 ◄ One cell

Cell ► grows.

2

3 ◄ Nucleus starts to divide.

4 ◄ Cell narrows in middle.

5

Two cells ►

3

Why you eat

Without regular supplies of food to use as fuel your body would soon stop working. Different types of food do different jobs, such as giving you energy or making you grow. To stay healthy you need to eat a good balance of all the types of food described below.

Proteins

Over ten per cent of your body tissue is made of protein so you need to eat protein to renew it and, if you are growing, to make more. The faster you are growing, the more you need. Protein is built up of chemical units called amino acids. Protein in food is broken down in your body into individual amino acids. These are then rebuilt in your cells to form the proteins you need. Good sources of protein are lean meat, fish, cheese, eggs, milk, nuts and beans.

Carbohydrates

These are built up of different sugars (including glucose) and give you most of your energy. You can either eat the sugars directly in foods such as fruit and jam or in the form of starch in foods such as potatoes, rice and bread. Starch becomes sugar inside your body. If you eat more carbohydrates than you need, the excess is converted into a substance called glycogen and stored in your liver and muscles. Or it is converted into fat. It is best to avoid eating sugar in drinks and in foods such as cakes, biscuits, sweets, chocolates and convenience foods. Besides turning to fat, it is bad for your teeth.

Fats

Like carbohydrates, fats provide you with energy. They also form parts of your cells, such as the membranes. Fat is stored in your body and helps to keep you warm. The fats you eat can come either from animals, in foods such as meat, milk, butter and cheese or from plants, in foods such as vegetable oils and nuts. Too much fat may play a part in heart disease.

Minerals

These are involved in vital chemical processes in your body. You need small amounts of about 20 different minerals. Calcium and phosphorus, found in foods such as milk and cheese, help to make your bones and teeth strong. Iron is needed by your red blood cells and is found in foods such as liver and green vegetables. A lack of zinc, found in nuts, fish and fresh vegetables, may cause skin rashes. You also need sodium chloride (salt). In general, people in developed countries eat more salt than necessary. This may be associated with high blood pressure.

Vitamins

You need small amounts of about 15 different vitamins so that essential chemical processes can take place in your body. A lack of any particular vitamin causes a specific illness. For example, if children do not have enough vitamin D they get an illness called rickets which stops their bones developing properly.

Fibre

Fibre, or "roughage", consists mainly of cellulose, which is a type of carbohydrate your body cannot digest. It is found in vegetables, fruit and wholemeal bread. Fibre is valuable because it is bulky and this helps to make the muscles of your intestines (bowels) work efficiently and so prevents constipation. Fibre may help to prevent serious diseases of the intestines, including cancer.

Water

You are losing water all the time in your urine (pee), in your sweat and when you breathe out, so you have to take in water to replace it. There is water not only in drinks but also in solid foods. Lettuce, for example, is nine-tenths water. You could stay alive longer without food than you could without water.

Vitamin	Good sources	Necessary for . . .
A	Milk, butter, eggs, fish oils, fresh green vegetables.	Eyes (especially seeing in the dark), skin.
B (really several vitamins)	Wholemeal bread and rice, yeast, liver, soya beans.	Energy production in all your cells, nerves, skin.
C	Oranges, lemons, blackcurrants, tomatoes, potatoes, fresh green vegetables.	Blood vessels, gums, healing wounds, possibly preventing colds.
D	Fish oils, milk, eggs, butter (and sunlight).	Bones and teeth.
E	Vegetable oils, wholemeal bread and rice, eggs, butter, fresh green vegetables.	Uses not yet understood.
K	Fresh green vegetables, liver.	Clotting blood.

Calories

The amount of energy that can be produced from different foods is measured in kilojoules or Calories*. Some foods have more Calories than others.

650 Calories
250 Calories
80 Calories
50 Calories

The number of calories you need depends on how much energy you use up. Here you can see approximately how many Calories you use doing different activities for an hour. If you regularly eat more Calories than you use up, you get fat. Some people naturally burn up calories faster than others, so they can eat more without getting fat. No one knows exactly why this is.

600 Calories
300 Calories
100 Calories
70 Calories

Getting fat

If you habitually overeat, the excess food is converted into fat and stored in special fat cells. The cells can increase in size and so you put on weight and "get fat". If you eat less than you need, your stores of fat are used up as energy and you get thinner. On average, fat people die younger than thin people. They are more likely to suffer from certain illnesses, including heart disease.

Fat cells

Teeth

There are 32 teeth in a full adult set and 20 in a set of first, or "milk", teeth. Your sharp front teeth, called incisors and canines, are for biting. The back teeth (premolars and molars) have knobbly surfaces for crushing and grinding the food when you chew. There are no premolars in milk teeth and some adults never grow their back four molars (wisdom teeth). Nobody really knows why humans develop two sets of teeth.

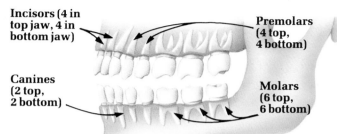

Incisors (4 in top jaw, 4 in bottom jaw)
Premolars (4 top, 4 bottom)
Canines (2 top, 2 bottom)
Molars (6 top, 6 bottom)

What are teeth made of?

Although teeth have different shapes and different jobs to do, they are all built in the same way. Your milk teeth fall out when your adult teeth grow up from underneath and weaken their roots.

Outer layer of enamel provides a strong biting surface. Enamel is non-living tissue and the hardest substance in your body.

Body of tooth is made of dentine, which is rather like bone.

Soft tissue called pulp contains blood vessels, which supply the tooth with food and oxygen, and nerves, which make it sensitive to pain and temperature.

Root is anchored in jaw-bone by thin layer of bone tissue called cement.

Crown
Gum
Root
Jaw-bone

Tooth decay

Everyone has bacteria (microscopic living creatures) in their mouths. If these get a supply of sugar from sweet foods, they multiply and a substance called plaque is formed. The bacteria produce acids, which eat into the tooth. If the hole is not filled by the dentist, it eventually reaches the pulp cavity and causes toothache. An infection or abscess may develop, or the tooth may become loose if the gum is damaged.

You can help to keep your teeth healthy by eating and drinking less sugary foods, cleaning them properly to remove plaque, using a fluoride toothpaste, which strengthens the enamel, and by going to the dentist for regular check-ups.

Acids make hole in tooth enamel.
Hole enlarges and reaches pulp cavity.

*1 Calorie = 1,000 calories.

Where food goes to

Before the food you eat can do its job, it has to be absorbed by all the minute cells in your body. First it has to be broken down so that it will dissolve. This process is called digestion and it takes place as the food travels through your digestive tract. The dissolved food then passes into your bloodstream and is carried to all the different parts of your body.

Digestion

Your digestive tract is a long tube which winds from your mouth to your anus (back passage). Most of your digestive organs are in your abdomen. This is separated from your chest by a large sheet of muscle called the diaphragm. Here you can see how food travels through the tract.

1 Your teeth bite and chew the food into small pieces. Saliva (spit), made by your salivary glands, moistens it so it slides down your throat more easily. Saliva contains the first digestive enzyme (see above). This starts digesting starch. (Your salivary glands swell up when you have mumps.)

2 The muscles of your tongue force the food back into your throat (pharynx) and your throat muscles guide it into your gullet (oesophagus). As you swallow, a flap called the epiglottis blocks off the top of the nearby windpipe so the food does not "go down the wrong hole" and make you choke.

3 The food goes down your oesophagus into your stomach. It does not slide down by gravity but is pushed along by muscles in the oesophagus. This process is called peristalsis and takes place all along your digestive tract. The sound you hear when your "stomach" rumbles is food and air being mixed up and pushed through the tract. In theory, peristalsis means that you could still eat and drink if you were standing on your head.

Salivary gland
Tongue
Epiglottis
Windpipe
Oesophagus

Normal position of epiglottis.
Epiglottis covers windpipe when you swallow.

Muscles in oesophagus contract.
Food is pushed along.

Enzymes

Chemical changes are taking place in your body all the time. These are speeded up by enzymes, which are special proteins made in your cells. There are several thousand different sorts of enzyme. Digestive enzymes help to break down and dissolve your food.

How food gets into your blood

The inner wall of the ileum is covered with thousands of tiny structures called villi which stick out like fingers. These give the tube a huge surface area for absorbing the food.

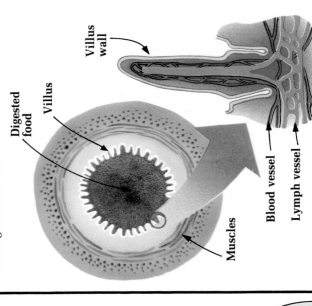

Villus wall
Villus
Digested food
Looking down the tube.
Muscles
Blood vessel
Lymph vessel

The walls of the villi are only one cell thick. The digested food passes through them and into the tiny blood vessels inside. The digested fats do not go directly into the blood vessels. They are absorbed into special "lymph" vessels and enter the blood later.

Being sick

You are sick when your diaphragm muscle and the muscles in the wall of your abdomen contract strongly and force partly digested food back up out of your stomach. It is stomach juice which makes vomit taste sour. There are many reasons for being sick, including eating too much, eating food that has gone bad and drinking too much alcohol.

Diarrhoea and constipation

Diarrhoea is often caused by an infection in the intestines or by food poisoning. Food travels through the intestines so fast that the water cannot be absorbed properly. If you have diarrhoea, you should drink extra fluid to make up for what you are losing. Constipation is often caused by not eating enough fibre.

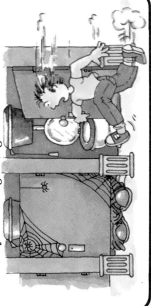

Appendix

The appendix has no function in humans, though in animals which eat grass it plays a part in digestion. An inflamed appendix (appendicitis) has to be taken out or it may burst and spread infection right through the abdomen.

Diaphragm

4

5

6

Large intestine

Gall bladder

7

Small intestine

8

9

Appendix

10

Anus

---

4 In your stomach the food is churned about and mixed with stomach juice. This contains enzymes which start digesting protein. It also contains hydrochloric acid, which helps to kill any bacteria swallowed with the food. A meal stays in your stomach for about four hours.

5 Your liver has several important jobs. One of these is to make a green liquid called bile. This acts rather like a detergent. It breaks up the fats you eat into tiny drops so that enzymes can work on them. Bile is stored in your gall bladder.

6 One of the jobs of the pancreas is to make a juice containing many different digestive enzymes. These work on all types of food.

7 The coiled small intestine is only about 4cm in diameter but it is about four metres long. In the first part, called the duodenum, the food is mixed with bile from your liver and with the juice from your pancreas.

8 By the time it gets to the second part of your small intestine (the ileum), most of the food is digested. It passes through the walls of the intestine into your blood. Your blood then carries the digested food to your liver for more processing before taking it round your body.

9 Water and any food which cannot be digested move on into your large intestine. Most of the water passes into your blood through the walls of the first part of the large intestine (the colon). Some of the water passes out of your body later as urine.

10 The more solid waste matter, called faeces, is stored further along your large intestine (in the rectum). The muscles of your rectum push it out through your anus when you go to the toilet.

Why you breathe

Food alone does not give your body the energy it needs. It first has to be combined with oxygen, which is a gas in the air. When you breathe in, oxygen goes into your lungs and from there is carried to all the cells in your body by your blood. Inside the cells the oxygen reacts with glucose (from digested carbohydrates) and the energy stored in the food is gradually released. This process is called respiration. The energy keeps your cells alive and working. During respiration, a waste gas called carbon dioxide, and water, are formed in your cells. You get rid of these when you breathe out.

1 Breathing

Your lungs and windpipe are known as your respiratory system. In this picture the left lung is shown cut open so you can see inside.

When you breathe in, air is sucked through your nose or mouth, down your windpipe (trachea) and into two passages called bronchi. One bronchus goes to the left lung, the other goes to the right. The bronchi gradually divide to form smaller and smaller passages, rather like tree branches.

Voice box (larynx)

Oesophagus

Windpipe (trachea)

Rib

Rib muscles

Bronchus

Heart

Diaphragm

2

At the ends of the smallest passages are bunches of air sacs called alveoli. These are like tiny balloons and fill with air when you breathe in. All together there are about 300 million alveoli in your lungs. Their total surface area is about 70 square metres, which is about 40 times the area of your skin.

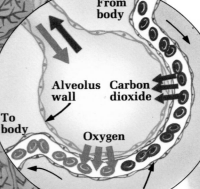

Alveolus

Bronchial tube

Blood vessel

From body

Alveolus wall

Carbon dioxide

To body

Oxygen

Blood vessel

3

The walls of the alveoli are only one cell thick. The oxygen from the air is able to pass through the walls and into the network of blood vessels which surrounds them. Your red blood cells carry the oxygen round your body. Your blood also carries back to the alveoli the carbon dioxide produced in your cells during respiration so that it can be removed from your body when you breathe out.

How cells release energy

Each of your cells contains two special chemicals. One, called ADP, acts like a flat battery. The other, called ATP, acts like a charged battery. When glucose and oxygen pass into the cell's mitochondria (its power stations), they react together, with the help of enzymes. This releases energy, which converts the flat ADP to charged ATP. The ATP then acts as a power supply for the rest of the cell. As its energy is used up, it becomes ADP again and goes back to the mitochondria for recharging.

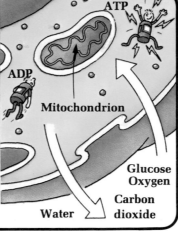

ATP

ADP

Mitochondrion

Glucose
Oxygen

Water

Carbon dioxide

1 How you breathe 2

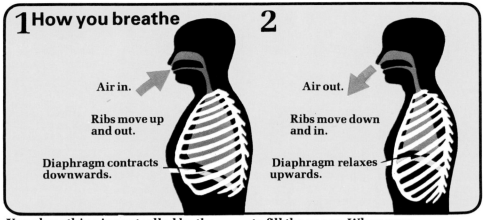

Air in.

Ribs move up and out.

Diaphragm contracts downwards.

Air out.

Ribs move down and in.

Diaphragm relaxes upwards.

Your breathing is controlled by the movements of muscles in your chest, in particular your diaphragm muscle and the muscles between your ribs. To breathe in, your diaphragm contracts downwards while your rib muscles pull your ribs up and out. This expands the space in your lungs, making the air pressure lower inside your lungs than outside your body. Air rushes in to fill the space. When your diaphragm relaxes upwards and your ribs move down and in, the space in your lungs is reduced again and air is squeezed out. Most people usually have about three litres of air in their lungs and exchange only half a litre of it on each breath. During exercise your body needs more energy, so you breathe faster and deeper to take in more air.

Coughing and sneezing

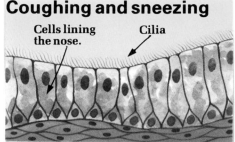

Cells lining the nose.

Cilia

A slippery liquid called mucus is produced in your nose and air passages. This warms and moistens the air you breathe so it can travel along the passages more easily. It also helps to trap dust particles. Tiny hairs called cilia gently waft the mucus away from your lungs towards your nose and throat. If particles irritate your nose, you sneeze them out. If they get into your lower air passages, you cough. When you have a cold, more mucus is produced. This also makes you cough and sneeze, and makes your nose run.

Talking

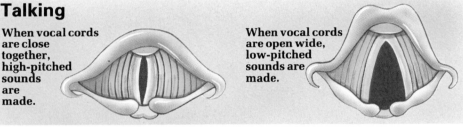

When vocal cords are close together, high-pitched sounds are made.

When vocal cords are open wide, low-pitched sounds are made.

Your voice box (larynx) is at the top of your trachea (see page opposite). When you breathe out, air passes between your "vocal cords". If there is enough air, the cords vibrate and this produces sounds. (These pictures show the vocal cords from above, looking down from the throat.) The muscles of your larynx can alter the shape of the cords. This produces different pitched sounds. By using the muscles of your pharynx (throat), mouth and lips, you form the sounds into words.

Hiccups

These are caused by your diaphragm contracting more violently than usual so that your in-breaths come in short gasps. The strange noise is caused by your vocal cords suddenly closing. Nobody knows why hiccups start but even unborn babies get them.

Smoking

Late teens

Early forties

Fifties?

Everybody's lungs gradually get blackened by breathing in dirty and polluted air but smokers are particularly likely to develop serious, and often fatal, diseases as a result of inhaling the dangerous chemicals in tobacco smoke. The chemicals irritate the air passages and increase the amount of mucus produced in them. This is one of the causes of "smoker's cough". The chemicals also make the cilia less efficient at clearing the mucus away and so it builds up, making the lungs more prone to infection. Smoking is one of the main causes of bronchitis (inflammation of the air passages) and 90 per cent of lung cancer is caused by smoking. Someone who smokes only five cigarettes a day is eight times more likely to die of lung cancer than a non-smoker. Smoking does not only affect the lungs. The chemicals also get into the blood, reducing its ability to carry oxygen and damaging the heart and blood vessels. Statistics show that if 1,000 children born today all take up smoking, 250 of them will be killed by smoking.

What blood is for

Your blood is your body's transport system. Pumped by your heart, it circulates continuously through all the different parts of your body. Its job is to carry vital substances, such as food and oxygen, to where they are needed and to collect up waste products for disposal. The body of an average-sized adult contains about five litres of blood.

Blood vessels

Your blood travels round your body in tubes called blood vessels. Put end to end, these would stretch for 96,560km, which is more than twice round the Earth. The picture below shows the main blood vessels.

Your blood goes from your heart into your arteries (shown below in red). These have thick, elastic walls because the blood pulses through them at high pressure. The arteries divide over and over again. Eventually they form a network of microscopic vessels called capillaries. These pass between the cells of all the tissues in your body. The capillaries gradually join up together again to form larger vessels called veins (shown here in purple). These carry the blood back to your heart. In your veins the blood flows slower and at lower pressure than in your arteries so their walls are thinner and there are valves to prevent it running backwards. Your heart and blood vessels are known as your circulatory system.

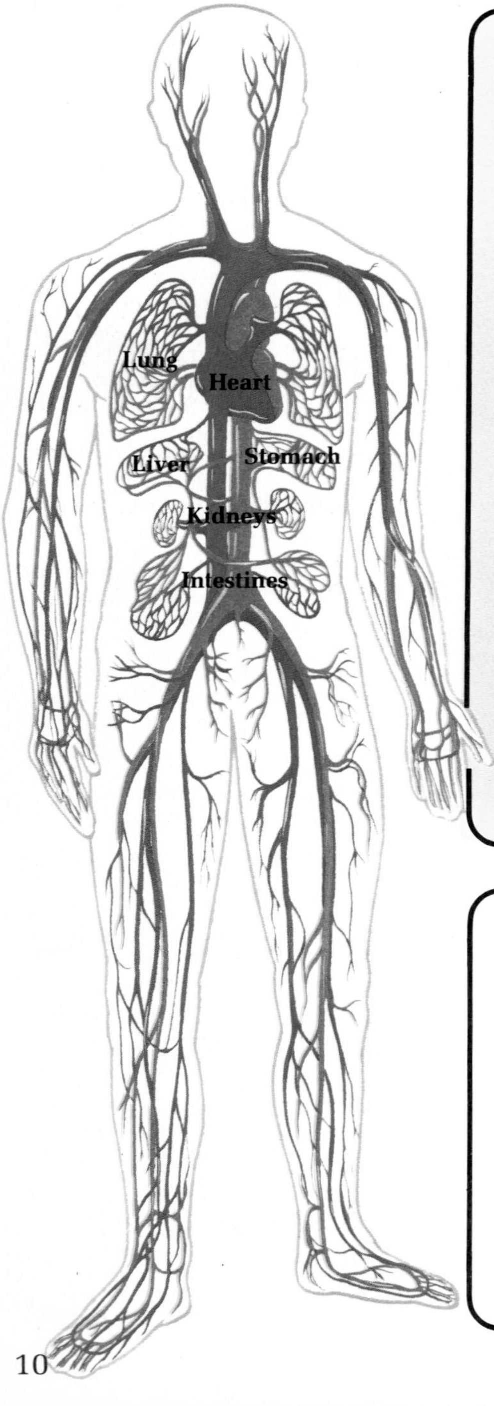

Lung
Heart
Liver
Stomach
Kidneys
Intestines

What is blood?

Blood consists of a mixture of cells floating in a straw-coloured liquid called plasma. Your blood cells are made inside the large bones of your body.

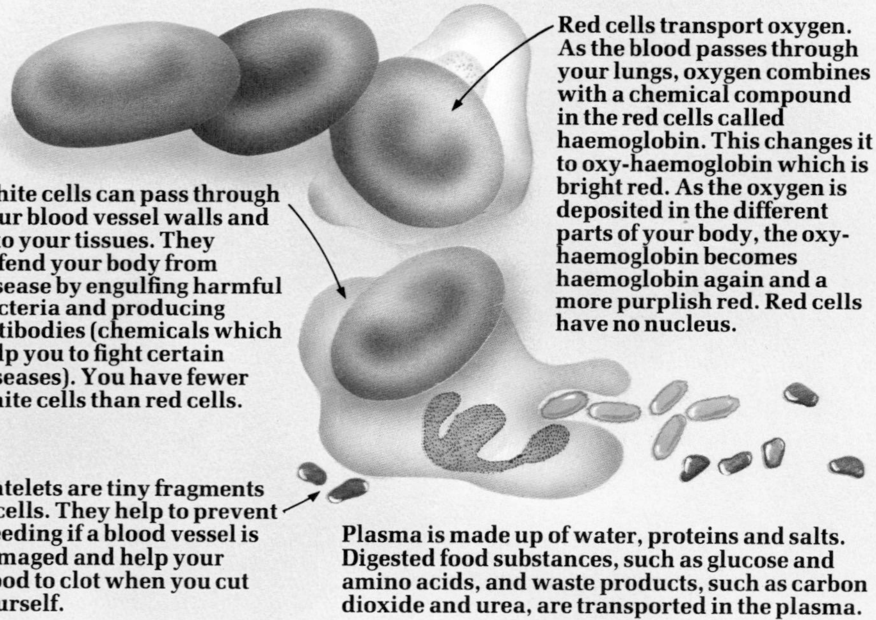

Red cells transport oxygen. As the blood passes through your lungs, oxygen combines with a chemical compound in the red cells called haemoglobin. This changes it to oxy-haemoglobin which is bright red. As the oxygen is deposited in the different parts of your body, the oxy-haemoglobin becomes haemoglobin again and a more purplish red. Red cells have no nucleus.

White cells can pass through your blood vessel walls and into your tissues. They defend your body from disease by engulfing harmful bacteria and producing antibodies (chemicals which help you to fight certain diseases). You have fewer white cells than red cells.

Platelets are tiny fragments of cells. They help to prevent bleeding if a blood vessel is damaged and help your blood to clot when you cut yourself.

Plasma is made up of water, proteins and salts. Digested food substances, such as glucose and amino acids, and waste products, such as carbon dioxide and urea, are transported in the plasma.

In your capillaries

The substances needed by your cells pass out of your blood when it is in your capillaries. The capillary walls are only one cell thick. Plasma and oxygen, from the red cells, are able to pass through the walls and into your tissue fluid. The tissue fluid carries the substances into the individual cells. It also carries waste products from the cells into the capillaries, or else into lymph vessels to be absorbed into the blood later via a vein.

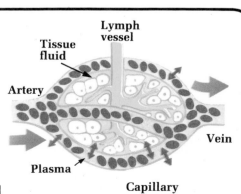

Lymph vessel
Tissue fluid
Artery
Plasma
Vein
Capillary

The heart

Your heart is slightly to the left of the middle of your chest, between your lungs. It is about the size of your fist and is made of muscle. As the muscle contracts, it pumps blood round your body.

The heart is divided into two halves, right and left. Each half has an upper chamber, called an atrium, and a lower chamber, called a ventricle. Four valves open and close as the heart pumps to ensure that the blood does not flow backwards. The beating sound you can hear if you put your ear to someone's chest is made by the valves slamming shut. The first beat is made by the valves between the atria and ventricles, the second by the valves between the ventricles and arteries. Doctors use stethoscopes, which make the beats louder, to help them detect heart abnormalities.

How a valve works

The valve on the right is the sort you have between the ventricles and arteries, and in your veins. Blood flowing in the right direction forces the flaps, or "cusps", open. If it flows in the wrong direction, they are forced shut.

Circulation

Your blood always circulates round your body in the same direction, as shown in this diagram. The whole circuit takes about 45 seconds.

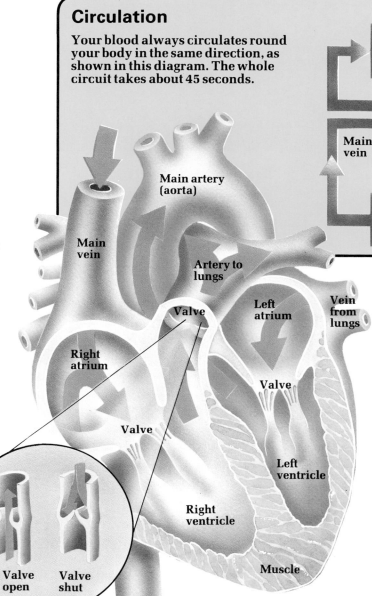

Main artery (aorta)

Main vein

Artery to lungs

Valve

Left atrium

Vein from lungs

Right atrium

Valve

Valve

Left ventricle

Right ventricle

Muscle

Valve open

Valve shut

Lungs

Aorta

Main vein

Heart

Rest of body

How your heart works

To keep pumping continuously, your heart needs food and oxygen, just like any other part of your body. It does not absorb these from the blood inside the chambers but from the capillaries of the "coronary" arteries which lie over its outer surface. A blockage in one of these arteries can deprive part of the heart muscle of blood. This is what happens in a heart attack. If a large part is affected, the whole heart stops working.

Coronary arteries

Pulse

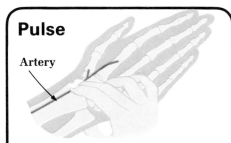

Artery

Every time your heart contracts, your arteries pulsate as blood surges through them. You can feel this at the wrist. The average adult pulse rate is 70 a minute when resting. This increases during exercise because the heart has to pump faster to provide more energy for the muscles.

Heart disease

Heart and circulatory disease is the main cause of death in countries with a high standard of living. The unhealthy lifestyle, which includes overeating, eating the wrong foods, lack of exercise, smoking and stress, makes people more likely to suffer from this type of disease.

Blood groups

Everybody's blood falls into one of four main groups, known as A, B, O and AB. These have different combinations of chemicals called antigens on the surface of the red cells and different antibodies in the plasma. When a blood transfusion is needed, the blood of the donor and patient has to be carefully matched. For example, blood in group A contains "anti-B" antibodies. This means that a person in group A cannot give blood to one in group B or receive blood from them. Mis-matching of blood can cause serious kidney damage to the patient.

About two-thirds of your body consists of water. This has to be kept at a constant level and evenly distributed throughout your cells. You take in water every time you eat and drink, and water is produced inside your cells during respiration. You lose water mainly in your urine, which is produced in varying amounts by your kidneys. In general, the more you drink the more urine your kidneys produce. If you are losing a lot of water, by sweating for example, they produce less. Your kidneys also help to control the level of substances such as salt in your body and they get rid of, or "excrete", waste products such as urea.

Kidneys and bladder

Your kidneys and bladder are known as your urinary system because they produce urine. Your kidneys are at the back of your abdomen, roughly on a level with your waist. The left kidney in this picture is shown cut open so you can see inside.

As your blood passes through your kidneys, any unwanted substances are separated out. This separated fluid, which is urine, passes down two tubes called ureters into your bladder. Your bladder is a muscular bag, which can store up to 400cc of urine. A tight band of muscle, called a sphincter, holds it shut. When you relax the sphincter, the muscles in the walls of your bladder contract and the urine flows into a tube called the urethra and out of your body. The urethra is longer in males than in females because it has to go to the end of the penis.

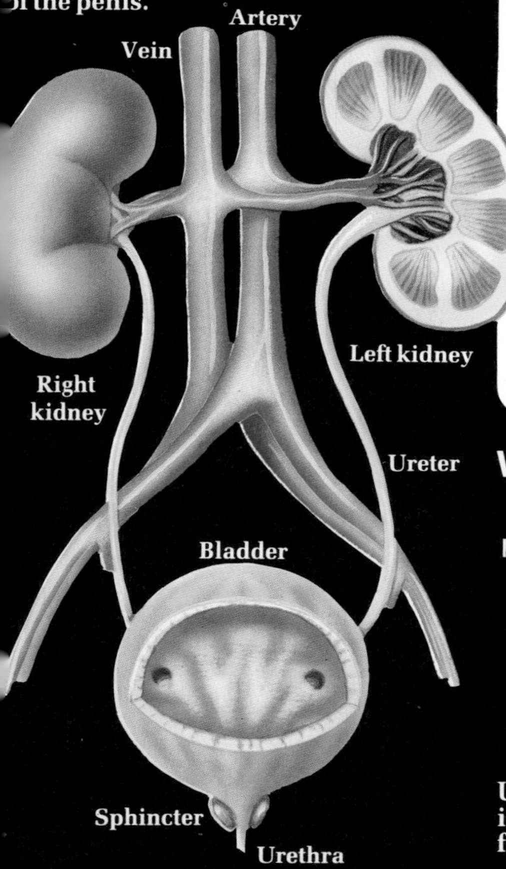

Artery

Vein

Right kidney

Left kidney

Ureter

Bladder

Sphincter

Urethra

Inside your kidneys

Each of your kidneys contains over a million microscopic filtering units called nephrons, like the one shown here. In all, the nephrons filter about 150 litres of fluid a day from your blood though only about 1.5 litres of urine is produced.

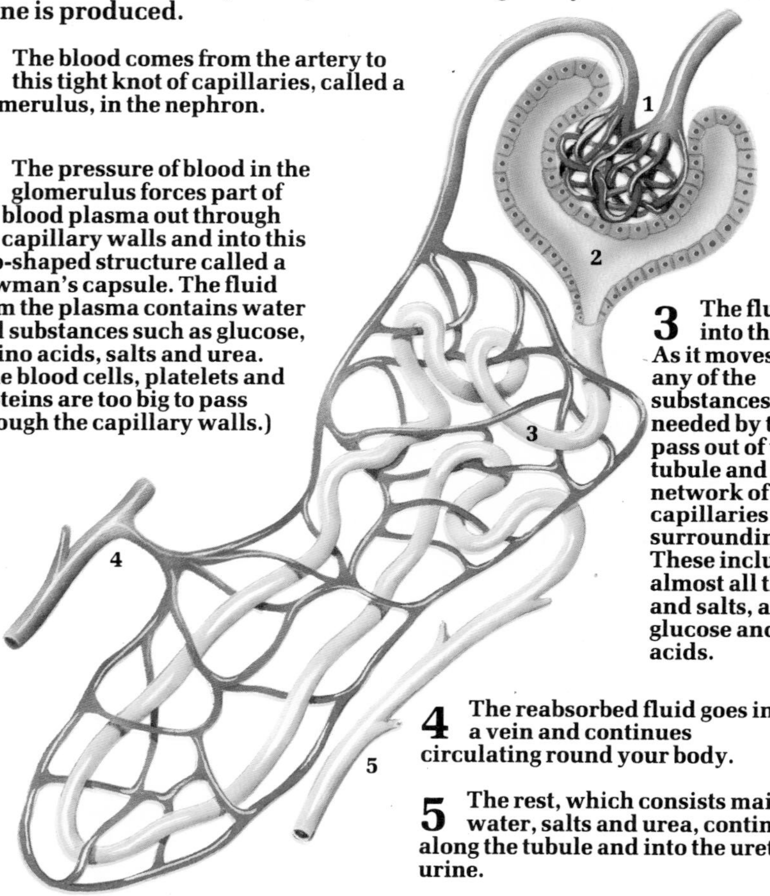

1 The blood comes from the artery to this tight knot of capillaries, called a glomerulus, in the nephron.

2 The pressure of blood in the glomerulus forces part of the blood plasma out through the capillary walls and into this cup-shaped structure called a Bowman's capsule. The fluid from the plasma contains water and substances such as glucose, amino acids, salts and urea. (The blood cells, platelets and proteins are too big to pass through the capillary walls.)

3 The fluid goes into this tubule. As it moves along, any of the substances still needed by the body pass out of the tubule and into the network of capillaries surrounding it. These include almost all the water and salts, and all the glucose and amino acids.

4 The reabsorbed fluid goes into a vein and continues circulating round your body.

5 The rest, which consists mainly of water, salts and urea, continues along the tubule and into the ureter, as urine.

What is urea?

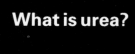

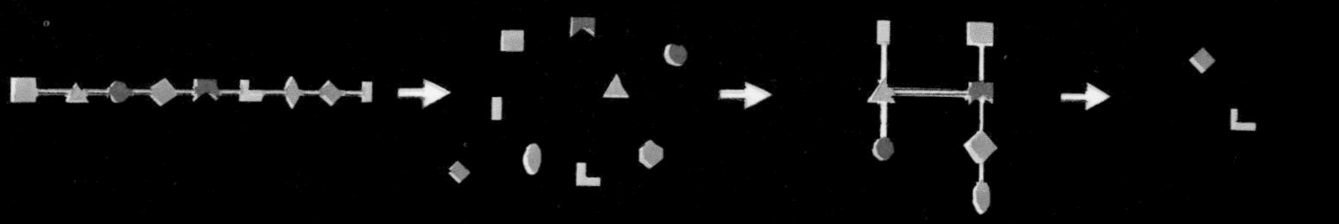

Food protein.

Protein broken down into amino acids.

Amino acids rebuilt to form body protein.

Surplus amino acids.

Urea is a waste substance produced in your body. It is made in your liver from any amino acids left over after the protein in your food has been broken down and rebuilt into new protein for your body.

Chemical control

Certain processes in your body are controlled by chemical substances called hormones. These are produced in groups of cells called endocrine glands and are carried all round your body in your blood. Different hormones act on different parts of your body. The picture on the right shows the main endocrine glands.

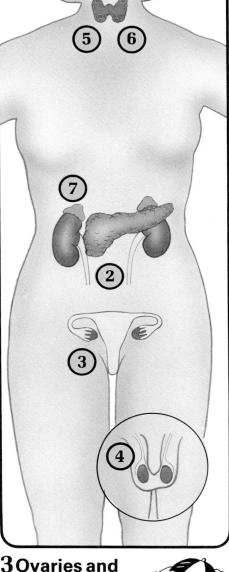

1 Pituitary

This is a pea-sized gland attached to the underside of the brain. It is partly controlled by the brain. The pituitary is sometimes called the master gland because many of its 11 hormones control the actions of other endocrine glands.

Growth hormone is produced by the pituitary. A child with too much may become a giant, one with too little may become a dwarf.

When a baby sucks at its mother's nipple, a hormone called oxytocin is released from the mother's pituitary. It travels to her breast, where it allows the milk to flow.

Antidiuretic hormone (ADH) from the pituitary helps to maintain the correct water balance in your body. It acts on your kidneys and regulates the amount of urine they produce.

2 Pancreas

As well as making digestive enzymes, the pancreas produces the hormone insulin. This regulates the level of glucose in the blood and the conversion of any excess into glycogen. Lack of insulin causes the disease diabetes. This can be treated by insulin injections or tablets.

3 Ovaries and 4 testes *

These glands produce the sex hormones. The female sex hormone, oestrogen, is produced in large amounts in females' ovaries and small amounts in males' testes. The male sex hormone, testosterone, is produced in large amounts in the testes and small amounts in the ovaries. The hormones are not

5 Thyroid

Your thyroid gland is in your neck, at the front of your trachea (windpipe). It uses iodine, which is one of the minerals in food and water, to make two hormones, thyroxine and T_3. These control the rate of respiration in your cells and are essential for the healthy development of new-born babies. If adults have too little thyroid hormone, they become sluggish. If they have too much, they become overactive.

6 Parathyroid

These are four tiny glands buried in the thyroid. They produce parathormone, which helps to regulate the balance of calcium in your blood and bones.

7 Adrenals

Your adrenal glands are just above your kidneys. The outer rim produces several hormones. One of the main ones, called aldosterone, controls the level of salt in your body.

The centre of the adrenals produces adrenaline. When you are afraid or angry, adrenaline pours into your blood and prepares you to take emergency action either by fighting or running away. Your stores of glycogen are converted back into glucose for energy, your breathing rate increases so you get more oxygen, your heart beats faster and your blood is directed towards your muscles.

produced in very large quantities until the age of puberty. This is about 11 in females and 13 in males, though it varies a lot between individuals. At puberty both sexes have a growing spurt and grow pubic hair and hair under the arms. Females' breasts develop, their hips widen, ova are released from the ovaries and menstruation (periods) begins. * Males grow beards, their larynx enlarges and their voice deepens, their shoulders broaden and sperm * are produced.

*You can find out more about these on page 27.

Your skin

Your skin is not just a bag to hold your body together. It is an important living organ with several different functions. It protects you from the changing conditions outside your body and from infection. It plays a large part in controlling your body temperature and, by responding to touch, it enables you to sense what is going on around you.* Your skin even plays a part in nutrition because, when it is exposed to sunlight, it makes vitamin D.

Over most of your body your skin is about 2mm thick, though over your eyelids it is only about 0.5mm thick and on the soles of your feet, where it gets a lot of wear, it is about 6mm thick. The skin is arranged in two main layers: the outer epidermis and the inner dermis. This picture shows your skin magnified many times.

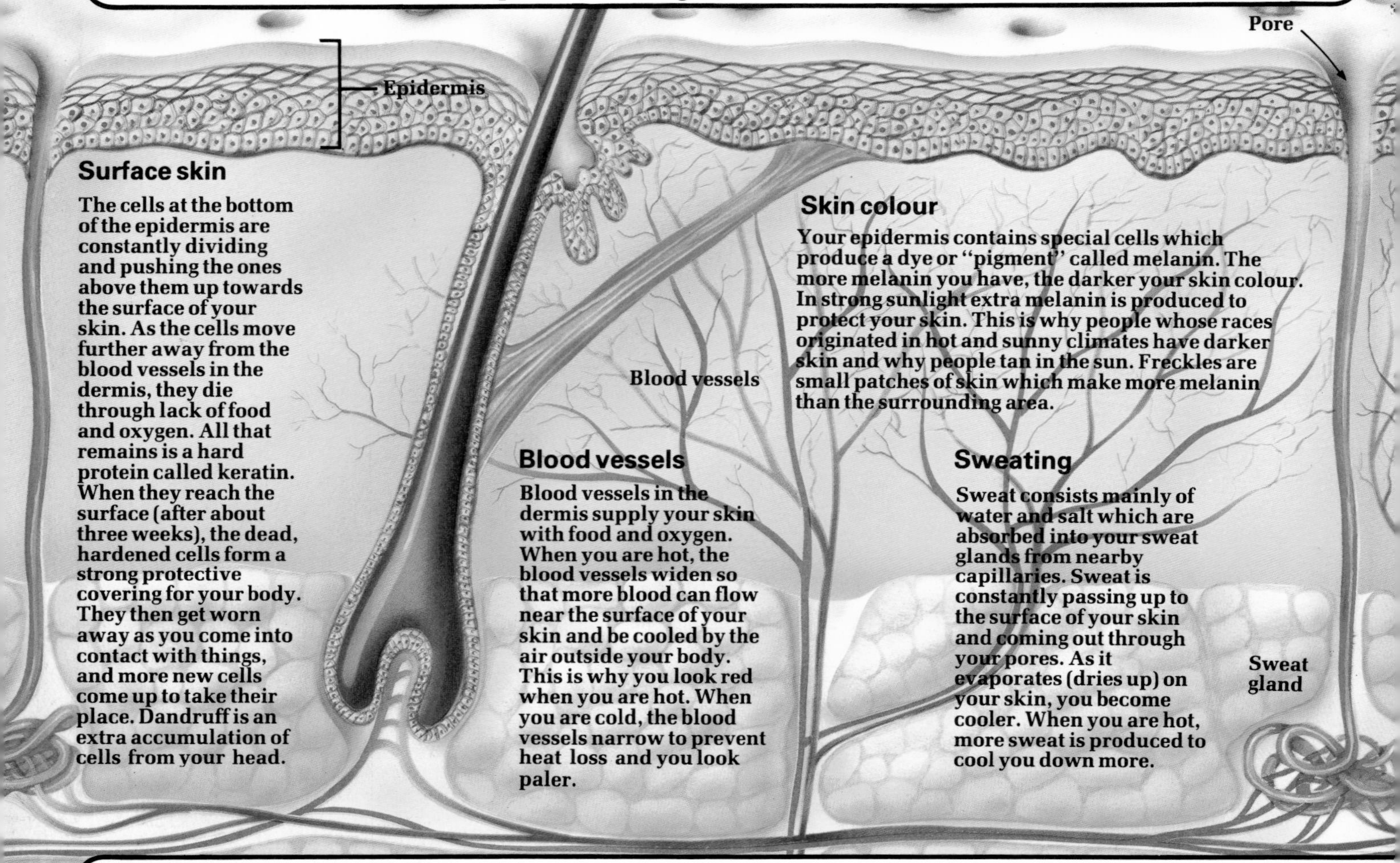

Pore

Epidermis

Surface skin

The cells at the bottom of the epidermis are constantly dividing and pushing the ones above them up towards the surface of your skin. As the cells move further away from the blood vessels in the dermis, they die through lack of food and oxygen. All that remains is a hard protein called keratin. When they reach the surface (after about three weeks), the dead, hardened cells form a strong protective covering for your body. They then get worn away as you come into contact with things, and more new cells come up to take their place. Dandruff is an extra accumulation of cells from your head.

Skin colour

Your epidermis contains special cells which produce a dye or "pigment" called melanin. The more melanin you have, the darker your skin colour. In strong sunlight extra melanin is produced to protect your skin. This is why people whose races originated in hot and sunny climates have darker skin and why people tan in the sun. Freckles are small patches of skin which make more melanin than the surrounding area.

Blood vessels

Blood vessels

Blood vessels in the dermis supply your skin with food and oxygen. When you are hot, the blood vessels widen so that more blood can flow near the surface of your skin and be cooled by the air outside your body. This is why you look red when you are hot. When you are cold, the blood vessels narrow to prevent heat loss and you look paler.

Sweating

Sweat consists mainly of water and salt which are absorbed into your sweat glands from nearby capillaries. Sweat is constantly passing up to the surface of your skin and coming out through your pores. As it evaporates (dries up) on your skin, you become cooler. When you are hot, more sweat is produced to cool you down more.

Sweat gland

Temperature control

Your body is gaining and losing warmth all the time. For instance, you absorb heat from the sun and from hot food and drink. Many of the chemical reactions in your cells, particularly in your liver and muscles, produce heat. You lose heat from any exposed areas of your skin when your body is warmer than your surroundings. Sweating is another way in which you are losing heat continually. Breathing cold air and eating cold food also use up body heat.

These gains and losses have to be balanced so that your body temperature stays stable at approximately 36.5-37°C. When you start to get too hot or too cold, your brain instigates certain changes to stabilize the temperature. These are widening or narrowing of the blood vessels in your skin, more or less sweating, goose pimples and shivering. Shivering works by increasing the activity in your muscles, which helps to produce heat.

Fever

No one really knows why you get a high temperature with certain illnesses. It is as though the brain's "thermostat" is temporarily reset at a higher level than normal. A high temperature is not an illness in itself, only a symptom of illness. The treatment depends on the cause.

* *To find out more about this see page 20.*

Hair

Your hair grows out of pits, known as follicles, in the epidermis. Cells at the root of the hair divide and push it upwards. As it grows further away from the blood supply, it dies and becomes hardened by keratin. Having your hair cut is painless because the hair is dead. About every two years, the cells in the follicle stop dividing and the hair falls out. You are losing hair from your head at the rate of about 50 a day. After a few months rest, the cells start to divide again and a new hair grows. When this does not happen, people eventually go bald. The colour of your hair depends on the amount of melanin in the cells. The shape of the follicles determines whether it is straight, wavy or curly.

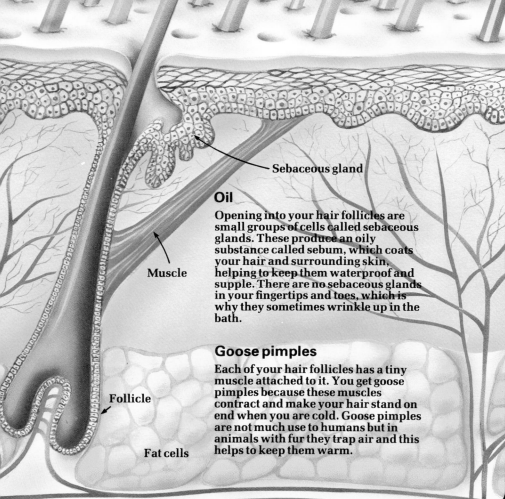

Sebaceous gland

Muscle

Follicle

Fat cells

Oil

Opening into your hair follicles are small groups of cells called sebaceous glands. These produce an oily substance called sebum, which coats your hair and surrounding skin, helping to keep them waterproof and supple. There are no sebaceous glands in your fingertips and toes, which is why they sometimes wrinkle up in the bath.

Goose pimples

Each of your hair follicles has a tiny muscle attached to it. You get goose pimples because these muscles contract and make your hair stand on end when you are cold. Goose pimples are not much use to humans but in animals with fur they trap air and this helps to keep them warm.

Cuts and bruises

When you cut yourself, the platelets and other substances in your blood help it to clot and form a scab. The scab helps to protect the damaged area until new skin grows over it. The new skin grows about 0.5mm a day. When the wound is healed, the scab falls off. A bruise is caused by blood vessels in your skin bleeding into the surrounding tissues.

Spots

Doctors think that spots, or acne, may be caused by changes in hormone levels, especially at puberty. Extra keratin is produced at the openings of the hair follicles and extra sebum in the sebaceous glands, which are most numerous on your face and back. The keratin and sebum accumulate at the openings and form blackheads, or they build up below the surface of your skin causing lumps and pimples. Acne can be improved by special creams from the doctor. Regular washing may help to remove the excess keratin and sebum and sunlight usually helps too. Greasy make-up makes spots worse. Some people find that cutting out foods such as chocolate helps, though there is no scientific evidence for this.

Nails

Nails are the remnants of claws and are formed in a similar way to hair. Each one develops from a row of dividing cells called a root. Your nails grow about 0.1mm a day and the part you can see is made of dead cells hardened by keratin.

Fingerprints

You have hair over almost the whole of your body. The palms of your hands and the soles of your feet are without hair but are covered with tiny ridges instead. This makes them extra sensitive. The patterns made by the ridges on your fingers are your fingerprints. They are formed months before you are born and no two people's are identical.

Information from outside

The information you receive about the outside world comes to you through special nerve cells called receptors. These respond to changes in your surroundings. When they are stimulated by light or sound, for example, they produce tiny pulses of electricity which travel along nerves to your brain. Your brain interprets the impulses and you become aware of what is happening. Many of the receptors are grouped together in sense organs such as your eyes or ears. On the next few pages you can find out how some of these sense organs work.

How you see

The picture on the right shows the inside of an eye viewed from the side, so you can see how it works.

Everything you look at is constantly reflecting rays of light. The rays enter your eyes and fall on the lining at the back of your eye, which is called the retina. Your retina contains receptor cells which are stimulated by the light. They send impulses to your brain, which interprets them so that you see.

1 Every time you blink and your eyelids cover your eyes, tears wash over the surface. The tears keep your eyes moist and help to keep them clean. You blink about 15 times a minute.

2 Your eyelashes help to keep specks of dust and dirt out of your eyes.

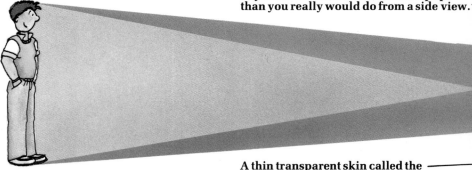

3 The image of the object you are looking at has to be in focus on your retina for you to see it clearly. For this to happen the rays of light have to be bent, or "refracted", when they enter your eye. Light from a near object has to be bent more than light from a distant object. A transparent disc, called the lens, plays an important part in focusing. Its shape is altered by the tiny muscles surrounding it depending on whether you are looking at something near or far away. This makes the light bend the right amount.

4 The image on the retina is upside down because the rays of light cross each other behind the lens.

The black dot in the centre of your eyes is called the pupil. It is really a hole through which the light enters.

The coloured part of your eyes surrounding the pupil is called the iris. It is muscular and alters the size of your pupils. This picture is slightly distorted so you can see more of the iris and pupil than you really would do from a side view.

A thin transparent skin called the conjunctiva covers the front of your eye and helps to protect it.

The proper name for the "whites" of your eyes is the sclera. This is the tough protective outer layer. Round the front of your eye it is called the cornea. The cornea is transparent where it passes behind the conjunctiva.

The centre of your eye, and the part between the cornea and the lens, are filled with clear fluids called humours. These maintain the spherical shape of your eye and play a part in focusing.

Your eyes are set in sockets of bone which help to protect them.

Glasses and contact lenses

These are extra lenses made of glass or plastic which can correct many cases of bad eyesight by helping to focus the image on to the retina.

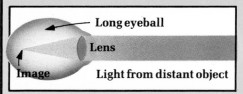

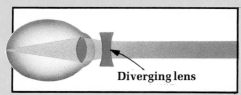

Short-sighted people cannot see distant objects clearly. This is usually because they have long eyeballs and the image of distant objects falls in front of the retina. Short-sightedness can be corrected by wearing lenses which make the rays of light diverge (bend outwards) before they enter the eyes.

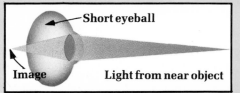

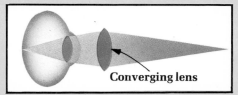

Long-sighted people cannot see near objects clearly. This is usually because they have short eyeballs and the image of near objects falls behind the retina. Long-sightedness can be corrected by wearing lenses which make the rays of light converge (bend inwards) before they enter the eyes.

How rods and cones work

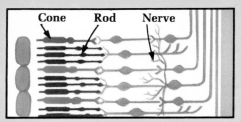

When light falls on the rods and cones in your retina it is absorbed by chemicals contained in them. This changes the structure of the chemicals and triggers off electrical impulses which travel along nerves to your brain. The light-sensitive chemical in rods is known as visual purple or rhodopsin. Vitamin A is used to form it. There are three different types of cone. Each type contains a chemical sensitive to red, blue or green light. All the other colours you see are made up of different combinations and proportions of these three.

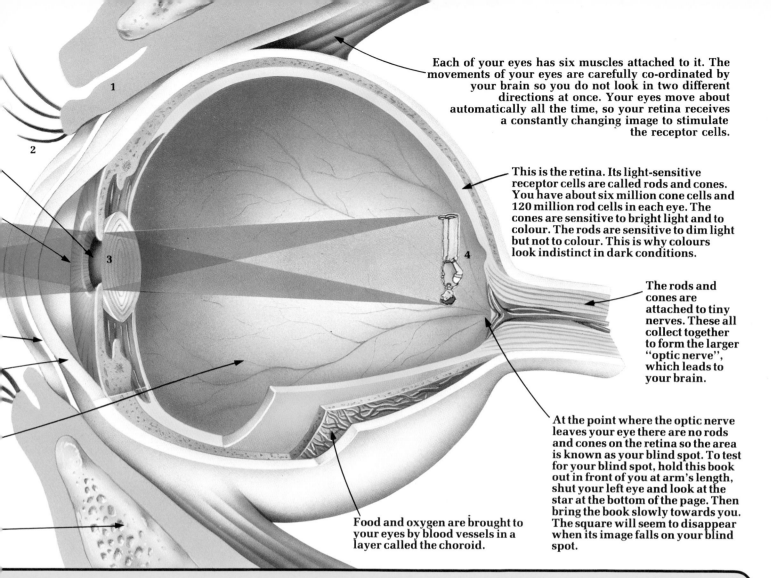

Each of your eyes has six muscles attached to it. The movements of your eyes are carefully co-ordinated by your brain so you do not look in two different directions at once. Your eyes move about automatically all the time, so your retina receives a constantly changing image to stimulate the receptor cells.

This is the retina. Its light-sensitive receptor cells are called rods and cones. You have about six million cone cells and 120 million rod cells in each eye. The cones are sensitive to bright light and to colour. The rods are sensitive to dim light but not to colour. This is why colours look indistinct in dark conditions.

The rods and cones are attached to tiny nerves. These all collect together to form the larger "optic nerve", which leads to your brain.

At the point where the optic nerve leaves your eye there are no rods and cones on the retina so the area is known as your blind spot. To test for your blind spot, hold this book out in front of you at arm's length, shut your left eye and look at the star at the bottom of the page. Then bring the book slowly towards you. The square will seem to disappear when its image falls on your blind spot.

Food and oxygen are brought to your eyes by blood vessels in a layer called the choroid.

Tears

Tears are being produced all the time by your "lacrimal" glands. They drain away into the back of your nose through your tear ducts. When you get something in your eye which irritates it, such as a speck of dust or onion juice, extra tears are produced to wash it away and the ducts overflow. No one knows why human beings cry when they are upset.

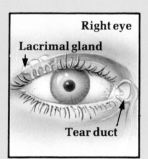

Right eye
Lacrimal gland
Tear duct

Why do you have two eyes?

Having two eyes increases your angle of vision and helps you to judge depth. Try shutting one eye and notice the difference. Although each of your eyes views the same object from a slightly different angle, your brain is able to combine the two separate images on your retinas into one single picture.

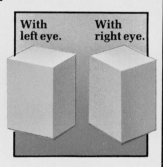

With left eye.   With right eye.

Pupil size

The size of your pupils varies automatically depending on how much light there is. When it is dark, the pupils expand to let in as much light as possible. In bright light they shrink to prevent damage to the retina. Try standing in front of a mirror and shining a torch in your eyes and you will see your pupils shrink.

Colour blindness

Colour blindness affects about eight males in every hundred but less than one female in every two hundred. It is probably caused by faulty cone cells and is usually inherited. Most men who are colour blind find it difficult to distinguish between red and green. Complete colour blindness is very rare.

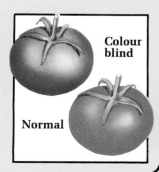

Colour blind

Normal

Hearing

Sound is really vibrations in the air. These stimulate receptor cells inside your ears to send impulses to your brain. Your brain interprets the impulses as sounds. What you can see of your ears is only one part: the outer ear. This leads to your middle and inner ears, which are safely protected within the bones of your skull.

1 The outer ear is more important in many animals than in humans. They can move their ears to "look for" the sounds. Although humans still have the muscles to do this, few people can make them work. Can you?

2 Your outer ear funnels the sounds down this tube, which is called the auditory canal. The canal is lined with hairs and produces wax. Occasionally this builds up and prevents people hearing properly but it can be syringed out safely and painlessly by the doctor.

3 Your outer ear is separated from your middle ear by a tightly stretched membrane called the ear drum. This vibrates when the sounds hit it.
It is not a good idea to poke anything into your ear. Even cotton buds or a handkerchief can damage your ear drum.

4 Your middle ear is filled with air and contains three tiny bones or "ossicles". These are called (from left to right as you look at this picture) the malleus (hammer), incus (anvil) and stapes (stirrup). The stirrup is the smallest bone in your body and is only about 3mm long. Any vibrations of your ear drum pass right along this chain of bones.

8 The impulses travel to your brain along this nerve, called the auditory nerve.

Eustachian tube

5 Your middle ear is separated from your inner ear by another tightly stretched membrane similar to the ear drum. This is called the oval window and vibrates when the stirrup vibrates.

6 Vibrations of the oval window are transmitted to a fluid in the outer channel of this coiled tube. The fluid is called perilymph and the tube is called the cochlea, which means snail. (This is a very simplified picture of the inside of the cochlea.)

7 The vibrations in the perilymph in turn set up vibrations in a second fluid, called endolymph, which fills the inner channel of the cochlea.
The inner channel contains the receptor cells, which have fine hairs attached. Movements in the endolymph pull on the hairs and trigger off electrical impulses in the cells. Some of the hair cells respond only to fast vibrations, which are produced by high-pitched sounds. Others respond only to slower vibrations, which are produced by low-pitched sounds. The louder the sound, the bigger the vibrations and the stronger the impulses produced.

Eustachian tube

The only way air can get into or out of your middle ear is through this tube, which leads to the back of your nose. When you swallow, chew or yawn the entrance to the tube opens and air can pass in or out. This allows the air pressure on both sides of your ear drum to remain equal. The pressure outside your ear sometimes changes suddenly, for example when you are in a lift or aeroplane. The popping sensation you sometimes get then is the pressure equalizing in your middle ear. Swallowing helps to equalize it quicker.

Balance

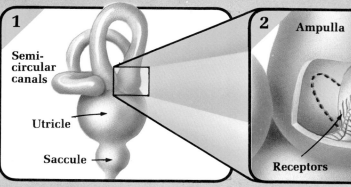

1 Semi-circular canals
Utricle
Saccule

2 Ampulla
Cupula
Receptors

These three semi-circular canals (see opposite page for their position in your ear) and the tiny sacs beneath them, called the utricle and saccule, are filled with endolymph and help you to balance. The sacs tell you what position your head is in and the canals tell you what direction it is moving in.

At the base of each canal is a swollen area called the ampulla. This contains receptor hair cells attached to a jelly-like particle called the cupula. As you move your head, the endolymph in the canals swirls about and pushes the cupula sideways. This pulls on the hairs and triggers off impulses to your brain.

Why do you have two ears?

Having two ears helps you to tell what direction sounds are coming from. This is because the sound hits one ear a fraction of a second before the other and produces stronger vibrations.

Loud noises

The chart below shows you the approximate loudness of certain sounds. Loudness is measured in decibels (dB). Repeated exposure to loud noise, say through headphones or at discotheques, can damage the receptors in your ears and make you deaf. This type of deafness cannot be helped by wearing a hearing aid.

Feeling dizzy

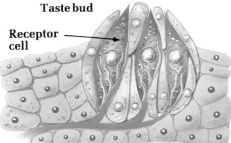

If you spin round and round and then stop, the fluid in your semi-circular canals continues to swirl for a while as though you were still moving. This confuses your brain

because your eyes and muscles are telling it that you have stopped. The result is that you feel dizzy. Travel sickness is also caused by the balance mechanism in your ears.

130dB	Jet aircraft	
110dB	Discotheque	
100dB	Pneumatic drill	
80dB	Heavy traffic	
60dB	Normal conversation	
20 dB	Whisper	

Taste

Taste bud
Receptor cell

Your taste "buds" consist of groups of receptor cells in your tongue which are sensitive to chemicals dissolved in your saliva.

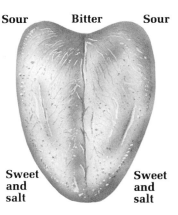

Sour   Bitter   Sour
Sweet and salt   Sweet and salt

Most of the buds are at the sides and back of your tongue. The buds in different areas respond to different tastes. You can only distinguish four basic tastes with your tongue: sweet, sour, salt and bitter. You use your sense of smell to detect more subtle flavours. That is why a lot of food seems to taste the same when you have a cold and your nose is blocked.

Smell

Receptor cells high up at the back of your nose are sensitive to chemicals dissolved in the mucus in your nose. You can smell more when you sniff because this draws air higher up so that more of the chemicals reach the receptors. Human beings can distinguish about 3,000 different smells.

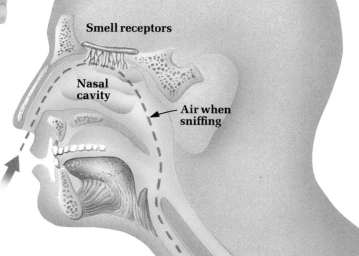

Smell receptors
Nasal cavity
Air when sniffing

Touch

In addition to doing its other jobs, your skin is an important sense organ with many thousands of receptor cells. In general, each receptor responds to only one type of sensation, such as heat, cold, light touch, pressure, pain or itch. This does not mean that all the cells responding to one type of sensation look the same. Here is a selection of receptor cells.

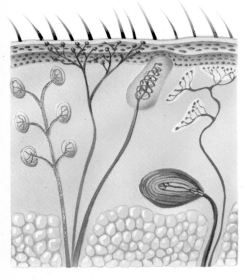

In the skin of some areas, such as your lips, fingers and the soles of your feet, you have many more receptors than elsewhere. Here you can see how the male human body might look if it was proportioned according to the sensitivity of its different parts. You can see why it is that even a tiny stone in your shoe often feels enormous and why it is sometimes difficult to find the exact spot of an itch in an area like your back.

The communications network

The information received by your senses has to be sent to your brain so your brain can sort it out and give your body instructions how to respond. The instructions as well as the information are transmitted in the form of electrical impulses along your nerves. Your nerves, together with your brain and spinal cord, make up your nervous system. Your spinal cord is a continuation of your brain which runs down your spine (backbone).

The nervous system

This is a simplified picture of the nervous system showing how nerves reach to all parts of your body. Each nerve (shown here in orange) consists of a bundle of nerve fibres. Each fibre is part of a nerve cell, or "neurone". Most of the cell bodies are in your brain or spinal cord, which are known as your central nervous system. Some of the fibres are very long, for example those stretching from your spinal cord to your feet.

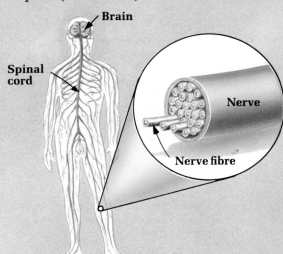

Brain

Spinal cord

Nerve

Nerve fibre

How nerves work

You have about 100 billion neurones in your body. There are three main types. Sensory neurones, which is a term sometimes used for receptor cells, carry impulses from your sense organs to your central nervous system. Motor neurones carry impulses back from your central nervous system to your muscles and glands. Connector neurones within the central nervous system pass the impulses from one cell to the next. The simplest types of responses you make to information provided by your senses are automatic ones, called reflex actions. Pulling your hand away from a prickly thistle is a reflex action. Below you can see how it comes about.

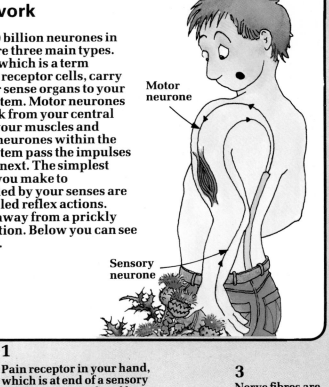

Motor neurone

Sensory neurone

1
Pain receptor in your hand, which is at end of a sensory neurone, is stimulated by thistle.

2
Electrical impulses travel along nerve fibre.

3
Nerve fibres are insulated by a sheath made of a fatty substance called myelin.

What is an impulse?

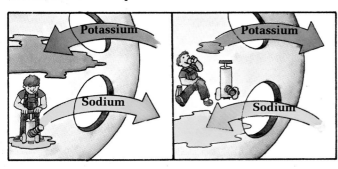

The electrical impulses in your body are caused by changes in the balance of the minerals sodium and potassium in your cells. Normally you have a lot of potassium inside your cells but not much sodium. This is because your cell membrane is constantly pumping sodium out into the surrounding tissue fluid. Outside the cells there is a lot of sodium and not much potassium. An impulse is produced by a momentary change in the cell membrane which allows sodium to pass into the cell and potassium to pass out. The impulse travels along your nerves at a speed of 120 metres per second. After it has passed, the normal chemical balance is restored by the sodium pump.

How impulses pass from one cell to another

Impulses cannot jump the tiny gaps between one cell and the next but are passed across chemically. The branches at the end of nerve fibres finish in "terminal buttons". These contain many energy-producing mitochondria, and pockets, called vesicles, which contain a chemical "transmitter". When an impulse reaches the buttons, the transmitter is released. It crosses the gap, which is called a synapse, to the dendrites of the next cell body and when enough has accumulated an impulse starts in this neurone.

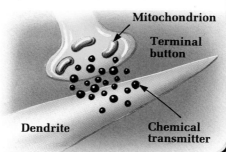

Mitochondrion

Terminal button

Dendrite

Chemical transmitter

Test your reflexes

Doctors use this test to see whether people's reflexes are working properly. Sit with your legs loosely crossed and ask someone to tap sharply just below your kneecap with the side of their hand. When they hit the right spot, your leg will jerk upwards. This is a reflex action.

Funny bone

Close to your funny bone, at your elbow, is a nerve which is less well protected than most. When you bang the bone you can feel an impulse shoot down your arm and make it tingle.

Autonomic nervous system

This is a secondary system of nerves. Although you are usually unaware of it, a series of automatic responses is taking place all the time in this system to control processes such as digestion, breathing and circulation. Many of the cell bodies of the neurones in the autonomic system are outside your brain and spinal cord in small groups called ganglia. The ganglia receive information from receptor cells in the various organs of your body and then send out appropriate instructions to muscles, such as your heart, and glands, such as your salivary glands. The system is self-regulating and helps to keep your body in a balanced state.

10 Branching end of motor neurone is embedded in the muscles of your arm. When impulses reach the muscles, they contract and pull your hand away from the thistle.

9 Impulses pass out of central nervous system along fibre of motor neurone.

8 Impulses pass across branching end of connector neurone to dendrites of the motor cell body.

4 Cell body of sensory neurone is in central nervous system.

6 The body of the next cell, a connector neurone, has these branches called dendrites. They pick up impulses from the sensory neurone.

5 Neurone has a branching end.

7 Connector neurone passes impulses on.

The human computer

The human brain is a bit like a computer. Your senses provide the input, your brain processes all the information, and the instructions sent to your muscles and glands are the output. The nerves throughout your body are like wires. The network of interconnecting neurones in your brain is far more complex and versatile, however, than the circuits of any computer, even though a computer can handle larger quantities of information. No computer can do anything until it has first been programmed by a human brain. The pictures on the right will give you an idea of how some of the different areas in your brain work. Very little is known about many other areas. They are probably to do with thinking, memory and decision-making.

Parts of the brain

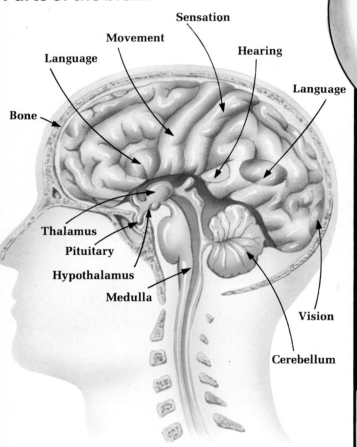

A section of the brain in this picture has been removed so you can see where some of the areas described on the right are positioned. Your brain is protected by the bones of your skull and by a thin layer of fluid which acts as a cushion around it. Your brain has a large number of blood vessels. The brain cells are active all the time, even when you are asleep, so they need a continual supply of food (in the form of glucose) and oxygen. If the cells are without oxygen for more than about four minutes, they are permanently damaged.

Movement

Conscious movements are controlled by the "motor" area. Motor neurones send impulses from here to the muscles in different parts of your body. The more precise the muscle movements, the more of the motor area involved. On the "map" of your body in the area, your hands and mouth take up the most space. The map is upside down because your feet are controlled by cells at the top of your brain and your face by cells lower down.

Language

Special language areas understand and process what you read or hear. They also send impulses to the nearby motor areas of the mouth and larynx in preparation for speech.

Smell

The smelling area interprets impulses from your nose with help from your memory.

Hypothalamus

The hypothalamus has several different jobs. It forms part of your autonomic nervous system and helps to keep conditions in your body constant. It regulates hunger and thirst, and body temperature. It also controls the release of many of the hormones from your pituitary gland (see page 13). Emotions, such as fear, anger and excitement, and also sex drive, are partly determined by the hypothalamus.

Pituitary

Thalamus

You feel pain in a part of your brain called the thalamus. Impulses then travel on to the sensation area so that you can tell where the pain is coming from. Pain helps to protect you by warning you of danger both from outside and inside your body. It often causes an automatic reflex action even before you are aware of the sensation.

Medulla

The medulla regulates essential functions such as heart rate and breathing and continues to work even when you are asleep. It also controls swallowing, coughing, sneezing and vomiting. Like the hypothalamus, the medulla is part of your autonomic nervous system.

Sensation

This area receives impulses from the receptors in your skin. As in the motor area, your whole body is mapped out in the brain cells, so that you can be aware of the exact spot of each sensation. The most sensitive parts of your body (see page 20) have the most space in your brain. The cells which appreciate taste are also in this area.

Hearing

The hearing area receives impulses from the cochlea in your ears. It can tell how loud a sound is from the strength of the impulses and what pitch it is by which cells in the cochlea are sending them. To tell which direction the sound is coming from, it compares the strength and timing of the impulses from each ear (see page 19).

Vision

Impulses from your retina travel to the vision area. Here the cells respond to particular simple patterns such as a straight line or a corner. Your brain then builds the patterns up into more complex images, probably by comparing and combining them with information in your memory stores.

Memory

Memories are stored in your brain in at least two stages, one for recent memories and one for more long-term ones. Nobody really knows how memory works. Initial short-term memory probably comes about because impulses travel round the brain cells repeatedly along certain pathways. For long-term memory and learning, a permanent change must take place in the chemical make-up of the cells or in the pathways.

Cerebellum

The cerebellum helps you to balance and co-ordinate your movements. It receives impulses from parts of the body such as your ears, eyes and muscles, integrates all the information and then adjusts the action of your muscles so your movements are smooth and accurate.

Two halves of the brain

1 The large, folded part of your brain is in two halves, which are known as the left and right cerebral hemispheres. Both hemispheres have corresponding areas for dealing with information from your senses and with movement. The nerves from the two sides of your body cross each other as they enter your brain, so that the left hemisphere is associated with the right side of your body and the right hemisphere with the left side.

2 Each hemisphere also has specialized areas. In right-handed people the left hemisphere controls the use of language and numbers, while the right hemisphere specializes in recognizing objects (including faces) by their shape and probably in appreciating music. In most left-handed people it is the other way round. 91 per cent of people are right-handed.

Sleep

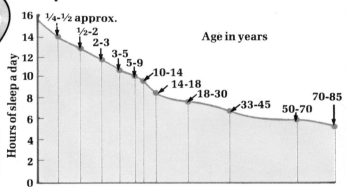

There are two kinds of sleep. One is known as active or rapid-eye-movement (REM) sleep, because your eyes move around even though they are closed. The other is known as quiet or non-REM sleep. Altogether you spend about 20 per cent of each night in active sleep and it is during active sleep that you dream. The activity in your brain can be measured by a machine called an electroencephalogram (EEG), which produces a pattern of waves. The waves produced during active sleep and when you are awake are similar. The reason for sleep and dreams is not really understood. In quiet sleep your muscles relax, and your heart and breathing rates fall, so this may be a period of recovery and repair for your body. Active sleep may be an important part of learning. The diagram above shows how people sleep less as they get older.

How you move

You are able to move because of the way your nervous system, muscles and bones all interact. Your nervous system sends impulses to your muscles, which are attached to your bones. The impulses make the muscles contract (shorten), this pulls on the bones and you move.

What is bone made of?

Only 30 per cent of your bones consists of living tissue. The rest is non-living tissue, mainly minerals. This is what makes the bones hard.

The inner part of the bone is arranged in a meshwork, which makes it both strong and light. It is sometimes called spongy bone.

Bone has a thin, tough outer layer called the periosteum. If you break a bone, cells in the periosteum multiply and grow over the break, joining the two parts of the bone together again.

Skeleton and muscles

On the right you can see the bones of the right side of your body and the muscles of the left side. Many of your muscles are arranged in layers over your skeleton. You have over 200 bones. As well as allowing you to move, they give your body a strong framework and help to protect your internal organs. For example, your rib cage protects your heart and lungs. You have over 600 muscles. Like your bones, they all have names. The buttock muscle, which is the largest, is called the gluteus maximus.

Many of your large bones contain a soft tissue called red marrow. Your red blood cells (5 billion a day) and your white blood cells are made in the marrow. Some bones also have yellow marrow, which contains fat cells.

This is a strong layer of compact bone. The living bone cells are arranged in rings around central canals containing blood vessels and nerves. Calcium and phosphorus are deposited by your blood among the cells. As well as making the bones hard, these minerals are needed for many of the chemical reactions in your body. Your bones act as a storage depot for them. Also among the cells are fibres of a protein called collagen. These help to make the bones resilient.

Cranium (skull)
Clavicle (collar-bone)
Scapula (shoulder-blade)
Sternum (breastbone)
Rib cage
Humerus
Radius
Ulna
Vertebrae (backbone)
Pelvis (hip-bone)
Femur
Coccyx (remnants of a tail)
Patella (kneecap)
Tibia
Fibula

1 Joints

The place where two bones meet is called a joint. Some joints, those of the bones in your skull for example, are fixed but most are moveable. There are several different types of moveable joint. Here are just three of them.

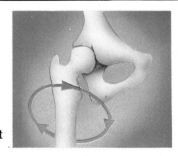

Ball and socket joints, at your hips and shoulders, move in all directions.

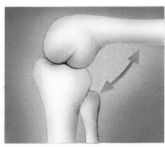

Hinge joints, at your knees and elbows, move in two directions only, like a door opening and shutting.

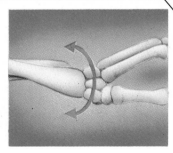

Pivot joints, at your wrists, twist so that you can turn your hands over.

How muscles work

The type of muscle that covers your skeleton is known as striped muscle because that is how it looks under a microscope. The type in organs such as your bladder, and in your digestive tract and blood vessels, is known as smooth muscle. Smooth muscle is controlled by your autonomic nervous system. Below you can see how striped muscle works.

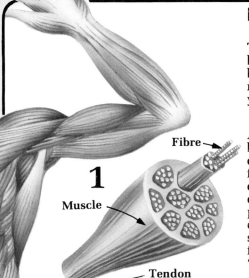

1 A muscle consists of bundles of long thin cells, often referred to as muscle fibres. The muscle and each of the bundles are enclosed in sheaths of the protein collagen. At each end of the muscle the sheaths join together to form a strong, flexible "tendon".

Fibre

Muscle

Tendon

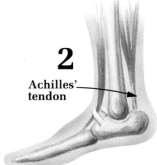

2 Tendons join your muscles to your bones. You can see and feel the largest tendon in your body (the Achilles' tendon) just above your heel. You can also see tendons on the inside of your wrist when you clench your fist and at the inside of your elbow when you bend your arm.

Achilles' tendon

3 Each muscle fibre has a motor nerve ending embedded in it and each fibre contains interlocking strands of two different proteins: actin and myosin. When an impulse reaches a fibre, a chemical transmitter is released. This releases energy in the cells' mitochondria and makes the strands of actin and myosin move closer together, so that the muscle becomes shorter (contracted) and fatter.

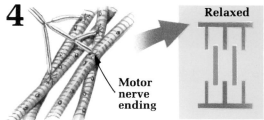

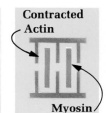

4

Motor nerve ending

Relaxed

Contracted

Actin

Myosin

5 The contracting muscle pulls on the bone to which it is attached and makes it move. The force of the movement depends on how many of the fibres contract at once. If you point your toe as hard as you can, your calf muscle will bulge out. This is because all its fibres are contracted. If you point your toe only slightly it will bulge less because fewer fibres are involved.

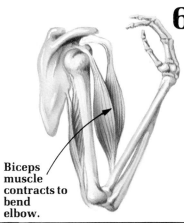

Biceps muscle contracts to bend elbow.

6 Most of your muscles are arranged in opposing pairs. For instance, as your biceps muscle contracts to bend your elbow, your "triceps" relaxes to allow the movement. When you want to straighten your arm again, the triceps contracts and the biceps relaxes. Special stretch receptors in your muscles let your brain know what your body is doing without your having to look at it.

Triceps contracts.

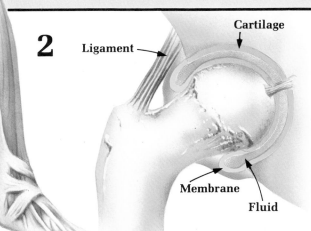

2

Ligament

Cartilage

Membrane

Fluid

The ends of the bones at a moveable joint are cushioned by pads of a smooth, rubbery protein called cartilage. (Your ear lobes and the squashy bit at the end of your nose are also made of a type of cartilage.) The joint is surrounded by a thin, slippery membrane. This produces a fluid which lubricates the joint. Without cartilage and fluid, your bones would grind against each other when you moved. The bones are held together by strong, flexible collagen fibres called ligaments. If a ligament is forced beyond its limit, it may tear. This is a sprain. If the bones slip out of place they are said to be dislocated. Someone who is described as being double-jointed does not really have two lots of joints, they just have extra-long ligaments.

Why exercise?

Exercise is an important part of keeping healthy. Without it muscles waste and are replaced by fat, joints stiffen up, and breathing and circulation become less efficient. There is an increased risk of becoming overweight and of developing certain illnesses, especially heart disease. Exercise alone is not enough to get the body really fit. It has to be combined with other aspects of a healthy lifestyle, such as eating a balanced diet and not overeating, smoking or drinking much alcohol.

How to get fit

Stamina, suppleness and strength are all different aspects of fitness. As you can see from the chart below, different sports vary as to which of these they develop. For example, yoga is excellent for suppleness and weightlifting for strength. The best all-round exercise is swimming. To get the benefit of any type of exercise you have to do it regularly. Be careful to build up the amount you do gradually as you get fitter. There is no point in getting completely exhausted, or in doing a sport you don't like. An important benefit of enjoyable exercise is that it helps you to relax and overcome stress, which can cause illness.

A = Stamina. B = Suppleness. C = Strength.

	A	B	C
Badminton	✳	✳	✳
Cycling	✳✳	✳	✳✳
Dancing (energetic)	✳✳	✳✳	✳
Football	✳	✳✳	✳✳
Gymnastics	✳	✳✳✳	✳✳
Ice skating	✳	✳✳	✳
Hill walking	✳✳	✳	✳
Horse riding	○	○	✳
Jogging	✳✳✳	✳	✳

	A	B	C
Judo	✳	✳✳✳	✳✳
Roller skating	✳✳	○	✳
Skipping	✳✳	○	✳
Squash	✳✳	✳✳	✳
Swimming	✳✳✳	✳✳✳	✳✳✳
Tennis	✳	✳✳	✳
Walking	✳	○	○
Weightlifting	○	○	✳✳✳
Yoga	○	✳✳✳	○

○ – no effect. ✳ – beneficial effect. ✳✳ – very good. ✳✳✳ – excellent.

Stamina

Stamina, or endurance, is the ability to keep doing something for a period of time without it becoming a strain. Even walking up a flight of stairs can be a strain for an unfit person and make their heart beat a lot faster than usual. In very simple terms, the fitter you are, the more exercise you can do without your heart rate rising substantially and the better you feel in general.

Muscle tone

Even when you are still, your muscles are not completely relaxed. Some of the fibres have to be contracted just to keep you sitting up. This slight state of tension is known as muscle tone. When people talk about "toning up", they mean firming and strengthening their muscles by exercise.

What is aerobics?

Aerobics means "with air". Aerobic exercise increases your ability to get oxygen round your body. To be aerobic, a sport has to be strenuous but not exhausting and you have to keep it up steadily and continuously (for at least 12 minutes at a time). Sports such as swimming, jogging and cycling can all be aerobic. Ones like sprinting and squash are not because they require short bursts of energy. These sports are anaerobic.

During aerobic exercise, your body makes a steady demand for more oxygen and you breathe deeply and more fully. Your heart works harder and over a period of time this strengthens it and makes it more efficient. Your circulation improves, with your blood vessels becoming more elastic and new channels opening up. All this increases your stamina and helps to reduce your risk of developing heart disease.

Getting tired

During aerobic exercise your muscles get a lot of their energy from the glucose in your bloodstream. During intense exertion your heart and lungs cannot get glucose and oxygen round your body fast enough so your muscles convert their own glycogen stores without oxygen (anaerobically). At the same time a substance called lactic acid is produced. As this builds up, your muscles start to tire and ache. This is one reason you cannot keep the exercise up for long.

Sex and babies

A baby develops when a female's ovum (egg cell) and a male's sperm cell meet and join together in a woman's body after a man and woman have had sex (sexual intercourse). The moment when the ovum and sperm join is called fertilization or conception. Together the two cells make one new cell. This grows and develops into a baby in the woman's womb. Both the male and female reproductive systems start working fully at puberty (see page 13).

1

1 Most of the female sex organs are in the lower part of the abdomen, between the bladder and the rectum.

2 The ovum is drawn into this tube, called an oviduct or Fallopian tube, by the fringed end. This is where fertilization usually takes place.

3 The egg passes into the womb (uterus). This is a hollow organ with thick muscular walls and many blood vessels. Its lining changes in response to changes in the levels of female hormones. Every month, from puberty to the menopause, it thickens in preparation for a fertilized ovum to embed itself in it. If the ovum is not fertilized, the lining disintegrates and the woman has a period (menstruates). The lining passes out of the vagina along with blood.

1 The ova are stored in the ovaries from birth. Every month, from puberty to the age of about 45, an ovum matures in one of the ovaries and is released. This is called ovulation. The time when ovulation stops is called the menopause.

4 The vagina is a stretchy tube leading from the uterus to the outside of the body. Glands in the lining produce a lubricating mucus.

5 Outside the female's body is the vulva. This consists of two folds of skin called labia (lips) which cover (from back to front) the opening of the vagina, the opening of the urethra (the tube from the bladder) and a sensitive mound of tissue called the clitoris.

2

Most of the male's reproductive organs are outside the abdomen. Inside it would be too warm for sperm production to be very efficient.

2 Two tubes, called sperm ducts, carry the sperm to the penis. The ducts open into the urethra. The sphincter muscle at the opening of the bladder prevents urine from passing down the urethra at the same time as sperm.

3 Two glands (the prostate and Cowper's) produce fluids which the sperm swim in. Semen is the mixture of sperm and the fluids.

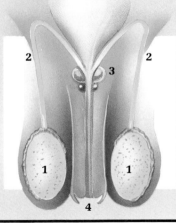

1 From puberty, sperm are produced in tiny tubes inside the testes. The sperm are stored in a coiled tube called the epididymis, which lies over the back of the testes.

4 The penis contains soft, spongy tissue and many blood vessels. The most sensitive part, at the tip, is called the glans. It is partly covered by a loose fold of skin called the foreskin.

3

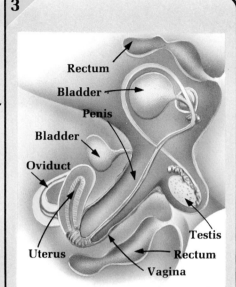

Rectum
Bladder
Penis
Bladder
Oviduct
Uterus
Testis
Rectum
Vagina

During sexual excitement the penis gets larger and stiff (erect) because it becomes congested with blood. The glands in the vagina increase their production of lubricating mucus. During intercourse, the penis fits inside the vagina. At the climax of intercourse (orgasm), muscles around the male's urethra contract, squirting (ejaculating) semen into the female's vagina and muscles in the female's vagina and uterus contract rhythmically. The sperm swim up through the uterus and into the oviducts. One ejaculation contains about 300 million sperm but only about 100 get as far as the oviducts before they die. If there is an ovum in one of the oviducts, fertilization may take place.

Contraception

There are several ways of preventing an ovum and a sperm joining and causing pregnancy. Some are more effective than others. After each method of contraception described below there is a percentage figure. This shows how many women in a hundred get pregnant using that method for a year. Without contraception, 80 per cent get pregnant.

THE PILL. These contain hormones, usually oestrogen and progesterone. They prevent ovulation and are prescribed by a doctor. (Almost 0%)

IUCD (Intrauterine contraceptive device). This is a small piece of plastic or metal which is inserted in the uterus by a doctor. It works partly by preventing an ovum from settling in the uterus. (2%)

CAP OR DIAPHRAGM. This is a thin, cap-shaped piece of rubber which the woman puts in her vagina, over the entrance to the uterus, before intercourse. To be safe, it has to be used with a spermicide (a cream which makes sperm inactive). (3% when used carefully)

CONDOM OR SHEATH (Johnny or rubber in slang). This is a thin rubber sheath which is put on to the erect penis to catch the semen. For extra safety the woman uses a spermicide. (3% when used carefully)

1

A baby starts to develop as soon as the ovum and sperm have joined together to form one new cell. First the cell divides to form two identical cells. These two cells then divide to make four, the four divide to make eight, and so on, until a solid ball of dividing cells is formed.

One sperm enters ovum (fertilization).

Ovum

Cell divides.

Ball of cells.

2

The ball embeds itself in the thickened lining of the uterus. As the cells continue to divide, they gradually become different from one another and start to develop into different tissues and organs. At this stage the future baby is called an embryo. After a month, when it is only about 5mm long, its developing heart is already beating. The embryo is contained in a protective bag of fluid called the amniotic sac.

3

After two months, all the main parts of the body are formed, though not yet fully developed. The embryo is about 3cm long and weighs about 1g.

While a baby is in the uterus, it gets its food and oxygen from a special organ called the placenta. This develops partly from the mother's tissues, partly from the embryo's, and contains blood vessels from each of them. The food and oxygen pass from the mother's blood vessels into the baby's across a thin separating membrane. They get into the baby's body through a vein in its "umbilical cord". Waste products from the baby's body pass out through two arteries in the cord and into the mother's blood. When a baby is born it is still attached to the placenta by the cord. Your navel (tummy button) is the remains of your umbilical cord.

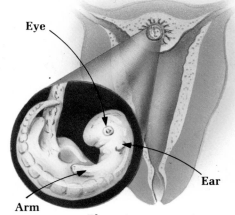

Eye

Arm

Ear

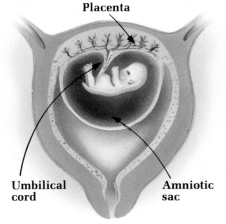

Placenta

Umbilical cord

Amniotic sac

Taking after your parents

A baby develops in the way it does because of two sets of "instructions", one in the ovum and one in the sperm. These instructions are in the chromosomes of the cells (see page 3). The ovum and sperm have 23 chromosomes each, making a total of 46 when they join together at fertilization. An exact copy of these 46 chromosomes is passed to every cell in the baby's body and stays with it for life. Because it has one set of instructions from each parent, it takes after both of them.

Chromosomes are made of a chemical called DNA (deoxyribonucleic acid). This looks rather like a twisted ladder. The rungs of the ladder consist of two pairs of small chemicals called adenine and thiamine, and guanine and cytosine. The order of the rungs varies and forms a code. A sequence of about 250 rungs gives the instruction for one particular characteristic, such as an enzyme, a hormone or a blood group. Each of these coded instructions is called a gene. There are hundreds of genes on each chromosome.

Which sex?

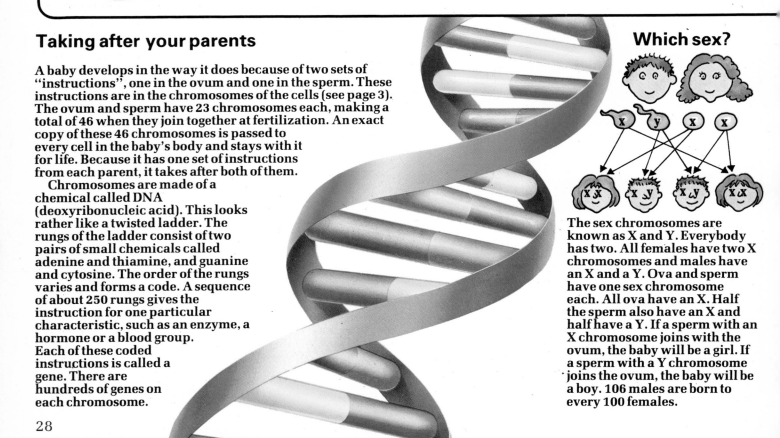

The sex chromosomes are known as X and Y. Everybody has two. All females have two X chromosomes and males have an X and a Y. Ova and sperm have one sex chromosome each. All ova have an X. Half the sperm also have an X and half have a Y. If a sperm with an X chromosome joins with the ovum, the baby will be a girl. If a sperm with a Y chromosome joins the ovum, the baby will be a boy. 106 males are born to every 100 females.

4

The baby continues to develop for another seven months. As it grows, the mother's uterus enlarges from its normal length of about 8cm and volume of about 3cm^3 to a volume of about 6,000 cm^3 (6 litres). The baby starts to move about and kick. It also sleeps, can hear loud noises and even suck its thumb.

5

Sometime during the last few months most babies settle into a head-down position in the uterus.

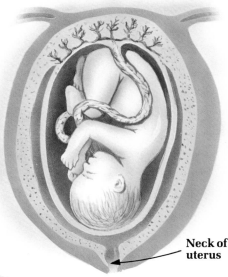

Neck of uterus

6

Most babies are born about 40 weeks after the date of the mother's last period. The process of giving birth is called labour. During the first stage, the muscles of the uterus start to contract, at first quite gently, then more and more strongly and frequently. This forces the baby downwards, so that its head stretches the neck of the uterus. This is the hardest part of labour and usually lasts about 12 hours. The amniotic sac usually bursts during this stage and the fluid flows out of the vagina.

The second stage is when the baby's head eventually starts to pass through the neck of the uterus. The mother helps by "pushing" and the baby passes into the vagina, which expands, and out of the body. This stage usually lasts about half an hour. Most new-born babies are about 50cm long and weigh about 3kg.

Finally, more contractions of the uterus force the placenta (now called afterbirth) out through the vagina.

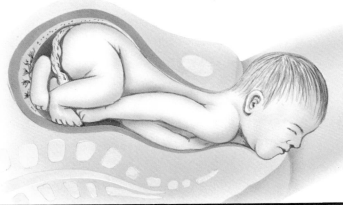

Hair colour

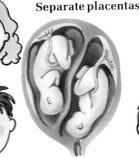

Most of your characteristics, your height and intelligence for example, are determined by many different genes and also by the conditions you grow up in. A few characteristics, such as the colour of your hair, are determined chiefly by one gene from each of your parents. The genes of the parents above could be combined to produce three different hair colours in their children. A dark hair gene is said to be "dominant" because it overrules genes for other hair colours. A fair hair gene is dominant over a red hair gene. To have red hair, you have to inherit a red hair gene from both your parents. Eye colour works in the same way. Brown is dominant over blue.

Twins

One birth in about 80 produces twins. There are two sorts. Non-identical, or "fraternal", twins are produced when two ova happen to be released at the same time and both are joined by separate sperm. These twins have different chromosomes, so they are not necessarily alike and can be of different sexes.

Identical twins are produced when the ball of dividing cells splits into two at a very early stage and each part goes on to develop into a separate baby. These twins are identical and always the same sex because they have identical chromosomes.

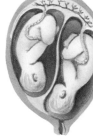

Twins usually have separate placentas.

Separate placentas

Shared placenta

Things that go wrong

There are many reasons for things going wrong in the human body. Here you can find out about some common types of diseases and ways of fighting them. The things you feel when you are ill, such as a headache or a pain in the abdomen, are the "symptoms" of your illness.

Congenital diseases

These are diseases that people are born with. They are often caused by faulty chromosomes. Babies who have Down's syndrome, for example, have 47 chromosomes in their cells instead of 46. This may make them physically or mentally handicapped.

Accidents and injuries

Most accidents happen in the home, on the roads and, to a lesser extent, in industry. The old and the very young are especially prone to accidents, the old to falls, for example, and babies to suffocation.

Cancers

These are the third most common cause of death in countries with a high standard of living, after accidents and heart and circulatory disease. A cancer is a disorder of cell growth. In normal tissues the cells divide and multiply only under carefully regulated conditions. A cancer cell (also called a malignant cell) is one that has undergone a change which frees it from this regulation. It divides and multiplies without control, damaging healthy cells in the process. As well as growing in one place to form a tumour (swelling), malignant cells can spread around the body and start up other tumours. (Not all tumours are cancerous. Some are fairly harmless.)

Cancers usually develop in older people though anyone may be affected. They can start in any part of the body. Some parts most commonly affected are the lungs, breasts, colon, skin and blood (this is called leukaemia).

TREATMENT. New discoveries are being made about cancer all the time and many people with the disease can now be cured. There are three main types of cancer treatment. Some tumours can be removed in an operation, some are damaged by radiation (radiotherapy), and some can be destroyed by very strong drugs (chemotherapy).

Degenerative diseases

These are caused by the body tissues gradually wearing out, or "degenerating", with use and old age. Loss of sight, deafness and arthritis (inflammation of the joints) can all be degenerative diseases.

Heart and circulatory disease

The formation of a blood clot in a blood vessel is called a thrombosis. This is one of the most common causes of a heart attack (see page 11). If the thrombosis is in one of the arteries to the brain, part of the brain is deprived of blood and is damaged. This is a "stroke". The symptoms, paralysis or loss of speech for example, depend on which area is affected.

BLOOD PRESSURE. This is the force with which blood is pumped through the arteries. (It is not the same as pulse, which is the rate at which it is pumped.)

People with persistently high blood pressure have an increased risk of heart attacks or strokes. Low blood pressure sometimes causes fainting when not enough blood reaches the brain. Fainting is a reflex action. When you fall over, gravity brings the blood back to your brain. It can also be caused by blood collecting in your legs when you stand still for too long.

Mental illness

There can be many reasons for mental illness. Stress from the environment is often part of the cause. Examples of mental illnesses are severe depression and anorexia nervosa (when young women stop eating properly because they are obsessed with being thin).

Environmental diseases

These are caused by harmful substances in the surroundings. The lung disease asbestosis, for example, is caused by asbestos dust. One of the dangerous chemicals in exhaust fumes is lead, which may interfere with the development of children's brains. Radiation, from nuclear bomb tests, for example, may cause cancers. It can also damage chromosomes and so harm future generations.

Infectious diseases

Most of these are caused by microbes, or micro-organisms, which are living things so small they can only be seen with a microscope. Not all microbes cause disease. Many are living in or on your body all the time quite harmlessly. Some are even used to make foods such as cheese, yoghurt and bread.

VIRUSES. These are the smallest microbes. They can only grow inside living cells. They invade your cells and use the cells' resources to multiply. This damages the cells and produces the symptoms of disease.

Many illnesses are viral. A serious one is polio; milder ones include colds, influenza (flu), measles, chicken pox, mumps, German measles, cold sores from herpes (type 1) and verrucae (a type of wart on the sole of the foot).

BACTERIA. These are single cell microbes, about 0.001mm long. They reproduce by dividing, sometimes very rapidly. A disease may be caused either by the harmful bacteria themselves damaging your tissues or by poisons (toxins) which they produce.

Bacterial diseases include TB (tuberculosis), typhoid, pneumonia, whooping cough, tonsillitis, tetanus, boils and some kinds of food poisoning.

HOW INFECTIOUS DISEASES SPREAD. Many infectious diseases spread through the air. An infectious person breathes, sneezes or coughs out microbes and another person breathes them in. Colds, flu and measles are spread in this way.

You can also get infections from food or water. Diseases such as typhoid and food poisoning are transmitted like this. Two ways food can be infected are by people and flies.

Many skin diseases, such as boils and warts, are transmitted by touch. Diseases spread in this way are called contagious diseases.

STD (SEXUALLY TRANSMITTED DISEASE). This is a group of contagious diseases which are also known as VD (venereal disease). They are caught by having sexual intercourse with an infected person. The microbes which cause the illnesses die quickly away from the warmth and moisture of the body so you cannot catch them from toilet seats, dirty sheets or towels. Gonorrhoea (known as clap) and herpes (type 2) are well known STDs. Most STDs can usually be cured if they are treated early. No cure has yet been found for AIDS. This is caused by a virus known as HIV which is transmitted in semen and blood. Many large hospitals have special STD clinics which give confidential advice and treatment.

The body's defences

Your body has several natural defences against disease. One of the most important is your white blood cells. Some of these engulf and destroy harmful bacteria, while others produce antibodies which fight various foreign invaders.

Some of the white cells which produce antibodies are formed in your lymph vessels, in lymph glands. When you have an infection more white cells are formed than usual, to help you fight the disease. This sometimes makes the glands swell up and you can feel them in your neck, armpits and groin.

Once your white blood cells have been stimulated to produce an antibody against a particular disease, they can produce it again very quickly if necessary. This is why you rarely get illnesses such as measles more than once. After the first attack, you become "immune".

Immunization

This is a way of making your body immune without it having to suffer the disease. The virus, bacteria or toxins which cause the illness are specially treated so they become harmless. They are then injected into you (or in the case of polio are swallowed). This makes your body produce antibodies against the disease and you are protected from it in the future.

Sometimes antibodies themselves are injected when there is no time for the body to learn to produce its own, during an epidemic for example.

Allergies

Some people develop antibodies to normally harmless substances such as pollen, feathers and food. The antibodies act against the person's own tissues and produce the symptoms of allergy.

Transplants

Many operations can now be performed to transplant tissues or organs (heart, kidneys, cornea) from one person to another. The main problem with transplants is that the white blood cells of the patient regard the foreign tissue as dangerous and produce antibodies to destroy it. Drugs can be used against the white blood cells but this then leaves the patient with very little resistance to infection. To help prevent tissue rejection donors are chosen with tissues as similar as possible to the patient's.

Drugs

Drugs are chemicals you can take to alter the way your body works. Many, such as aspirin, relieve symptoms; others, such as anti-cancer drugs, can cure disease. An important group of drugs is antibiotics, including penicillin. These can kill or stop the growth of many of the bacteria which cause infectious diseases.

EVERYDAY DRUGS. Coffee, tea and cola drinks all contain stimulants (drugs which speed up your body processes). Nicotine, in tobacco, is a drug which acts on the nervous system. (See page 9 for more about smoking.) Alcohol also affects the nervous system, including the brain. People who drink a lot of alcohol can become physically as well as psychologically dependent on it.

All drugs, including these everyday ones, can cross the placenta in pregnant women and harm the developing baby in various ways.

DRUG ABUSE. This is when drugs are taken in ways and doses not intended by doctors. Drugs which act on the nervous system to alter mood are the ones most commonly abused. People who take them frequently may become both psychologically and physically dependent. There is a danger of overdose and of serious long-term side effects. The main types are strong pain killers, such as heroin, morphine and cocaine; sedatives (sleeping drugs) including barbiturates and diazepam (valium); and stimulants including amphetamines and LSD (acid).

Glue sniffing has an effect similar to alcohol. Dangers include unconsciousness, vomiting and choking, with possible long-term damage to the kidneys and nervous system.

Cannabis (also called pot, hash, grass, marijuana) also makes you feel "high". Its long-term side effects are not yet known.

Kidney machines

People with kidney failure can use kidney machines to filter their blood. The blood is fed down a tube from one of the patient's blood vessels and into the machine. It passes alongside a bath of special "dialysis" fluid. The waste, and excess water and salts, pass into the fluid and the clean blood is returned to the patient's blood vessel. This takes many hours and has to be done several times a week. A strict diet also has to be followed.

Looking inside the body

There are various ways a doctor can see inside a person's body and so diagnose illnesses more easily.

X-RAYS. These are a type of electromagnetic ray which can pass through body tissues. If X-rays are directed at the body and a photographic plate is placed behind it, an image is produced on the plate. The X-rays pass through soft tissues easily and these show up black. They are partly stopped by bones, which show up white.

ULTRASOUND SCANNERS. Ultra high frequency (UHF) sound waves are bounced off the different organs. The waves make a pattern, which is displayed on a screen and can be interpreted by the doctor. This is a useful way of examining babies in the uterus because it is harmless.

CAT (COMPUTERIZED AXIAL TOMOGRAPHIC SCANNERS). X-rays are directed at the body from several different angles at once. A computer helps to interpret the images produced and a "slice" through the body is shown on a screen.

MAGNETIC SCANNERS. These are just being developed. An electromagnet makes the body produce radio waves and a computer builds up an image from them.

Index

First published in 1983 by
Usborne Publishing Ltd,
Usborne House, 83-85 Saffron
Hill, London, EC1N 8RT.
Copyright © 1991, 1983
Usborne Publishing

The name Usborne and the
device 🜊 are Trade Marks of
Usborne Publishing Ltd. All

Printed in Italy

THE USBORNE YOUNG SCIENTIST
MEDICINE

Pam Beasant
Designed by Iain Ashman

Edited by Tony Potter
Consultant editor Dr. Gillian Strube
Consultants Drs. Val and Mike Patton

Contents

Illustrated by Iain Ashman, Adam Willis, Stuart Trotter, Chris Lyon, Martin Newton, Michael Saunders, Gerry Browne, Tony Smith and Mark Longworth

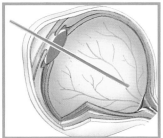

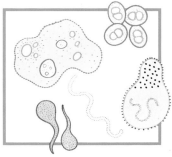

What is medicine?

Medicine is the study of how the body is cured when it goes wrong, how it is kept healthy and how illness is prevented. On these two pages you can find out about the subject of medicine.

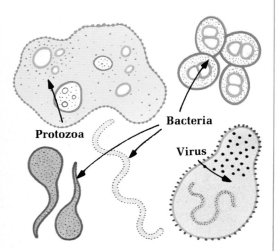

People become ill for many reasons. Mostly it is because germs invade their bodies and multiply. Some of these germs are shown above and you can find out more about them on pages 8-9.

Many diseases in the past spread because people lived in unsanitary conditions in crowded houses where germs spread very quickly.

Modern sewage works

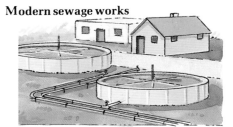

The development of sewage systems and the supply of clean drinking water have done more than anything else to improve the health of everybody.

Over the last fifty years, medicine has become a sophisticated science using techniques and equipment which are sometimes borrowed from other fields, such as space research. Laser surgery, for instance, uses concentrated beams of light to cut through the skin cleanly during an operation.

A laser beam being used in surgery.

Health and medicine are very different around the world because of factors such as climate, environment and food. You can find out about this on pages 26-27.

What is the body made of?

When people study medicine, they first learn what the body is made of and how a healthy body works.

1 Your entire body is made of billions of tiny units called cells. They work together all the time to keep it functioning properly.

2 There are different kinds of cells, each with a different job to do; for instance red blood cells carry oxygen around your body and nerve cells send messages of sensation and pain to your brain.

A single skin cell

Red blood cells

Tissue

3 Your body has layers of tissue, which are groups of cells of similar type, such as skin and muscle.

Medical people

There are many different kinds of medical people including family doctors, specialists and different kinds of nurses. Midwives, for instance, are nurses who are experts at delivering babies. The picture on the right shows some of the main people involved with medicine. There are also people whose jobs take them into the field of medicine, such as epidemiologists (who study why outbreaks of disease happen) and health officers (who check the cleanliness of restaurants, for instance).

Doctor

Midwife

The specialist doctor in charge of a hospital unit is called a consultant.

Nurses work shifts to run hospital wards 24 hours a day.

Physiotherapists help people to move properly after an illness or accident.

When you become ill your body reacts by showing symptoms such as a headache, diarrhoea or vomiting. You can find out more about symptoms on the next two pages.

When you are ill you see a doctor who has a general knowledge of all types of illness. He or she decides what is wrong after examining you and asking lots of questions. This is called making a diagnosis – find out how it is done on pages 14-15.

Sterile (germ-free) clothing   Surgeon

The doctor will treat you according to the diagnosis – perhaps with pills or an injection, or you may be sent to hospital for tests or to be examined with a view to operating.

Acupuncture needles

Sometimes people prefer to have alternative forms of treatment for their illness. There are many different alternative therapies available, such as acupuncture, which has been practised for centuries in China. Find out about this on pages 18-19.

The doctor can prevent some illnesses by giving an injection which makes you resist them. This is called immunization – find out more about it on pages 12-13.

Vegetables   Bread   Fruit   Fish

You can also help to prevent illness yourself by eating a balanced diet and taking exercise.

4 It also has organs, which are groups of tissue. Your heart, liver, stomach and lungs are all examples of organs.

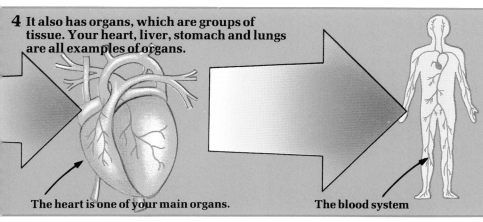

The heart is one of your main organs.   The blood system

5 Groups of organs which work together are called systems. Your heart and veins, for instance, make up your circulatory (blood) system which keeps the blood flowing round your body.

    You also have a special system called the immune system which is a complicated mass of organs and chemicals whose job it is to fight illness. You can find out about this on pages 10-11.

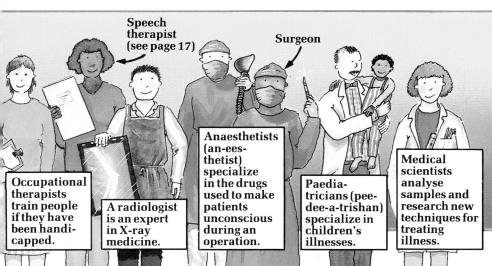

Speech therapist (see page 17)   Surgeon

Occupational therapists train people if they have been handicapped.

A radiologist is an expert in X-ray medicine.

Anaesthetists (an-ees-thetist) specialize in the drugs used to make patients unconscious during an operation.

Paediatricians (pee-dee-a-trishan) specialize in children's illnesses.

Medical scientists analyse samples and research new techniques for treating illness.

Specialists are experts on one part of the body or one group of illnesses. Each has a special name which is sometimes long and difficult to pronounce because it is taken from Greek or Latin. Cardiologists, for example, are experts on heart disease, and haematologists (hee-mo-tolo-jists) specialize in blood disorders. Many specialists work in hospitals, which are divided into units for each branch of medicine. Some travel to patients' homes to give treatment, and others work in clinics and health centres.

3

About illness

Most illnesses are caused by tiny particles called germs coming into your body. These live off substances in cells which you need to keep healthy. You then start to feel ill because your body cannot function in its normal way.

Your body reacts when ill by showing symptoms such as a temperature, a cough or a headache. Each illness has its own particular combination of symptoms which is how you or a doctor knows what is wrong with you. On these two pages, you can find out how your body reacts to illness.

Germs

Germs live in your body all the time, are present in the food you eat and are also in the air. Most of them are harmless. Germs multiply in most places, but prefer warm, damp or

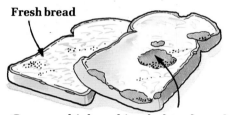

Fresh bread

Germs multiply making the bread mouldy.

dirty conditions. When certain germs multiply in food, the food goes bad and when they multiply in you they can cause illness. There are many kinds of germs and you can find out about them on pages 8-9.

Your defences

Your body is prepared for an invasion, or infection, of germs and starts to fight them immediately. This is done by a network of organs* and chemicals called the immune system which destroy and control germs.

Your immune system will recognize an illness you have had before, such as measles. It will fight the germs and kill them off before they have any effect.

Immune system

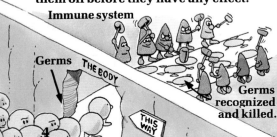

Germs THE BODY

THIS WAY

Germs recognized and killed.

Before the symptoms

Most illnesses take some time to secure their hold on the body. This is called the incubation period and can vary from a few days to several months. When it is finished, the symptoms of the illness appear.

This person has caught 'flu (influenza) but feels fine.

Two days later the symptoms start.

Follow the squares on the board to find out how illness develops and how your body reacts by showing symptoms.

Being sick

Being sick, or vomiting, is caused by a number of things from food poisoning to over-eating. Whatever the reason for being sick, however, the same things are going on inside your body when it happens.

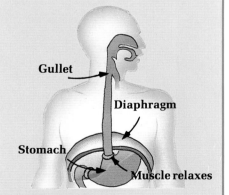

Gullet

Diaphragm

Stomach

Muscle relaxes

When you are sick, the lining of your stomach becomes irritated, making your stomach contract violently at the same time as the muscle at the end of your gullet relaxes. Your diaphragm also contracts, pushing against your stomach and forcing everything in it up your throat and out of your mouth.

Diarrhoea

Diarrhoea is when all the solid waste inside the bowel becomes runny and liquid. It is usually caused by a stomach upset, such as food poisoning. Food does not go through the normal digestion processes, and only a little is absorbed by the body. Diarrhoea causes a loss of water, glucose and minerals.

VOMITING

You eat some bad food

START

HEADACHE

Stay in bed for a day

Feeling marvellous - go to a party

Friend has measles

Headache

A headache is caused by pressure around your brain. The pain is caused by the blood vessels in your brain contracting then expanding. A headache can happen for many reasons. It may be due to an infection, or because the muscles in your neck and scalp become tense.

Normal size blood vessels

Expanded blood vessels causing a headache.

4

*See page 3.

Sneezing

Sneezing is your body's way of getting rid of anything irritating your nose. A cold, for instance, makes the inside of your nose inflamed and you sneeze to relieve it. If you are allergic* to anything, such as pollen, then you will sneeze to get rid of pollen particles in your nose.

Coughing

Coughing is called a reflex action which means that your body does it automatically. You cannot help coughing if you breathe in dust, or choke on food. Coughing stops anything from getting into your lungs and makes you swallow or spit it out instead. If you have a cold, for instance, mucus builds up in your air passages, and you cough to get rid of it.

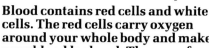
How blood defends you

Blood contains red cells and white cells. The red cells carry oxygen around your whole body and make your blood look red. There are fewer white cells, but they are a very important part of your body's defence system. If you cut yourself, lots of red and white blood cells go to the area and the white cells eat any germs that may be getting into the cut. There are also particles called platelets in blood which help it to clot. This is why a cut always stops bleeding after a while.

White blood cell

A germ being destroyed by a white blood cell.

Sometimes cuts or spots become infected by germs. When this happens pus forms. Pus is made of dead white blood cells which gather in the area round the cut or spot. The more germs that enter the area, the greater the number of white cells that go into action. It is better to leave a small cut uncovered as this allows a dry crust called a scab to form which also protects the cut from germs.

Dead white blood cells forming pus in a cut.

What is pain?

Pain is a symptom of illness because your body is telling you there is something wrong with it.

Pain is part of the system inside you which responds to touch, taste and smell (called the sensory system). Tiny fibres, called nerves, send messages to your brain when something is painful. Your brain identifies the site, and sometimes the cause of the pain.

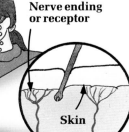

Nerve ending or receptor

Pain message going to brain.

A sharp leaf

Skin

Feeling run down

Meet someone with a cold

DIARRHOEA

Develop cold

SNEEZE AND COUGH

TEMPERATURE

Getting better

HEALTHY AGAIN

RASH

Develop measles

Temperature

Your normal body temperature, even in cold weather, is 37°C (98.4°F). Having a temperature means that your body temperature has gone higher than this.

39°C   Thermometer

This is a high temperature.

A temperature is often caused by an infection such as 'flu. When the 'flu germs damage healthy cells, they release certain chemicals which make you feel feverish and hot.

Rash

A rash is a skin irritation caused by an infection or allergy. For example, when you have measles, tiny blood vessels in your skin called capillaries, are damaged and release chemicals which cause a rash. The damaged capillaries cause an increase in blood to the skin, making it look red.

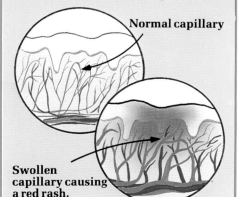

Normal capillary

Swollen capillary causing a red rash.

*An allergy is an abnormal reaction to normally harmless substances.

5

Things that go wrong with the body

Although many illnesses are caused by germs, there are lots of other reasons why people become ill. For example, babies can be born with an illness inherited from their parents.

On these two pages, you can find out about some of the main kinds of illnesses there are. On pages 8-9 you can find out about infections – the germs that cause them and how they spread.

Blood circulation disorders

Blood circulates constantly in the body, pumped by the heart. It carries oxygen which every cell, organ and system in the body needs to function. Oxygen is distributed from the lungs to main blood vessels (arteries) and from there to small arteries, then to small blood vessels (capillaries) and then to cells. Many diseases arise from the blood-flow being obstructed, which restricts the oxygen supply. This can result in reactions ranging from a faint to a heart attack (see opposite).

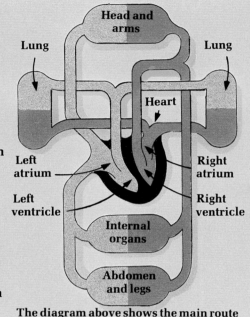

The diagram above shows the main route of the blood through the heart and round the body.

A pacemaker is a battery-powered electrical generator, inserted into the chest and attached to the heart with a fine wire. It regulates the beat of a heart not pumping properly.

Wire to heart

Heart disease

Heart disease is a disorder in the main arteries on the surface of the heart (coronary arteries). It happens because a fatty substance called cholesterol is deposited inside the arteries making them narrower and narrower, restricting the blood-flow. Heart disease is not necessarily dangerous in itself, but it can lead to a heart attack, or a condition called angina which gives the sufferer acute chest pains after exercise.

Heart attacks

A heart attack is a lack of blood to part of the heart. It happens for various reasons. There might be a blood clot in one of the coronary arteries, for instance, or a narrow segment of diseased artery might become too narrow for the blood to get through. A heart attack causes severe chest pains and sometimes the person collapses.

Strokes

A stroke is the result of an interruption of the blood supply to parts of the brain. This deprives the cells of oxygen and means they cannot work properly. These are usually the cells that control movement, speech and vision. In many cases people who have had a stroke lose some or all of these faculties for a while, but wholly or partially recover them after a few months. In severe cases, however, the sufferer can be left handicapped or die.

Industrial diseases

Industrial diseases affect workers in mines, chemical plants, factories and anywhere where there is a risk of breathing in excessive amounts of dust or chemical pollution over a number of years. They are usually diseases of the lung and respiratory systems. Miners, for example, often suffer from forms of bronchitis through breathing in coal dust which has been circulating in stale underground air. You can find out more about industrial diseases and how they affect health and the environment on pages 26-27.

Cancer

In general, cancer refers to the uncontrolled division and spread of faulty cells in the body, which destroy healthy cells. The disease can take many forms – it can cause growths called malignant tumours, for example. It can start in any part of the body. The pictures below show sections of two lungs – one with healthy cells and one with cancerous cells. People who smoke are much more likely to develop lung cancer. Many forms of cancer are now treated successfully, as long as they are spotted before they start to spread to other areas of the body.

Workers are given chest X-rays routinely in some factories containing a high level of dust.

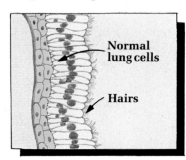

Normal lung cells

Hairs

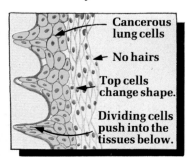

Cancerous lung cells

No hairs

Top cells change shape.

Dividing cells push into the tissues below.

Hereditary diseases

Diseases can be inherited from parents in the same way that eye and hair colour is inherited from them. These are called hereditary diseases. The unborn child is formed in the mother's womb with the disease.

A disease called haemophilia is carried, but not suffered, by some women. They can pass it on to male children who actually suffer the disease. The blood of a haemophiliac boy does not clot easily and even a small cut can bleed dangerously.

A woman carrying haemophilia has a 1 in 4 chance of giving birth to a boy who suffers from the disease. Before looking at the chart which explains this, find out in the paragraphs on the right how a child is formed.

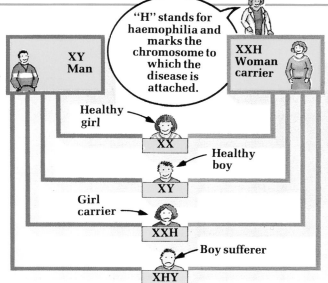

"H" stands for haemophilia and marks the chromosome to which the disease is attached.

XY Man

XXH Woman carrier

Healthy girl — XX

Healthy boy — XY

Girl carrier — XXH

Boy sufferer — XHY

A child is formed by two cells; an egg cell from its mother and a sperm cell from its father. A part called a sex chromosome from each cell determines the child's sex. An egg cell always gives an X chromosome and a sperm cell either an X or a Y chromosome. A girl is made from 2 X chromosomes and a boy from an X and a Y chromosome.

Haemophilia is carried by one of the woman's X chromosomes.

Illnesses needing surgery

Some illnesses are caused by infections in an organ, or growths in the body which cause obstructions. These illnesses can often be completely cured by surgery to remove the diseased tissue. Operations can also repair damaged veins, replace joints, remove blood clots and transplant organs that are faulty. A common illness needing surgery is appendicitis. You can find out about on the right.

Your appendix has no function in your body so you do not miss it if it is removed.

Large intestine

Small intestine

Appendix

Animals such as rabbits have a large appendix to help them digest grass.

Appendicitis

Appendicitis happens when a small, tail-shaped part of the intestine, called the appendix, suddenly becomes swollen and inflamed. The appendix is at the end of the small intestine. Nobody knows why it should become inflamed.

An infected appendix is removed in hospital. On pages 20-21, you can find out how this operation is done. If the appendix is left it can burst, spreading infection through the intestines and leading to a dangerous illness called peritonitis.

Deficiency diseases

Deficiency diseases happen because the body is lacking (deficient) in some of the things it needs. Mostly they are caused by poor diet but sometimes they happen because the body is unable to manufacture certain substances. A condition called iron-deficiency anaemia is caused by a lack of iron in the red blood cells. This can happen when people do not eat food which contain iron such as green vegetables.

Malnutrition

Malnutrition is an extreme and preventable deficiency disease caused by inadequate nourishment of any kind. It is widespread in countries which do not have enough food for their inhabitants. Malnutrition affects the growth and development of the body, increasing the body's reaction to infection and lowering its resistance to germs.

AIDS

AIDS stands for Acquired Immune Deficiency Syndrome. It is an extremely serious disease which attacks the immune system, leaving the sufferer unable to fight infection. AIDS is caused by a virus known as HIV (human immuno deficiency virus). HIV can be transmitted sexually or by drug abusers sharing needles.

About 15% of the world's population suffers from malnutrition. Two-thirds of these live in South East Asia.

No cure has yet been found for AIDS, so it is important to prevent the spread of HIV.

Iatrogenic diseases

Iatrogenic diseases are those caused by doctors, medicines and forms of treatment designed to cure illnesses. These diseases are not intended, but happen through the careless administration of medicines, or mistakenly diagnosing an illness, or through the side-effects of medicines given for another disorder.

In the early 1960s, a drug called thalidomide was given to some pregnant women to relieve morning sickness. It prevented the normal growth of limbs in some of the babies – a side-effect unforeseen by doctors and scientists.

People who receive radiotherapy for cancer often suffer nausea and hair-loss caused by the treatment.

Infections

Infections are illnesses that spread from person to person. Mumps, measles, colds and 'flu are all examples. Infections are caused by four main kinds of germs. These are viruses, bacteria, protozoa and fungi. Germs are parasites, which means they live off healthy cells and multiply there. They move or are carried to the body in different ways and enter the body by several routes.

Here, you can find out about the germs that cause infections and how they spread.

Viruses

Viruses are so small that they cannot be seen under an ordinary microscope. Different viruses cause illnesses such as colds, 'flu and chickenpox. The virus particles

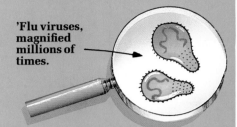

'Flu viruses, magnified millions of times.

burrow into healthy cells and live off them to produce more virus particles. The healthy cells die and the virus moves on through your body to find more cells to live off.

Bacteria

Bacteria (singular bacterium) are tiny single-celled creatures found everywhere. They reproduce by dividing into two when they reach a certain size. This is called fission. Some can damage tissues in the body

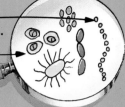

Streptococcus causes sore throats.

These bacteria also have Latin names.

and produce poisonous chemicals which make you ill.

Some bacteria can be useful too. For example, one kind lives in humans and produces a substance called vitamin K which helps blood to clot.

How germs get into the body

Germs are breathed in through the nose. To protect you, your nostrils are lined with fine hairs which catch most of them before they enter your body and make you ill.

Nose

Mouth

Germs can also enter the ears and the eyes, causing infection.

The mouth is a gateway for germs. They enter your body in food and drink, and when you breathe in through your mouth.

Diseases can be passed from one person to another during sexual intercourse. These are called sexually transmitted diseases (STD) or venereal diseases (VD). Many cause a discharge and itching in the groin*. They are often treated at special clinics.

Groin

Skin

Your skin is a natural barrier to germs, but they can enter the body through a cut or scratch, or if an insect which is carrying germs pierces your skin by stinging or biting you.

Some infections can also enter here which are not sexually transmitted; for example, a urinary tract infection such as cystitis (inflammation of the bladder), which causes pain when weeing.

How infections spread

This picture shows some of the ways in which infections spread from one person to another.

Droplet method

When you have an infection such as 'flu, the virus lives in your nose and throat. It is passed to other people when you breathe out, cough or sneeze. The viruses are in drops of liquid in your breath. This is the droplet method of spreading infection.

Contact

Some infections are spread by direct contact. A condition called herpes causes a sore, usually around the mouth or the groin. If someone touches it, or touches something the infected person has used – such as a towel – the virus causing herpes can burrow into their skin and the illness develops. This is the contact method of spreading infection.

8   *See pages 30-31 for a diagram of the sexual organs.

Fungi

Mushrooms, toadstools and mould are all different types of fungi (singular fungus). Certain kinds of fungus can grow on the body too and cause infections.

Athlete's foot is caused by particles

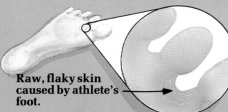

Raw, flaky skin caused by athlete's foot.

called ringworm fungus which grow between the toes, making the skin flaky and crusty. These are picked up in places with damp floors such as swimming baths. Athlete's foot is treated using ointment or powder.

Protozoa

Protozoa (singular protozoan) are another type of germs. They are tiny single-celled animals rather like bacteria. Most of them are completely harmless but some can cause disease.

This protozoan can cause dysentery.

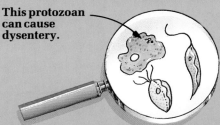

One kind of protozoan can live in the human intestine and cause a disease called dysentery, for which the symptoms are vomiting and acute diarrhoea. Dysentery is quite rare in most parts of the world.

Worm infections

Infections are also caused by different types of worms. One of them is the hookworm, which lives in water and soil in some countries. People can be infected by them if they walk bare-

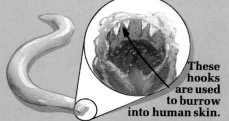

These hooks are used to burrow into human skin.

footed. The worms eggs, called larvae, burrow through the skin of feet and ankles and are carried through the blood system. There they develop into adult worms, which cause the illness.

Water-borne infections

Water can carry infections, especially in places where there is no sewage system or clean water supply. A river, for example, might be used by a whole village as drinking water and as a place to wash. If people with an infection use the river as a toilet, germs are passed into the water where they live and develop. The infection is then passed to people using the river for other purposes.

Cholera is an example of a disease passed on by contaminated water. People can die from the terrible diarrhoea it causes.

This man has an infectious disease.

The water is contaminated by him and these people are in danger of catching the disease.

What is an epidemic?

An epidemic is a large outbreak of one infectious disease. The most recent and serious examples are the outbreaks of a bacterial infection called legionnaires' disease, first diagnosed in 1976. The disease is dangerous because it causes pneumonia which can lead to death.

How insects carry disease

Insects such as flies, fleas and mosquitos can infect people with germs picked up, for example, from animals. This is called the vector method of spreading disease.

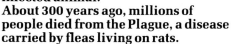

Flies

A fly can pick up germs in dirty places such as rubbish dumps. The germs stick to the fly's feet or hairy body. When the fly lands on some food, the germs are passed onto it and can infect the person who eats it.

Sticky legs

Fleas

Fleas feed on animals by sucking their blood. They also bite humans and can pass on disease from an infected animal.

About 300 years ago, millions of people died from the Plague, a disease carried by fleas living on rats.

Mosquitos

A type of mosquito which lives in hot, swampy countries carries protozoa germs (see above) which produce a disease called malaria in people bitten by the mosquito.

Piercer

How your body fights illness

Your body is an amazing fighting machine designed to combat the germs and hazards in the world. It heals when you cut it and will fight most germs successfully.

The picture on the left is colour coded to show which main systems work together to prevent germs from making you ill. For example, the stomach is part of the alimentary canal which contains substances which destroy germs.* There are also lumps called lymph nodes, situated all over the body, which produce chemicals to kill germs.

Each system is described individually below. You can find out opposite how the same systems help to heal broken bones and cuts.

1 Alimentary canal

The alimentary canal is lined by mucous membrane which is wet and slippery. Its main function is to break down the food you eat into useful substances. It also protects you from illness because the juice in your stomach contains acids which kill many germs.

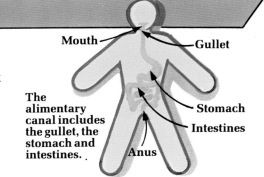

Mouth
Gullet
Stomach
Intestines
Anus

The alimentary canal includes the gullet, the stomach and intestines.

2 Warning systems

There is a complicated network of nerves inside you. Their job is to send messages to your brain which identifies sensations such as smell, pain, heat and noise. Without such a system, your body could be damaged without you realizing. The nervous system acts as a warning system about injury and illness.

How nerves work

Each nerve fibre under your skin is called a receptor because it receives sensations. The nerves send messages in the form of pulses of electricity which reach your brain in a fraction of a second.

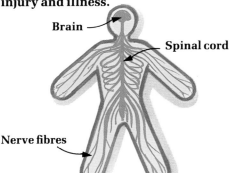

Brain
Spinal cord
Nerve fibres

Nerve cells

Your nervous system is made up of nerve cells which vary greatly in shape and size. Most of them are situated in your brain and the top of your spinal cord. Attached to each cell are long fibres which reach all parts of your body. Some of the nerve-endings are just beneath your skin while others are attached to muscles and organs. There are lots of them in your hands, feet, and round your mouth.

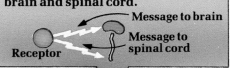

When you prick your finger on a pin, the receptor sends a lightning message to the nerve centres in your brain and spinal cord.

Message to brain
Message to spinal cord
Receptor

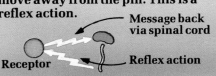

Your brain sends a message via the spinal cord telling your finger to move away from the pin. This is a reflex action.

Message back via spinal cord
Reflex action
Receptor

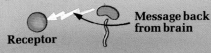

Your brain searches your memory and sends back a message identifying the pin as the cause of pain.

Message back from brain
Receptor

The alimentary canal is shown in gold.

The nervous system is shown in green.

The lymph nodes (see opposite page) are shown in blue.

The blood system is shown in red.

10

The alimentary canal is part of the digestive system.

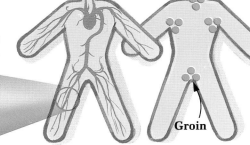

Your blood contains special white blood cells called lymphocytes. When germs penetrate your blood system, lymphocytes produce chemicals called antibodies to fight them. The antibodies attach themselves to germs and either neutralize or destroy them.

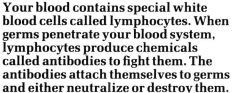

Antibodies

Germs

Lymph nodes

Groin

Lymphocytes are made in your bone marrow and in small swellings called lymph nodes which are all over your body, especially in your neck, armpits and groin. The main function of lymphocytes is to produce antibodies.

You produce antibodies in response to particular germs. The antibodies you produce against one kind of illness will not be effective against another.

How bones heal

When you break a bone, a blood clot forms in much the same way as over a cut. Capillaries move in and supply blood to the damaged bone which it needs to start the healing process. Special cells called osteoblasts, which make bone, move into the area and reproduce quickly, knitting the broken ends of the bone together. This process takes from a few weeks to months depending on where and how the bone is broken.

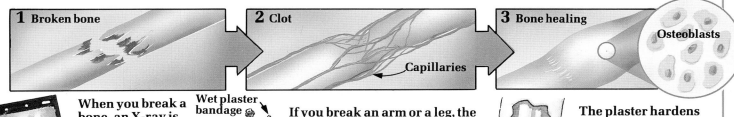

1 Broken bone

2 Clot

Capillaries

3 Bone healing

Osteoblasts

X-ray

Break

When you break a bone, an X-ray is taken so that the doctor can see exactly where it is broken and how badly.*

Wet plaster bandage

If you break an arm or a leg, the doctor will soak in water a bandage impregnated with plaster, then wrap it around the broken limb.

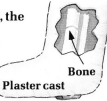

Bone

Plaster cast

The plaster hardens to form a tube in the shape of your arm or leg so that the broken bone is held together in the right position.

Cell replacement

Your body is constantly manufacturing new cells to replace those that have died. A red blood cell, for instance, has an average life of only four months.

Food provides the basic nutrients needed to make new cells. The speed of this process varies. For example, new skin grows within a few days, while bones and organs take weeks to heal. Some cells, such as muscle cells, cannot be replaced if they die. This is why it is important to keep them in good working order through exercise.

A cell dividing

How cuts heal

When you cut yourself, the blood round the cut clots, hardens and forms a scab. New tissue begins to grow underneath the scab, pulling the cut skin together. The scab gradually shrinks, then falls off when the new tissue has repaired the damaged skin.

Graze

Scab

Deep cut

Suture

Knot

Sometimes if a cut is very deep, the doctor might stitch it up to help the skin knit together more quickly and stop the bleeding. This is done with a short, curved needle and special sterile thread called suture. The stitches are put in one at a time and individually knotted. This makes the stitch strong, and easy to remove. During an operation, dissolving stitches are sometimes put into the tissue below the skin, as well as ordinary ones in the skin itself.

Getting better

The period when your body is recovering from illness or injury is called convalescence.

Convalescence is especially needed after a serious illness, or an accident which involves the loss of a lot of blood. This can put the body in a state of shock, which means that it stops functioning properly, and the healing process takes longer to begin.

Preventative medicine

Preventing illness is just as important as curing it. Doctors, medical scientists and health officers spend much of their time looking for ways of controlling and wiping out illness. This is called preventative medicine.

One of the most important aspects of preventative medicine is dealing effectively with sewage and rubbish and providing clean drinking water. Other aspects of preventative medicine include regular medical check-ups and immunization.

On these two pages you can find out how lots of people work to keep you healthy and what you can do to look after your own body.

► People used to empty waste on to the street. This allowed germs to breed freely and infect drinking water.

Sewage works purify and dispose of toilet and kitchen waste.

Public health

Health officers are appointed by the government to visit factories, shops and restaurants, checking that conditions are clean and the food is fresh and safe to eat. Spot checks are carried out and samples of food taken away to be analysed in a laboratory. These safeguards help to prevent outbreaks of food poisoning and other infections.

A health officer checking a restaurant.

Check-ups

Check-ups are carried out in schools and clinics to look for early signs of illness. This is called screening and is an important part of preventative medicine because doctors may spot and be able to treat an illness before it develops. For example, babies can be screened to make sure their hips are not dislocated. Any dislocation can be treated so the baby does not have difficulty later when it is learning to walk.

Some illness may be prevented by having check-ups.

Immunization

One of the most important parts of preventative medicine is immunization against disease. This is when the doctor gives you a vaccine, which is a small amount of substance which usually causes a disease. It makes your body produce antibodies to kill those particular germs. Should you later come in contact with that disease, your body will recognize it and produce the antibodies to kill it before you get ill. You are then said to be immune to that disease.

Soon after birth, you are given your first set of vaccines to protect against diseases such as polio, which can affect limb growth. After a few years you might be given a further dose, called a booster, to make sure you are still immune. Vaccines against some diseases, such as measles, last for life.

Your body reacts to vaccines in different ways, and they travel round the body at different rates, depending upon how they are given. You might be given an injection, be pricked by a puncher with lots of small sharp needles on it, or be given tablets, or drops on sugar lumps.

Vaccine on sugar lumps.

Tablets containing vaccine.

These sharp needles scratch your skin. The vaccine then enters your bloodstream.

Developing immunity

All babies are born with some immunity to disease which is passed on from their mother through the placenta. This immunity lasts for about six months. When it wears off, babies can only become immune by suffering a disease, which produces antibodies naturally, or through vaccination.

Vaccines are prepared from chemicals called antigens, taken from animals and people who have suffered the disease. They are made from samples of blood collected from blood donors, for example. Vets collect similar samples from animals.

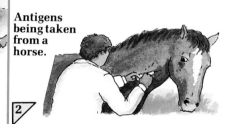

Antigens being taken from a horse.

Vaccines are also prepared from samples of the disease itself collected in the same way as antigens, or cultured in a laboratory. The sample is weakened using heat or chemicals so that it is just strong enough to make the body produce antibodies, but not the disease.

People can also become immune to a disease by being given ready-made antibodies extracted from other people which the body adopts as its own.

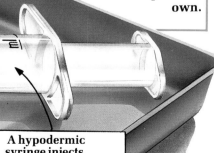

A hypodermic syringe injects vaccine straight into your bloodstream through a vein.

Why you need to be immunized

Placenta

The baby receives food through the placenta. Rubella can cross it and infect the baby.

Sometimes there is a special reason to be immunized against particular illnesses.

It is very important, especially for girls, to be immunized against rubella (German measles). Although it is not a serious disease, it can damage an unborn child if a pregnant woman catches it. Rubella is caused by a virus which damages the cells of the mother and baby. This affects the baby's growth and it can be born disabled.

Sometimes when you go abroad vaccines are needed against diseases not found in this country. This is both to protect you and to ensure that you do not bring any infection back home and start an epidemic. *

It is very important not to take animals from one country to another. They can carry infections too. One of the worst is rabies, for which there is no cure. People catch rabies by being bitten by infected animals.

Keeping yourself healthy

There are several things you can do yourself to keep healthy, such as eating a balanced diet, taking lots of exercise and avoiding things which damage your body such as smoking. (Never inhale the fumes of substances such as glue. They can damage organs and even kill.)

Fats

Fats provide more energy than carbohydrates, and also vitamins, some of which you cannot get any other way.

Cheese

Protein

Protein is broken down and becomes acids called amino acids which your cells use for growth, and to repair tissues.

Meat

Carbohydrates

Carbohydrates provide energy which you need for any physical activity. Some energy is made into heat, maintaining your body temperature of 37°C (98.4°F).

Bread
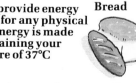

It is a good idea to exercise as much as possible to keep your body in good working order. Exercise helps to keep your heart pumping efficiently and keeps your muscles strong. It also increases your lung capacity so that more oxygen gets into your body, and it helps you to burn off excess food. One of the best exercises is swimming because it uses all parts of your body at once.

Different food contains different substances needed by your body. These are protein, vitamins, minerals, water, fat, carbohydrate and roughage. The chart below lists the main foods in a balanced diet, and how they help your body.

Water

Water makes up about 70% of your body weight. It is contained in most food. Without any food or water you would die within days.

Water

Vitamins

Vitamins are chemicals which your body needs to work efficiently but cannot make itself.

Fruit

Minerals

Minerals are used in the construction of body tissues.

Vegetables

Fibre

Fibre adds bulk to your diet and helps your waste products to keep moving.

Beans

Bran

As part of preventative medicine, doctors educate people about the effects on their bodies of smoking, alcohol and drugs. They encourage and help people to avoid these things or give them up.

*See page 9.

Going to see the doctor

People usually go to the doctor if they have had an accident, or need advice, a check-up, medicine, or an immunization. If they are ill, the doctor will ask questions and examine them to find out what is wrong. This is called making a diagnosis.

The doctor uses special equipment to examine a patient, such as a sphygmomanometer to measure their blood pressure (see opposite page). When a diagnosis has been made, the doctor decides how to treat the patient. If medicine is needed, the doctor writes a prescription, which is an authorization to the chemist to provide the medicine. Prescriptions ensure that dangerous medicines are controlled.

What is the doctor's job?

Doctors have to have a thorough knowledge of a healthy body to recognize the symptoms of an illness.

It helps to be a good listener and sympathetic towards people because an accurate diagnosis depends mainly on what the patient says.

There are thousands of different kinds of medicines available. The doctor has to choose the right one for the patient and make sure they have no allergies* to any medicine, such as penicillin.

Sometimes the doctor will send patients to a specialist for a second opinion, or to hospital for tests or an operation.

The doctor has to keep up-to-date with all the new medicines and techniques available to give the patient the best treatment possible.

Making a diagnosis

The doctor fits together the answers to questions like a jigsaw puzzle to make a diagnosis. She starts by asking about the general health and past illnesses of the patient. This is called taking a case history and it helps the doctor to know if a patient is prone to any illnesses. Below you can find out how a doctor diagnoses appendicitis.

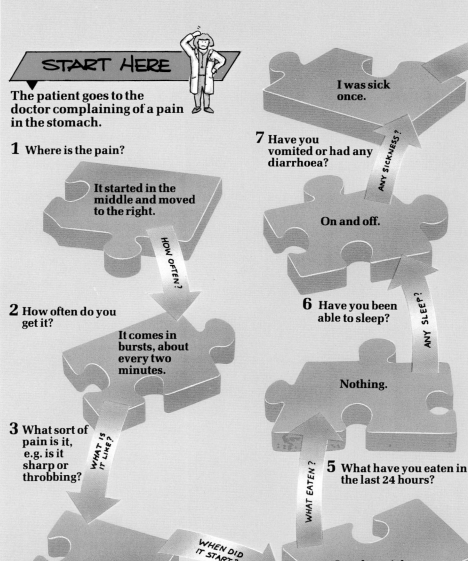

START HERE

The patient goes to the doctor complaining of a pain in the stomach.

1 Where is the pain?

It started in the middle and moved to the right.

HOW OFTEN?

2 How often do you get it?

It comes in bursts, about every two minutes.

3 What sort of pain is it, e.g. is it sharp or throbbing?

WHAT IS IT LIKE?

It is a very sharp pain.

WHEN DID IT START?

4 When did the pain start?

Late last night.

WHAT EATEN?

5 What have you eaten in the last 24 hours?

Nothing.

ANY SLEEP?

6 Have you been able to sleep?

On and off.

ANY SICKNESS?

7 Have you vomited or had any diarrhoea?

I was sick once.

A general examination

On the right you can find out what happens when the doctor checks a patient's body to find out if there is anything wrong. This is called a general examination.

8 Have you had a temperature?

Yes

TEMP-ERATURE?

OTHER PAINS?

9 Do you have a pain anywhere else?

No

ANY PILLS?

10 Have you taken any medicine?

Two aspirins.

Then the doctor will feel the patient's stomach all over. This hurts, but it is necessary for the doctor to find the tender part.

YOU HAVE APPENDICITIS

At this point the doctor might suspect that the patient has appendicitis and send them to hospital to have their appendix removed. You can find out about this operation on pages 20-21.

The doctor looks inside the eyes with a thin torch to make sure there are no infections or eyesight defects.

A different torch is used to check the ears to make sure there is not too much of a substance called wax which clogs up ears and affects the patient's hearing.

The doctor might look in the mouth to check the tonsils, and check there is no swelling in the patient's throat.

The doctor checks the patient's weight to make sure they are not too light or too heavy for their height.

The doctor takes the patient's pulse by putting three fingers over the main artery in the wrist. The pulse beats are then counted to see if the patient's blood is flowing at the normal rate.

The doctor listens to the patient's chest with a stethoscope. This is to make sure the heart and lungs are working properly.

The feet may be checked in case there is athlete's foot or a verruca.

Other equipment

The doctor also has lots of other equipment which might be used during an examination. For example, a blood pressure kit, syringes and needles for taking blood samples or giving immunizations (see page 12),

Syringe

sharp knives, a stick like a lollipop stick to take samples from the throat, and a hammer to tap the joint just below the knee-cap to check the patient's reflexes – if their knee jerks then all is well.

Blood pressure kit

Blood samples

Many infections can be detected in the blood. This is because invading germs use the bloodstream to move around the body. A small sample of blood taken from the arm is enough to show if germs are present. It can also show deficiencies in the blood, such as too few red blood cells which causes a condition called anaemia.

Urine tests

Infections can be present in urine. Sometimes this can be seen by the doctor without sending a sample for analysis. There might be blood present, for example, or the urine might be a dark or pale colour, or have an abnormally thick consistency. A condition called diabetes is caused by too much sugar in the body which is detected in the urine.

Blood pressure

Blood pressure is the force with which your heart pumps blood around your body. It is measured on a sphygmomanometer and recorded as two numbers written like a fraction. The top number, called the systolic, measures the pressure when the heart is pumping. The second number, called the diastolic, measures the pressure in between heart-beats when the heart is relaxed.

Treating illnesses and injuries

Often your body will cope with an illness and you will get better without any help from medicines or doctors. Sometimes, however, you may need some medicine, or advice from a doctor on how to get better more quickly. The doctor might tell you to cut down on certain food such as chips, or do some special exercises, for instance. You can find out on these two pages about medicines and treatments. On pages 18-19, you can find out about alternative forms of treatment to those described here.

About medicines

There are many different kinds of medicines, and they can be taken in different ways. Some are swallowed while others are injected or inhaled, or given in drops in the eyes and ears, or in tablets pushed up the back passage (rectum*).

Injection

Tablet

Ear-drop

Penicillin in mould, killing bacteria.

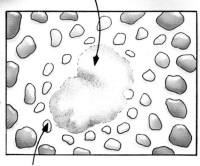

White neutralized bacterium

How medicines work

Medicines called antibiotics work directly on bacteria, either preventing them from multiplying, or killing them completely. They are used to treat many illnesses from ear infections to pneumonia. ▶

Analgesics dissolve in your stomach and travel round your bloodstream.

Some medicines relieve ▲ symptoms of illnesses such as pain or fever, but do not actually kill the germs. They are called analgesics and include aspirin. Analgesics work in different ways; for instance by blocking the chemicals in your body which trigger pain fibres.

Some medicines are used to replace substances lacking in the body. Vitamin D, for instance, is needed for the proper growth of limbs. It can be given as medicine to people who lack it in their diet. ▼

This food contains vitamin D.

Overweight people often have high blood pressure.

Medicines called anti-hypertensives are used to bring down high blood pressure. High blood pressure is dangerous because it causes the heart to overwork and increases the risk of strokes.

Medicines are dangerous and are carefully controlled by doctors and chemists. Many can only be obtained if a doctor prescribes them with strict instructions as to when and how often

DANGER

they should be taken. You should never touch any medicines without the knowledge of an adult. If they are mis-used they could make you very ill and even kill you.

All medicines act differently on the body. For this reason some have to be taken after a meal, and others on an empty stomach; some need to be mixed with water and others swallowed whole. It is always

important to follow the instructions on a medicine label very carefully as they are harmful unless correctly taken. If you do not complete a course of antibiotics, for instance, the bacteria may survive. They can then

build up an immunity to the substances in the antibiotic so that a dose in the future would be useless. A complete course of antibiotics kills all the bacteria.

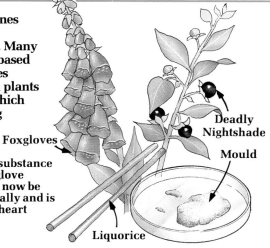

Most medicines are made in laboratories. Many of those are based on substances contained in plants and herbs which have healing properties.

Foxgloves

Digitalis is a substance found in foxglove leaves. It can now be made artificially and is used to treat heart disease.

Deadly Nightshade

Mould

Liquorice

Belladonna, or atropine, comes from a plant called deadly nightshade. An extraction from it is used to dry up saliva (spit) before an operation*.

Liquorice lines the stomach and is used to treat stomach ulcers caused by too much acid.

Penicillin is extracted from mould and it kills bacteria germs.

Problems with medicines

Some medicines cause side-effects or allergic reactions. Common side-effects are vomiting, rashes, diarrhoea, sleepiness and indigestion. The doctor has to weigh the advantages against the disadvantages when prescribing medicines. If, for example, an illness is not serious and the medicine for it can cause side-effects just as unpleasant as the symptoms, then it is not worth taking the medicine. With more serious illnesses such as cancer, other medicine is given to control the side-effects of the medicines for the cancer.

Physiotherapy

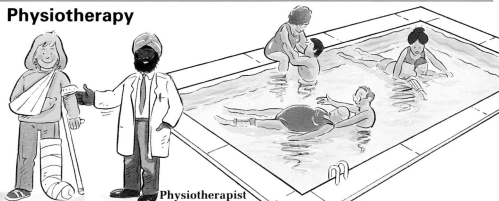

Physiotherapist

Physiotherapy consists of treatment given by specially trained people to anyone who cannot move properly. It is important because muscles start to waste away if they are not used. A physiotherapist uses massage, heat treatment, electrical treatment, and teaches special exercises.

After a stroke, for example, a physiotherapist will begin treatment quickly to prevent paralysed muscles causing a leg or an arm to shorten, and to teach the patient to use other mucles to do the job of those that have failed. The exercises may be carried out in a swimming pool.

Occupational therapy

Occupational therapy means giving people activities to help them overcome disabilities that they may have been born with, or to help them recover from a serious illness or accident. In doing the activities, patients learn how to cope with everyday tasks with as little help as possible. The activities range from handicrafts such as knitting to improve concentration or relieve depression, to practising familiar activities such as making tea.

Many people find some everyday tasks very difficult after an accident or illness. Occupational therapy units therefore often have kitchens where patients can practise cooking and other skills that they may have been able to do easily before. Sometimes special equipment is needed such as mixing bowls that stick to work tops. These are helpful if someone is not able to use both hands easily.

The occupational therapist may make a visit to the patient's home to see if anything can be done to make it safer and easier for the patient to manage. For instance, replacing steps with a ramp is very important for a person in a wheelchair.

Some activities are taught to improve concentration or coordination.

Special diet

Some illnesses are treated by a special diet. For example, in people with diabetes the level of sugar in the blood cannot be controlled properly by the body. Some diabetics can be treated solely by a diet low in sugar and high in fibre.

Rest and exercise

Your body needs rest to recover from any illness and return to its full strength. After an injury such as a broken bone, however, exercise may be necessary even if it is painful. This is because muscles and bones become weak if they are not used. Inactivity can also stop your blood flowing as quickly as it should. This can cause blood clots to form which restrict the blood-flow.

Speech therapy

Speech therapy is used to help people who have speech defects or difficulties. After a stroke, for example, a speech therapist can help the patient recover speech through special voice exercises.

*See pages 20-21.

Alternative medicine

On these two pages you can find out about some treatments which have not traditionally been used by family doctors. Together, they are called complementary, or alternative medicine and they are often used alongside conventional treatments.

There are hundreds of different kinds of these treatments, some of which have been established for thousands of years. Some involve taking medicines, or remedies, which are made entirely of natural ingredients. One, called osteopathy, uses massage and manipulation of bones, joints and muscles.

Herbs are crushed to make medicine.

Osteopathy

Another, called acupuncture, uses fine needles which are pushed into the skin at certain places. The theory of most forms of alternative treatment is based on the idea that the body should contain a fine balance of things to stay healthy. When ill, the whole person should be treated and not the symptoms of a particular illness as in conventional medicine. In China, the theory is expressed in symbols called yin and yang. Together they represent all the functions of the body and mind and stand for the perfect balance of positive and negative forces. When they are unbalanced, through eating the wrong food, for example, then you become ill. Many alternative treatments are based on the ideas of people who were conventional doctors but developed their own theories about how people should be treated. Now, many therapists are not doctors but are trained in one alternative treatment.

Yin Yang symbol

Going to see a natural therapist

Natural therapists take a case history and make a diagnosis just like ordinary doctors. The procedure for doing this is slightly different though. For instance, a therapist might ask much more detailed questions about yourself and your past, some of which do not seem to have anything to do with your illness. They will also note the way you walk and talk, and whether you are shy or outgoing. This is because the therapist believes that you must be treated as a whole, not just your illness, and that each individual responds to a different kind of treatment.

The therapist notes this man's slouch as well as his symptoms.

Acupuncture

Acupuncture is an ancient Oriental treatment based on the idea that all things contain a life force called Chi. Chi flows along invisible lines in the body called meridian lines. On these lines are hundreds of invisible points called pressure points. An acupuncturist acts on these points mainly by applying needles. They might also use finger pressure, heat, lasers or ultrasound. The treatment is not always in the same area as the illness. For example, someone with a kidney complaint might be given treatment in their ear by an acupuncturist.

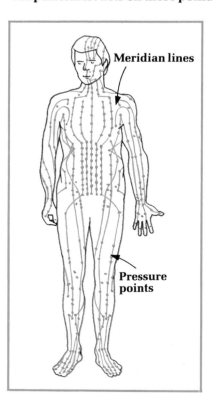

Meridian lines

Pressure points

An acupuncturist decides which parts of the body need to be treated and sticks fine needles into the pressure point areas. Surprisingly, this does not hurt at all because the

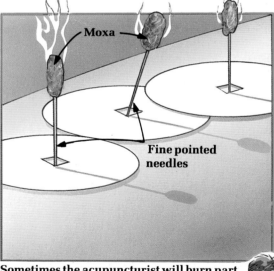

Moxa

Fine pointed needles

Sometimes the acupuncturist will burn part of a dried mugwort plant called moxa on the ends of the needles. This generates soothing heat down the needles and into your body and is called moxibustion.

acupuncturist knows exactly where and how to stick in the needles. This requires much experience and training and you should never try it yourself.

Homeopathy

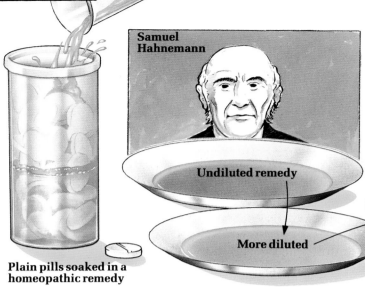

Homeopathic medicine is based on the principle that symptoms of illness are caused by the body's fight against it and not by the illness itself. This is generally known as the "like cures like" theory because, in healthy people, homeopathic medicine actually causes the symptoms you are trying to treat.

Plain pills soaked in a homeopathic remedy

Samuel Hahnemann

Undiluted remedy

More diluted

More diluted

Remedy ready for use, extremely diluted.

Homeopathic medicine was founded about 200 years ago by a German doctor called Samuel Hahnemann. Experimenting with alternative remedies was not new, but Hahnemann discovered that the remedies worked much better if they were extremely diluted – sometimes so that hardly a drop of the medicine remained. Many conventional doctors found this hard to accept and it was a long time before homeopathy was established.

Osteopathy

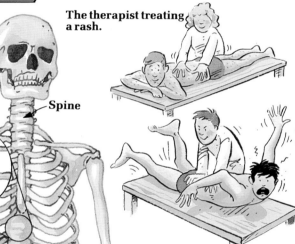

Osteopathy is concerned with the manipulation of joints, particularly in the region of the spine. It was founded by a doctor called Andrew Taylor Still over a hundred years ago. It is based on the idea that we become ill if any part of the spine is out of place. The theory developed because the spine and spinal cord are central to the body's structure and the nervous system *

Spine

Spinal cord

The therapist treating a rash.

The high velocity thrust

Many people go to an osteopath if they have "ricked" their back, and they are treated by a simple manipulation of the spine. But the osteopath's field is wider and they can treat rashes, stomach upsets and headaches, for example, by manipulation of the joints.

The actual manipulation can be quite vigorous; one technique is called "the high velocity thrust". Others are very gentle, coaxing the tissues of the patient to respond. The osteopath decides on a different technique for different patients.

Psychological therapies

Many alternative treatments are based on the idea that the mind can control illness; that it is caused by a depressed or anxious mental state and can be cured by an effort of will. These treatments are called psychological therapies and are close to the branch of medicine called psychiatry.

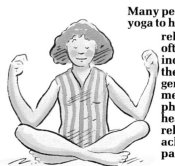

Many people do yoga to help them relax. They often find it increases their general mental and physical health and relieves aches and pains.

Sigmund Freud developed psychoanalysis about a hundred years ago. This involves talking to a patient in a special way to draw out of them things that are troubling them, making them depressed and ill. The patient often experiences a sense of release through this and finds that their health improves.

Many of Freud's ideas have now been changed or rejected altogether, but he is the father of the now extensive branch of psychological medicine.

Hypnotherapy

It has been known for thousands of years that people can be put into a trance, rather like walking in your sleep. This is called hypnotism and is a psychological therapy. The idea behind hypnotherapy is that the patient relaxes and answers truthfully all the questions asked by the therapist. This allows a diagnosis to be made. Further sessions are used to reduce pain, or to enable a patient to stop worrying, helping the symptoms of an illness go away.

Hypnotism is most effective when the patient's illness is related to stress.

*See pages 10-11.

Operations

Operations range from heart transplants, which take hours, to having a wart removed, which only takes seconds.

All operations are part of the branch of medicine called surgery. They are usually carried out in hospitals by specially trained doctors called surgeons in a room called an operating theatre. This is kept free of germs and has all the equipment to deal with major operations. On these two pages you can find out what happens during an operation to remove the appendix, called an appendicectomy.

An operating theatre is called a theatre because it used to be built as one. Students used to watch the operations in tiered seats all around. Now they watch them on special video screens.

Reasons for operating

Most operations are straightforward and many can be done in less than half an hour. For example, a surgeon might do several tonsil operations (tonsillectomies) a day. Other operations are exploratory; the surgeon opens someone up to find out what is wrong with them.

Emergency operations are carried out, for example, after road accidents, or because of infections such as appendicitis which must be dealt with immediately.

Preparing for an operation

Although the idea of an operation may be frightening, techniques and equipment are so sophisticated that there is no need to feel nervous. Follow the steps on the right to find out what happens during an appendicectomy.

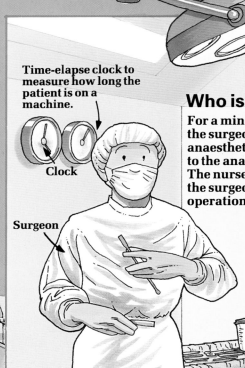

Time-elapse clock to measure how long the patient is on a machine.

Clock

Surgeon

Who is in the operating theatre?

For a minor operation, it is only necessary to have the surgeon and one nurse present, and an anaesthetist who monitors the patient's response to the anaesthetic and regulates their breathing. The nurse is there to pass instruments to the surgeon and generally assist at the operation. At a major operation there will be a surgeon and a junior surgeon and possibly a student as well as two nurses, the anaesthetist and some technicians to help operate some of the sophisticated equipment in the operating theatre. The surgeon's team is called a firm.

There is a large selection of cutting instruments; some small and thin for delicate surgery and others large and strong for cutting through bone, for example.

Everyone in the firm wears completely sterile clothes; a gown, rubber boots, gloves, a cap, and a mask over their mouths. This is to prevent the spread of germs. All the instruments used are also sterilized.

There are sterile containers where the surgeon puts samples that are sent to the laboratory for analysis.

A range of cotton swabs are used to wipe up blood from the patient, and needles and suture for sewing up the wounds.

1 The patient is not given anything to eat or drink for several hours before the operation. It can be dangerous if there is food in his stomach while he is unconscious (anaesthetised). If he is sick during the operation, any food could make him choke.

Never be afraid to ask a doctor or nurse any questions if you are having an operation.

2 A hospital doctor sees him to make sure he is ready. This doctor will probably be present at the operation. Sometimes the surgeon who will operate will come and see him too to explain what is going to happen.

20

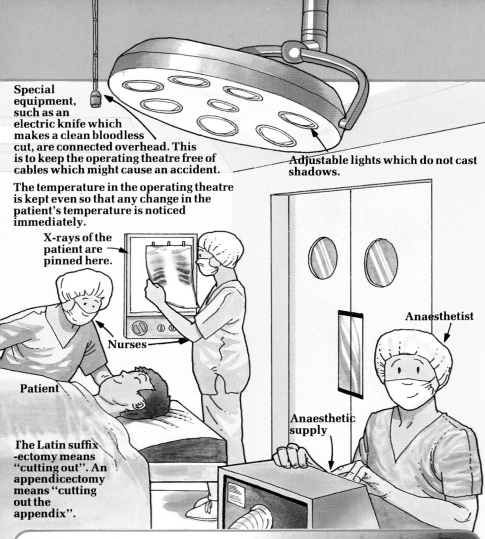

Special equipment, such as an electric knife which makes a clean bloodless cut, are connected overhead. This is to keep the operating theatre free of cables which might cause an accident.

Adjustable lights which do not cast shadows.

The temperature in the operating theatre is kept even so that any change in the patient's temperature is noticed immediately.

X-rays of the patient are pinned here.

Nurses

Anaesthetist

Patient

Anaesthetic supply

The Latin suffix -ectomy means "cutting out". An appendicectomy means "cutting out the appendix".

The operation

The surgeon makes a cut about 8cm (3in) long in the skin on the right hand side of the abdomen using a very sharp knife called a scalpel.

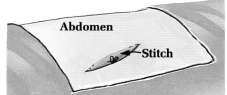

Abdomen

Stitch

The skin and tissue underneath it opens up and the surgeon can then see the appendix attached to the end of the small intestine.* He puts a stitch at the top of the appendix and pulls it tight to cut off the blood supply, then slices off the appendix with another sharp knife.

Suture

Appendix

The surgeon then sews the tissue together using dissolving suture. Finally the skin is sewn up with ordinary suture. The appendix is put in a sterile container and sent to the laboratory for analysis. This is necessary as doctors are still unsure what causes appendicitis.

Unless the appendix is very badly infected, the operation only takes about ten minutes.

The operation is now complete. The anaesthetist administers a drug which reverses the anaesthetic and the patient wakes up after a few minutes in the recovery room.

After the operation

The patient might feel a bit sick when he wakes up, which is just the after-effects of the anaesthetic. He might feel thirsty too because the pre-med dries out the mouth. If he tries to move too much immediately, the area round the stomach will feel stiff and sore. The next day, however, he will have to get up and start using his muscles again so that they do not stiffen up.

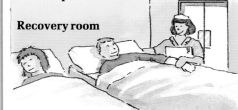

Recovery room

In the past

Only just over a hundred years ago, operations were carried out with no anaesthetic at all. Conditions were very unhygienic and many patients died because of germs picked up on the operating table. In 1865, a doctor called Joseph Lister used a spray disinfectant called carbolic during operations to kill the germs in the air. This was the basis of modern germ-free surgery.

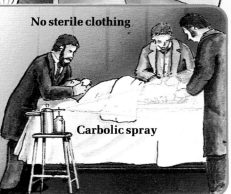

No sterile clothing

Carbolic spray

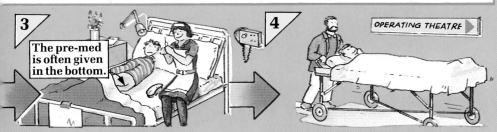

3

The pre-med is often given in the bottom.

A nurse will give the patient an injection, or a syrup, to make him drowsy and relaxed and to dry up excess fluids in the mouth. This is called a pre-med.

4

OPERATING THEATRE ▶

The patient is dressed in a loose gown and wheeled to the operating theatre on a trolley. The anaesthetic, usually administered in the form of an injection, is given before the patient goes into theatre.

*See page 7.

How a hospital works

A hospital is run by a team of doctors, nurses, administrators, technicians, porters, cleaners, cooks, laundry workers and many more. It is a complicated organization of units, each of which specializes in one kind of illness or treatment. There are also departments in a hospital for physiotherapy and occupational therapy, and laboratories where scientists analyse samples taken from patients.

A team of administrators is in charge of the smooth-running of the whole hospital, while doctors and nurses are in charge of all the patients. The senior hospital doctors are specialists in one type of illness or area of the body. A paediatrician, for example is a specialist in children's illnesses. On these two pages you can find out about the different departments of a hospital.

Reasons for going to hospital

Some people only visit the hospital when they need treatment or the use of special equipment. They go to a special section of the hospital called out-patients.

Usually about half the patients in hospital need an operation. They are called surgical patients.

Some people visit special clinics in the hospital. Pregnant women, for example, visit the ante-natal clinic where they are given a check-up.

Exploratory operations and other tests are done in hospital. One of these is a lumbar puncture in which spinal fluid is drained from the spine through a long needle to test it for diseases such as meningitis.

Others go when they have had an accident and need emergency treatment. They are taken to the accident-emergency unit, sometimes by ambulance.

Units in a hospital

There are lots of different units in a hospital. Each has a special name and a specialist doctor in charge called a consultant. You can find out below what the units are called and what goes on in them.

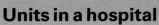

Geriatrics	This unit specializes in the care of old people.
Haematology	Blood disorders are treated here.
Intensive care	This unit looks after the seriously ill.
ENT	ENT stands for Ear, Nose and Throat and specializes in those parts of the body.
Maternity	Where babies are born.
Cardiology	This unit deals with heart disorders.
Radiography	Where X-rays are taken, and X-ray treatment is given (see page 24).
Renal	Kidney diseases are treated here.
Physiotherapy	This is where people improve mobility after an illness or accident.
Psychiatry	This unit deals with mental illness.
Outpatients	Where people go who do not have to stay in the hospital to be treated.
Paediatrics	Children's diseases are treated here.
Blood bank	Blood from donors is stored here for those who need transfusions.
Orthopaedics	This unit specializes in bone disorders.
Pharmacy	The medicines taken by the patients are prepared here.
Dermatology	Skin diseases are treated here.
Operating theatres	This is where the operations are performed.

Wards

Each hospital unit is divided into wards, which are rooms containing two rows of beds. Some wards hold one or two patients, while others hold up to fifty at a time.

Curtains

Each bed in a ward has curtains that are pulled round it if the patient needs some privacy.

There is a room in each ward where the nurses keep supplies such as bedpans (which are used by patients unable to walk to the toilet), and medicines.

Each ward is run by a senior nurse called a sister who organizes the duties of the junior nurses and is responsible for giving the treatments prescribed by the doctor.

Hospital for the healthy

Hospitals do not just look after ill people. For example, there is usually a maternity section where babies are born. This is kept apart from other units so that new babies do not come into contact with infectious illnesses.

Births are supervized in hospital by midwives and

doctors, called obstetricians, in case anything goes wrong. Premature babies (those born early) are put in machines called incubators which regulate the air temperature, acting a bit like the mother's womb, until the baby can manage on its own.

Out-patients

Out-patients often go to see specialists who are based in the hospital. The specialist examines and treats them in the same

way as a family doctor does, but if they need to be admitted to the hospital, the specialist can arrange it immediately.

Out-patients sometimes visit hospital to use special equipment, such as NMR (nuclear magnetic resonance) scanning equipment. This is especially useful for diagnosing back problems and brain disorders by producing pictures.

scanner image

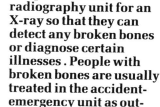

Doctors sometimes refer out-patients to the radiography unit for an X-ray so that they can detect any broken bones or diagnose certain illnesses . People with broken bones are usually treated in the accident-emergency unit as out-patients.

Running the hospital

The hospital managers are in charge of all these things. They control the hospital's money and decide what to spend it on after discussion with the medical staff. They are also in charge of paying the salaries of the people employed by the hospital.

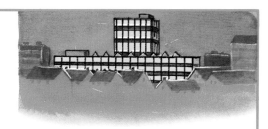

Hospitals are extremely expensive to run. They also have to run smoothly and efficiently and need a constant supply of equipment.

The managers also make sure the hospital has, for example, enough back-up electricity generators to deal with emergencies such as power cuts. Many life-saving machines depend on electricity.

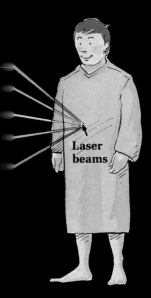

Laser beams

Many of the latest advances in medicine use technology developed for non-medical purposes. Lasers, for example, are used in industry for drilling, cutting, welding and engraving. They are also used in surgery to make bloodless cuts and perform delicate operations. On these two pages you can find out about some of the technology which has revolutionized medicine over the last hundred years.

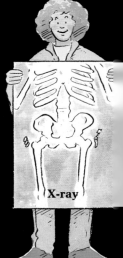

X-ray

Looking inside the body

To make an accurate diagnosis of some illnesses without surgery it is essential to be able to see and photograph inside the body. There are now many techniques for doing this, some of which are also used to treat any abnormalities found.

Pictures of the inside of the body were first taken using X-rays in 1895. These enabled doctors to see if bones were broken or growths developing.

About X-rays

X-rays are part of the "electromagnetic spectrum", which includes light, radio waves and microwaves. These "waves" travel at the same speed, but their wavelengths are different, giving them different properties. Unlike light waves, X-rays can travel through the flesh of the body, but are absorbed by bone, in particular the calcium in them. When X-rays are directed at the body a shadow of the bones appears on a

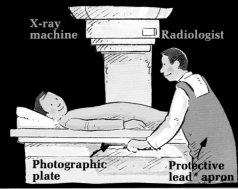

X-ray machine — Radiologist

Photographic plate — **Protective lead* apron**

photographic plate behind it. If exposed for too long, X-rays destroy the body's tissue. With care, they can be used to destroy diseased tissue in people suffering from cancer. This is called radiotherapy.

People who specialize in X-ray medicine are called radiologists. They wear protective clothing because continual exposure to X-rays is dangerous.

Lasers inside the body

Lasers are often used in conjunction with an endoscope – a tube about as thick as a finger which is pushed into the patient's body, often down their throat. Endoscopes are used to see and remove things, such as growths, inside the body. They consist of glass fibre (fibre optic) cables which are made of hair-like strands of glass, through which ordinary light and laser light can be passed. Each cable has a different function. One, for example,

is used to light the body, and another to suck out samples for analysis.

A doctor guides the endoscope at one end, watching its progress through a magnifying glass. The inside of the body is reflected onto the glass from the light-reflecting fibre optic cables. A pincer at the other end grasps the growth. The doctor can then send a laser beam down one cable to destroy the growth and seal, or cauterize, the wound.

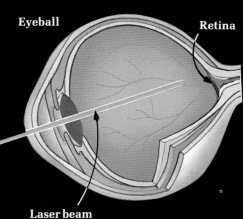

Eyeball — **Retina**

Laser beam

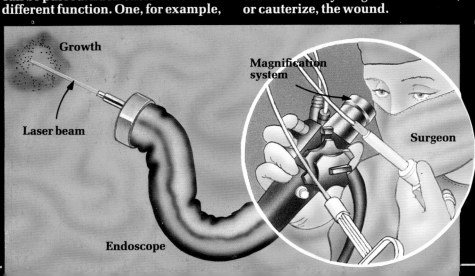

Growth

Laser beam

Magnification system

Surgeon

Endoscope

Lasers are also used in eye surgery, which is a particularly delicate organ to work on. The intense laser light beam is directed straight through the eyeball, like ordinary light, to the part which needs surgery. If the patient has, for example, a detached retina, the laser welds the retina back in place with a tiny heat scar.

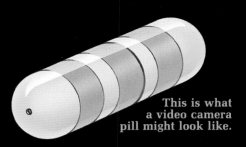

This is what a video camera pill might look like.

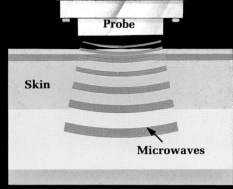

Probe

Skin

Microwaves

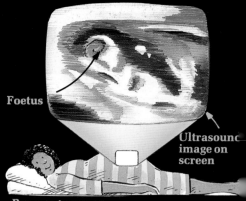

Foetus

Ultrasound image on screen

Pregnant woman

Video cameras

One of the new techniques being developed at the moment is a video camera which looks exactly like a pill and can be swallowed like one. It travels through a patient's body, transmitting pictures and information on the temperature and acidity of the patient's body to the doctor. This is done through a radio transmitter inside it.

Waves inside the body

A new process using microwaves detects defects in tissue through a probe inserted into the body. At the moment, the microwaves only penetrate 4mm (⅙in) into the body, but a more powerful probe is being developed.

Ultrasound is a technique which uses sound waves to detect, for example, that an unborn child (foetus) is growing normally. It is used in place of X-rays on pregnant women, as doctors believe it is safer for the foetus.

New operations

Sophisticated operations, such as organ transplants, depend on machines that have been developed to imitate one or several of the body's functions.

A transplant operation means removing a diseased organ from a patient and replacing it with a

healthy one, usually taken from someone who has recently died from some other cause. Kidney, liver, heart, lung and cornea transplants have so far been performed.

The main danger of a transplant operation is the possibility of the patient's body rejecting the new

organ in the same way as the body reacts against invading germs. Medicines are given to supress the immune system so that the patient does not form antibodies to fight the organ. This makes the patient very vulnerable to other infections until the organ is accepted.

The heart-lung machine

This is a heart-lung machine to which a patient is connected during open heart surgery (which means the heart is opened up). Blood from the main arteries and veins is diverted through the machine while the surgeon works on the heart. The machine imitates the heart and lungs by pumping the blood round, supplying it with oxygen and removing carbon dioxide.

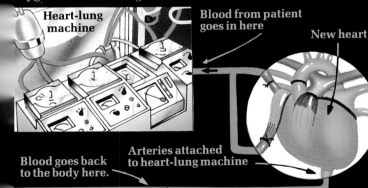

Heart-lung machine

Blood from patient goes in here

New heart

Blood goes back to the body here.

Arteries attached to heart-lung machine

Microsurgery

Microsurgery is performed with the aid of a microscope. It is used for delicate operations which involve joining tiny blood vessels and nerves after an accident, or after they have been cut by the surgeon to reach another part of the body. It is often used for operations on the eye, and during organ transplants. It is essential in brain surgery (neurosurgery), where the centres which control all the body's functions are closely packed together and the surgeon has to see exactly where he is working.

Microsurgery has also made it possible to re-join limbs that are accidentally severed. In some cases, surgeons can sew the limb back on, re-connecting all the nerves, muscles, ligaments, tendons and blood vessels, so that, with physiotherapy, the limb works almost as efficiently as before.

Using a microscope to see, a surgeon suspends a metal ring round a small vein to hold the suture in place while the ends are being joined.

Breakthroughs in the laboratory

Many medical advances are chemical ones, made "behind the scenes" in the laboratory by scientists who have developed amazing new tests and medicines. For example, all newly born babies

A modern laboratory

are tested for thyroid deficiency – a condition which stunts a child's growth and leaves them with irreperable brain damage. Through a simple test, the condition can now be detected in time to treat the affected children, who then develop completely normally.

Health and the environment

People's health depends on what job they have, where they live, how much money they have and what their habits are. Someone who smokes, drinks too much alcohol and has a bad diet is likely to be less healthy than someone who does not.

All the things around you, natural or man-made, are your environment. On these two pages, you can find out how environment affects the health of individuals and whole populations.

Health at work

Some jobs involve working in places which have a high level of dust or toxic fumes which pollute the air. Mines, factories, chemical plants, laboratories and X-ray units in hospitals are all examples of working environments which are potentially dangerous to health. Coal dust in mines can cause pneumoconiosis, silica dust in quarries causes silicosis, and asbestos dust causes asbestosis. These are all diseases of the lung which develop over a number of years. Safety precautions are strict in working places at risk. In some factories workers wear special filter masks to avoid breathing in dust and fumes.

Protective clothing in a nuclear power plant

This sign denotes a radioactive area.

Overshoes containing lead.

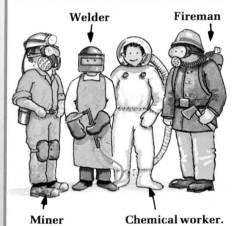

Welder

Fireman

Miner

Chemical worker.

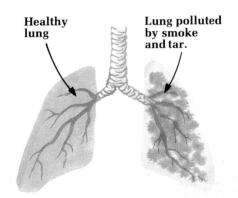

Healthy lung

Lung polluted by smoke and tar.

In nuclear power stations where they are dealing with radioactive materials, the workers have to wear full protective clothing – even lead overshoes in case the floor is radioactive. These safety precautions, however, cannot eliminate the risks completely.

Man's effect on the environment

Every country in the world is affected by the problem of pollution. Poisonous substances escape from cars, factories and chemical plants. Pollution does not disappear, it goes into the air and circulates there, sometimes travelling hundreds of miles. It can change the environment and even affect the chemical composition of the atmosphere. The health of whole populations could be at risk if pollution increases.

To keep pollution under control, measures have been introduced such as making cities smokeless zones, introducing lead-free petrol, and fitting exhaust filters on cars. There is still the long-term problem of how to dispose of the enormous quantities of waste from chemical plants, some of which is radioactive, and how to prevent disasters such as spillages from oil tankers. These things have a direct effect on the health of those who live nearby, including plants and animals.

Sea-bird trapped in an oil-slick.

Passive smoking

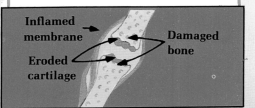

Smoking is a form of pollution and a very dangerous habit, causing diseases such as bronchitis and lung cancer. Smokers are not the only ones at risk. If a non-smoker works in a room full of smokers, they can contract the same diseases (although it is less likely). This is called passive smoking.

Living conditions

Poor sanitation*, dampness and overcrowded living conditions in the home contribute to the development of illness. A disease called tuberculosis (TB), which is a bacterial infection (usually of the lungs), is easily spread in overcrowded communities. Rheumatism, a condition which stiffens joints, is more likely to affect people who live in damp houses, or near the sea where there is dampness in the air.

The picture below shows a rheumatic knee-joint.

Inflamed membrane → Damaged bone
Eroded cartilage

The World Health Organization

The World Health Organization (WHO), keep a constant up-to-date supply of information on the state of health of people from every country. It gives specialist advice to governments of countries that have a health problem (such as how to control the spread of disease after a natural disaster). It also campaigns to control infections such as malaria, through immunization and drainage of swamps where disease-carrying mosquitos live.

The WHO also organizes educational programs to teach people about nutrition, sanitation and immunization – three of the most important factors in disease control.

Climate

The climate of a country refers to its temperature, and whether it is dry or has a lot of rain. Climate affects health in several ways. Hot countries, for instance, attract many insects which carry disease, such as mosquitos.

Jungles grow in hot, moist climates.

Swamps attract mosquitos.

Most areas of the world have variable climates. Countries very far north or south of the equator, however, have long summers or winters and this can affect health. In parts of Northern Russia, for instance, there is so little daylight during the winter that the children need to be exposed to ultra-violet light from a machine every day. This is to provide the vitamins which are usually made by the skin after contact with the sun, and which are essential for bone growth.

Diet

The food people eat affects their health. A poor diet causes deficiency diseases such as rickets which stunts the growth of bones. It deprives the body of the basic nutrients it needs to make antibodies to fight germs. This leads to low resistance to infections which are mild in people with a good diet. In some countries, for example, measles is a serious disease, killing many children who are malnourished.
In many countries, there is no shortage of food, but people become ill through eating "junk food" such as cakes, chips and fizzy drinks. This food is not nutritious and tends to make you overweight which is also unhealthy. People who eat too much, drink too much alcohol and smoke are more likely to develop heart disease.
In countries where the diet is basic but nutritional, people tend not to develop illnesses such as appendicitis and stomach ulcers.

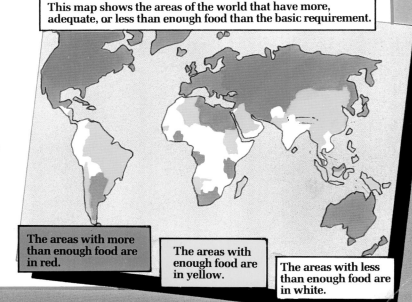

This map shows the areas of the world that have more, adequate, or less than enough food than the basic requirement.

The areas with more than enough food are in red.

The areas with enough food are in yellow.

The areas with less than enough food are in white.

*See pages 12-13.

First aid

First aid means the first help given to someone if they are ill or have an accident. This ranges from giving them "the kiss of life" (artificial respiration), to putting a plaster over a cut.

Here, you can find out how to give some basic first aid, such as putting on a bandage, and how to deal with an emergency. A doctor should be consulted if an injury looks serious.

This picture shows useful things to have in a family medicine chest.

Scissors

Safety pins

Sticky plasters (air-strip so that the air can get to a cut through the holes).

Antiseptic ointment

Bandage

Needle

DANGER

All medicines are dangerous. Never play with medicines and never take any medicine without asking an adult first.

Splinters

A splinter is a tiny sliver of wood that gets wedged into the skin, usually your hand. Unless it is very tiny, it is best to remove it in case it is dirty and causes infection.

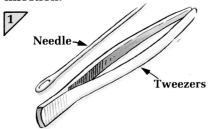

1

Needle

Tweezers

Remove a splinter using a needle and a pair of tweezers. Clean them with antiseptic liquid before use.

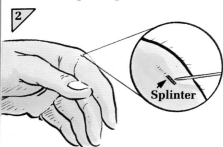

2

Splinter

Use the point of the needle to work free one end of the splinter without piercing the skin if possible.

3

Using tweezers, gently pull out the splinter and then wash the area with antiseptic liquid (or dab on some antiseptic ointment).

Cuts

These steps show how to deal with a bleeding cut. If the cut is deep it should be seen by a doctor as it might need stitches.

1

Press firmly on the cut for three to five minutes using your hand, cotton wool, tissue, or a towel. This is to stop the bleeding.

2

Wash the cut gently using cotton wool and warm water, then dry it using a clean towel or tissue.

3

Put a piece of air-strip sticky plaster over the cut for a few days to keep it germ-free. Take the plaster off at night and replace it with a clean one in the morning. This allows air to reach the cut which helps it heal quickly.

Using a bandage

If a cut is very dirty, or covers a large area, it is best to wash it carefully then put a bandage on it with a lint dressing. The steps below show you how to bandage an arm. You can use the same procedure for a leg cut.

1

Clean the wound with warm soapy water and cover it with gauze, or a piece of lint, smooth side down.

2

Make sure the arm is slightly bent. Take the bandage and wrap it round the arm firmly but not tightly. Cover the area 15cm (6in) above and below the cut.

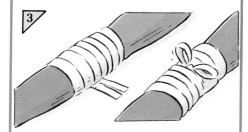

3

Cut about 20cm (8in) down the centre of the free end of the bandage. Tie the cut ends together in a bow over the cut area.

Holes to allow air to the cut.

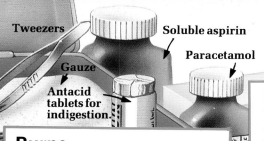

Tweezers

Soluble aspirin

Paracetamol

Gauze

Lint

Nose drops for stuffed up noses.

Antacid tablets for indigestion.

Burns

Minor burns, which affect only the top layer of skin, heal very quickly although they can be very painful when they happen. If small blisters appear on a burn, they should not be burst.

1

Run the burnt area under the cold tap to cool it and help prevent blisters forming.

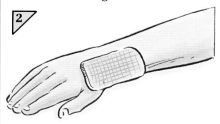

2

Cover it with something clean and dry, such as a tissue or a towel.

3

Superficial burn

Deep burn

If the burn is small with little blisters, keep it covered and dry for a few hours. See your doctor if it covers a large area or is deep and covered with dead skin.

Bruises

The "black and blue" colours of a bruise are caused by blood gathering under the skin which comes from tiny blood vessels which burst when you knock them hard.

Most bruises have to be left to heal up by themselves. They will hurt for a few days so it is best to avoid situations when they might be knocked.

Fainting

Fainting is caused by a lack of oxygen to the brain which makes you fall over. This is the body's way of getting the head down so that blood can travel back to the brain easily. It should only last for a minute or two. It is usually caused by hot weather, tiredness, lack of food, or standing still for too long.

If someone feels faint, sit them on a chair, put their head between their legs and fan the back of their neck until the feeling passes. It helps if they then sip a glass of water.

If someone actually faints, turn them on their side and make sure they can breathe properly. Loosen any tight collars and buttons round the neck. The picture above shows the exact position to put someone in who is unconscious – it is called the recovery position.

At an accident

Do not move someone who has had an accident and cannot move themselves as they might have broken a bone. Make sure they can breathe properly, try to stop heavy bleeding by applying pressure to the area, and get help quickly if the person is unconscious or in a lot of pain. Especially never move anyone who has hurt their back.

Artificial respiration

Artificial respiration means blowing into the lungs of someone who has stopped breathing, to start them working again. This should never be practised on people breathing normally.

1

Clear the patient's mouth of any objects such as chewing gum, false teeth, vomit or blood. Tilt their head back with the chin pushed forward. This is to clear the airways. Put your hand under the chin, open the mouth, and pinch the nostrils firmly together.

2

Take a deep breath and completely cover the patient's mouth with your own. Blow deeply into the lungs and repeat quickly four times to fill up the lungs with air.

3

Wait for the chest to fall. If the patient does not start breathing, repeat artificial respiration until they do or until help arrives.

You should always tell an adult or a doctor if someone hurts themselves badly. In serious cases, these are the three most important things to do until help arrives: make sure the patient can breathe easily, stop heavy bleeding and check that the person is conscious.

Sprains and twists

A sprained ankle means that the ligaments which hold the bones together have been overstretched. This can happen quite easily. It usually causes the ankle to swell up and will be painful for a few days. All painful sprains should be seen by a doctor in case the bone is broken as well.

Atlas of the body

When people study medicine, the first subject they learn is the structure of the human body. This is called anatomy. The pictures below show the main bones, organs and external features of a female and a male human body. You can use these as a reference guide as you read through the book.

2 Inside the body

In the pictures below, the male and female body show organs that are common to both, such as the heart, liver and lungs. They also show two of the body's systems – the blood system and nervous system. The female's sexual organs are the only difference between the bodies – they are labelled with an asterisk (*) to distinguish them.

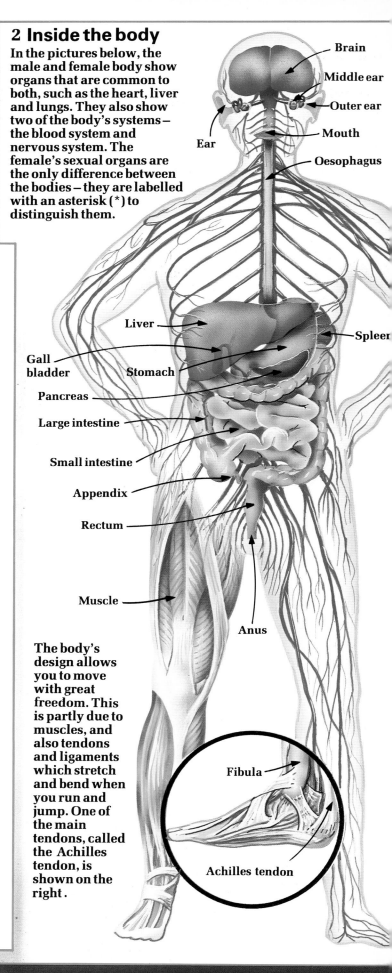

Brain
Middle ear
Outer ear
Ear
Mouth
Oesophagus
Liver
Spleen
Gall bladder
Stomach
Pancreas
Large intestine
Small intestine
Appendix
Rectum
Muscle
Anus
Fibula
Achilles tendon

The body's design allows you to move with great freedom. This is partly due to muscles, and also tendons and ligaments which stretch and bend when you run and jump. One of the main tendons, called the Achilles tendon, is shown on the right .

1 Outside the body

The pictures below show the external features of a male and female body. The main differences between them are in the sexual organs. Other external differences are that a woman has breasts and wider hips. A man has slightly broader shoulders, a less well-defined waist, and hairier skin, especially on his face.

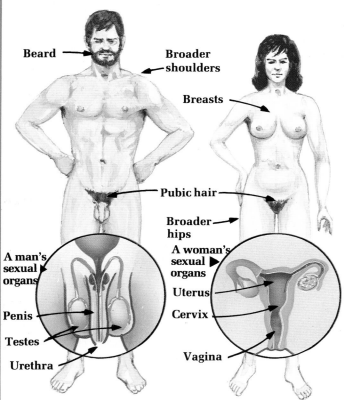

Beard
Broader shoulders
Breasts
Pubic hair
Broader hips
A man's sexual organs
A woman's sexual organs
Uterus
Penis
Cervix
Testes
Urethra
Vagina

Sexual organs

A woman's sexual organs are inside the body while a man's are on the outside. The big picture on the right shows where the woman's sexual organs are positioned – they are labelled with an asterisk (*).

Men are usually stronger than women because their muscles are more developed. Women, however, often live longer than men and are more resistant to diseases such as heart disease.

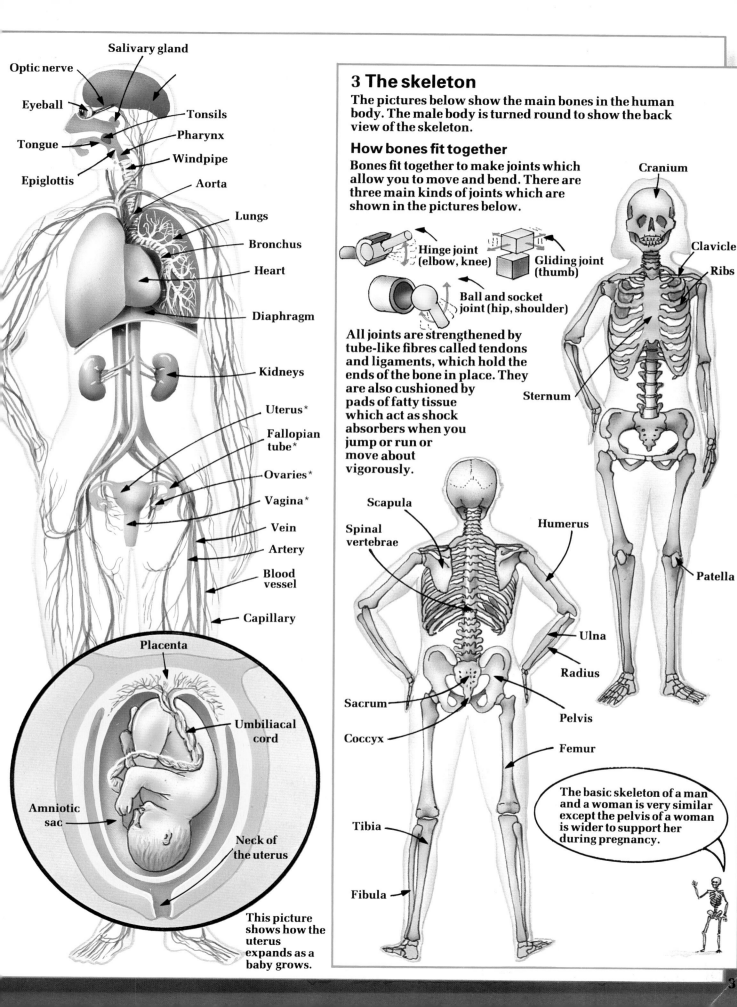

Salivary gland

Optic nerve

Eyeball

Tongue

Epiglottis

Tonsils

Pharynx

Windpipe

Aorta

Lungs

Bronchus

Heart

Diaphragm

Kidneys

Uterus*

Fallopian tube*

Ovaries*

Vagina*

Vein

Artery

Blood vessel

Capillary

Placenta

Umbiliacal cord

Amniotic sac

Neck of the uterus

This picture shows how the uterus expands as a baby grows.

3 The skeleton

The pictures below show the main bones in the human body. The male body is turned round to show the back view of the skeleton.

How bones fit together

Bones fit together to make joints which allow you to move and bend. There are three main kinds of joints which are shown in the pictures below.

Hinge joint (elbow, knee)

Gliding joint (thumb)

Ball and socket joint (hip, shoulder)

All joints are strengthened by tube-like fibres called tendons and ligaments, which hold the ends of the bone in place. They are also cushioned by pads of fatty tissue which act as shock absorbers when you jump or run or move about vigorously.

Cranium

Clavicle

Ribs

Sternum

Patella

Scapula

Spinal vertebrae

Humerus

Ulna

Radius

Sacrum

Coccyx

Pelvis

Femur

Tibia

Fibula

The basic skeleton of a man and a woman is very similar except the pelvis of a woman is wider to support her during pregnancy.

31

Index

First published in 1985 by Usborne Publishing Ltd, Usborne House, 83-85 Saffron Hill, London, EC1N 8RT, England.

Printed in Belgium.